Balkan Anschluss

Central European Studies

Charles W. Ingrao, senior editor
Gray B. Cohen, editor

Balkan Anschluss

The Annexation of Montenegro and the Creation of the Common South Slavic State

Srdja Pavlović

Purdue University Press
West Lafayette, Indiana

Copyright 2008 by Purdue University. All rights reserved.

Printed in the United States of America.

ISBN 978-1-557-53465-1

Library of Congress Cataloging-in-Publication Data
Pavlovic, Srdja, 1961–
  Balkan Anschluss : the annexation of Montenegro and the creation of the common South Slavic state / Srdja Pavlovic.
    p. cm.
  Includes bibliographical references and index.
  ISBN 978-1-557-53465-1 (alk. paper)
  1. Montenegro—History. I. Title. II. Series.
  DR1835. P38   2007
  949.745'01—dc22
                                            2007051921

Contents

Introduction   1
   Tribal or National Consciousness?   5
   The Writings on the Podgorica Assembly:
   The Magic Circle of Historiography   13

Chapter One   29
   Historical Background: Poets and Warriors
   Independent Montenegro: The History of an Idea   48

Chapter Two   65
   Montenegro during World War I:
   Saving the Dynasty or Saving Serbdom?
      The Montenegrin Treaty with Serbia: Generals without an Army   68
      The Role of the Serbian Envoy in Montenegro   72
      The Capitulation of Montenegro   75

Chapter Three   87
   The King in Exile
      Montenegro, the Great Powers, and the Paris Peace Conference   94
      Montenegro and Italy   95
      "God Is High Above Us and Russia Is Far Away"   97
      France and Montenegro   98
      The Lion and the Eagle   106
      The United States and the Montenegrin Question   109
      The Politics of the Fait Accompli   111

Chapter Four 119
   The Montenegrin Committee for Unification
      Program and Proclamation 121
      Diplomatic Activities 122
      The Newsletter *Ujedinjenje* and the Battle of Spilled Ink 123
      The Montenegrin Committee and the Allied Subsidies
         to King Nikola 127
      Activities among the Montenegrin Students 128
      The Issue of the Prisoners of War 130
      The King Strikes Back 132
      Preaching to the Choir: Toward Annexation 138

Chapter Five 145
   The Preparation for the Great People's Assembly in Podgorica
      The Activities in Montenegro: United We Stand! 147
      God's Messengers 154
      Winter of Discontent: The Christmas Uprising 163

Conclusion 175
   Abiit ad Plures: The New State Is Born
      Montenegro: Polity in Turmoil 176

Appendix 1 181

Appendix 2 185

Appendix 3 187

Bibliography 189

Index 207

Introduction

The establishment of the first common state of the South Slavs was announced in Belgrade on December 1, 1918, at the time when the map of Europe was redrawn. The new state was the product of attempts by the international community to deal with the dissolution of the Austro-Hungarian monarchy and the Ottoman state, as much as it represented the fulfillment of desires of the South Slavs.[1] From the point of view of the Great Powers (Russia, France, and Great Britain), the common South Slav state came into being as the result of many compromises. Those compromises were made in order to honor the principle of self-determination while trying to satisfy the local and regional powers' growing appetite for new territory. At the end, some of the decisions were in violation of that declared principle. Montenegro is a case in point. From the perspective of many South Slavs, the creation of the Kingdom of the Serbs, Croats, and Slovenes represented the materialization of an old dream. That dream, however, meant different things for different South Slavic groups.

The political elite in Serbia envisaged the new state as the territorial expansion of their own state and as the just reward for their considerable and successful war effort. Croats and Slovenes viewed the new state as leveling the political playing field and as the legal framework that would allow them to preserve and manifest their cultural distinctiveness and political aspirations. Montenegrins were hoping to contribute to the common state in a more constructive manner as one of its constitutive elements. These conflicting desires meant that not everybody was fully satisfied with the structure and the manner in which the new state was created. As time progressed it became apparent to other South Slavs that Serbia, supported by the Great Powers, would play the main role in designing the state structure and influencing its internal dynamics. Ivo Banac rightly pointed out that "the superior power of Serbian government led to the unification that did not meet even the basic desires of those who wanted a federal state organization."[2] In the case of Montenegro, such realization came rather late and at a high price in human lives. The text that follows characterizes the events that took place in Montenegro at the end of 1918 as annexation by Serbia rather than as the unification of the two states. Although arguing in favor of using the term *annexation* in describing the events, I have used both terms throughout. By doing so I have tried to acknowledge that Montenegrins do not have a uniform view on this issue. I have used the term *unification* when describing and analyzing the views of those who supported the union and the term *annexation* when representing either my own findings and conclusions or referring to the sentiments of those Montenegrins who opposed the manner in which this matter was handled.

At the end of World War I, Montenegro was annexed by Serbia, thus effectively strengthening its position vis-à-vis other South Slavs and its World War I Allies. The unification of Montenegro with Serbia, which was proclaimed on November 25, 1918, in Podgorica by the Great People's Assembly of the Serbian People in Montenegro, represents one of the most important and hotly contested issues of recent Montenegrin history. This event marked the disappearance of the 400-year-old Montenegrin state and formalized its annexation by Serbia, drawing in blood a deep demarcation line between its citizens. These negative consequences for the Montenegrin state were the product of a combination of economic, political, and military factors, both domestic and international. From the time of annexation forward, manifestations of the political and cultural distinctiveness of Montenegro and its peoples were reduced to a minimum and were colored by the events that took place during and after the Podgorica Assembly. In spite of the later divisions along party lines, the common denominator of the Montenegrin political reality was (and to a great extent still is) the passionate disagreement between the so-called Greens and Whites (Zelenši and Bjelaši) or, respectively, the opponents and advocates of the 1918 annexation/unification. The contested character of the decisions made by the Podgorica Assembly affected the Montenegrin political scene, conditioned the nature of the relations between Serbia and Montenegro for decades to come, and defined the character of the common South Slav state. On a broader level the Podgorica Assembly also indicated numerous ailments that characterized the relatively short and somewhat turbulent existence of the Kingdom of the Serbs, Croats, and Slovenes (later renamed the Kingdom of Yugoslavia) and raised the question about the viability of any common state in those parts of the Balkan Peninsula.

The policies of the period and the events surrounding the annexation of Montenegro became a contested political issue and over the years acquired the character of a debate among intellectuals, historians, and politicians, both in Serbia and in Montenegro. Montenegrin historiography searched for answers by revisiting the issues of Montenegrin identity and the nature of the ideology of the time, as well as by arguing for or against a particular national paradigm. The debate over the significance of the Podgorica Assembly corresponds somewhat to the modern-day dilemmas of many Montenegrins who, throughout the twentieth century, kept searching for the right place and the optimal legal framework for their state and constantly questioned its structure. While attempting to cope with recent traumatic experiences, many Serbs and Montenegrins used historical memories of events that occurred during the first decades of the twentieth century as the basis of their arguments and counter-arguments. This gave a new lease on life to the events from the past and made them the topic of contemporary debates.

The participants in this long and spirited debate were many and could be broadly divided into two groups along the old fault lines separating Greens from Whites. They were politicians, lawyers, economists, historians, and writers, and many were contemporaries of the events they wrote about. The central issues they debated were the questions of the legality of the Podgorica Assembly, the legitimacy of its resolution, and its being a representation of the popular will of Montenegrins.

The body of work on this topic in English is relatively minor. Within the English-speaking scholarly environments, the Montenegrin Question and the Podgorica Assembly have been addressed only in passing and in the context of a dynastic struggle between Cetinje and Belgrade. English-speaking authors have been concerned with the larger context of the creation of nation-states among the South Slavs and with the balance of power between the two major players in the region, Serbs and Croats. Montenegro was discussed only as a relatively insignificant segment in the process of much larger geopolitical changes in the Balkans.[3] The scarcity of material in English, the general nature of the existing material, and the conflicting assessments of the position of Montenegro among the South Slavs are some of the reasons behind this text and, to a great degree, determine its narrative form. Moreover, the consensus was (and is to this day) that the Montenegrins and Serbs are but one nation sharing a common language, religious beliefs, and traditional values. Many scholars are quick to include Montenegrins together with Serbs and point out that the region was, for centuries, a refuge for the remnants of the defeated Serb nation, whereas the Montenegrin state represented only a "peripheral extension of Serbia."[4] Others maintained that the argument about shared religious beliefs denotes a contested territory because "Orthodoxy alone can not for any length of time paper over other factors of division. . . . Montenegrin Orthodoxy has resisted, and still resists, incorporation within a Serbian church."[5] As for the books written on the Podgorica Assembly and published in Serbia and Montenegro, they all shared a common feature: the perception of Montenegrins as ethnic Serbs.

This book aims at answering a central question with respect to relations between the Kingdom of Montenegro and the Kingdom of Serbia in the period between 1910 and 1919: were the unification of Montenegro and Serbia in 1918 and the subsequent establishing of the Kingdom of the Serbs, Croats, and Slovenes in accordance with popular sentiment in Montenegro? My central hypothesis is that the unification of late 1918 was an act of annexation of Montenegro by Serbia and that it occurred with the political blessing of the Entente and, further, that the Podgorica Assembly represented the final act of the long process of the appropriation of Montenegro. It should be said, however, that Montenegro's annexation occurred not only as the consequence of the policy of Serbia and the Great Powers but also because of a considerable sympathy within Montenegro for the union with Serbia. Many people in Montenegro were in favor of a common South Slavic state, and this sentiment, and the union with Serbia, were based on the principle of equality between the two states. The analysis that follows therefore focuses on the interplay between external and internal forces that played a role in the annexation.

In order to answer these questions and explain the internal dynamics of the process, it is necessary first to outline a broader historical framework. The first chapter provides an overview of the stages of development of the Montenegrin state. It is followed in chapter 2 by an analysis Montenegro's role in World War I. Chapter 3 discusses the period following the capitulation of Montenegro in January 1916 and analyzes the relations between the Montenegrin government in exile and the Great Powers. It also elaborates on both the gradual marginalization of King Nikola by his World War I allies and the lack of will on the part of the international community (the external factor) to support Montenegrin postwar independence and sovereignty. Chapter 4 focuses on activities of the Montenegrin Committee for Unification (the internal factor) in preparation for the final act of annexing Montenegro. The evidence presented in this chapter sheds light on the interplay between the external and internal factors and strongly indicates that the whole undertaking was guided and financed by the Serbian government. The crux of this book is the critical assessment of the preparations for the Podgorica Assembly (Great People's Assembly of the Serbian People in Montenegro), the event that marked a turning point in relations between Montenegro and Serbia, as well as in the development of the future common state of all South Slavs (chapter 5). I have also critically analyzed the role played by the Montenegrin King Nikola Petrović and his government in exile in the final months before the assembly. Chapter 5 elaborates on the dynamics of the assembly sessions in Podgorica, including procedural matters, such as the election of the delegates, the question of the legality of this political gathering, and the critical evaluation of the political campaign in Montenegro that preceded the assembly. The analysis of the assembly sessions casts serious doubts on the legality of the decision-making process and indicates that the resolution adopted in Podgorica was the crowning moment in the protracted effort of the Serbian Karadjordjević dynasty to achieve primacy among the South Slavs and to dominate the future common state. Furthermore, the decision to unify Montenegro with Serbia was never officially acknowledged by any institution of the Kingdom of Serbs, Croats, and Slovenes or by any foreign government. I also address the postassembly situation in Montenegro and the opposition movement known as the Christmas Uprising. The analysis of this armed uprising, its scope, and its long-lasting effects undermines the argument of the unionists that the people of Montenegro all agreed with the manner in which the Montenegrin state was dismantled.

In preparing this book I have examined substantial archival material related to the political, economic, diplomatic, military, and cultural relations between Montenegro and Serbia, as well as documents relevant to the assembly and events surrounding it. I have undertaken a critical evaluation of a number of primary sources ranging from the official documents of political and cultural organizations to private correspondence and journals and to memoirs. Primary sources also include newspapers of the period, periodicals, and visual material (photographs, posters, postage stamps), as well as the catalogs of various publishing organizations in Serbia and Montenegro. Those primary sources are located in several archival collections in Montenegro and Serbia, the United Kingdom, and Italy. Moreover, I have critically evaluated a number of secondary sources in Serbo-Croat, English, and Italian that are related to the main subject of this book. Those secondary sources include memoirs and personal journals of those who took an active part in the assembly sessions, as well as scholarly works by historians.

My intention is to broaden the field of analysis by introducing an alternative discourse through research on the internal dynamic of the Montenegrin political landscape and the contesting visions of its future. Recognizing the "handicap of heterogeneity"[6] of the visions of the future South Slav state means rethinking the conventional perception of South Slav history. It also means revisiting the issues that have been unjustly marginalized by the existing scholarship. The importance of such an approach also lies in the fact that this heterogeneity of political, cultural, and ideological concepts between the elites in Montenegro and Serbia is not a thing of the past. The present political instability in the region indicates that old and unresolved ideological differences and long-standing political rivalries between Montenegrin and Serbian elites lie at the core of current political confrontations in the region.

Tribal or National Consciousness?

Any debate over the political significance of the Podgorica Assembly inevitably turns into a discussion of the Montenegrin identities because the two are connected to the point of inseparability. Due to this interconnectedness, it is necessary briefly to address the question of Montenegrin identities. The question is relevant to the main topic of this book because one of the central premises of the Podgorica Assembly and the entire process of annexation in 1918 was the assumption of oneness between Serbs and Montenegrins.

The case for the Montenegrin state's independence and sovereignty might be easier to argue, but resolving the issue of identities in Montenegro of the period is a daunting task. An examination of this aspect of Montenegrin history should begin by addressing the issue of the national awareness of its population in the past. This is an important point of departure because it deals with the issue of "ancestral land" and "temporal continuity" and with the application of modern analytical categories such as nation and national identity to periods prior to the emergence of these concepts. Did the seventeenth- and eighteenth-century Montenegrin tribes think of themselves in national terms, and were they aware of the existence of such a level of identification?

Even though Montenegrin history and tradition provide numerous examples of Montenegrin identification with Serbs, it would be safe to argue that such identification was of a general, non–nation-specific nature and had more to do with the notion of shared religious beliefs than with ethnic/national awareness among the Montenegrin tribes of the period. The persistent inclusion of Montenegrins within the Serbian ethnos is usually rationalized by invoking the shared language and religious beliefs of Montenegrins and Serbs and elevating the importance of certain common features of their respective traditional cultures. I would argue that such an approach is based on projecting the concept of national consciousness back in time in order to establish historical continuity for the presence of a particular nation in the region. Such a methodology rationalizes the notion of a "lost ancestral land" that has to be reclaimed. In modern times, the urge to repossess the "cradle" of one's civilization from an unwanted "other" has often resulted in significant demographic changes and forced population movements.

Seventeenth- and eighteenth-century Montenegrin society was characterized by occasional voluntary cooperation at the intertribal level. However, these temporary tribal alliances had little to do with the modern concept of national identity and more to do with military aims, primarily fending off Ottoman forces. There can be no question about the primacy of tribal autonomy in Old Montenegro and Brda over the powers of the central authority in Cetinje.[7] Furthermore, almost all the Montenegrin tribes (with the exception of those from Katunska Nahija) at one time or another assisted neighboring Ottoman forces against other tribes from the area.[8] In the Montenegro of the period, it was the tribe and not the state/central authority that provided almost exclusively the mechanisms of horizontal identification for individuals. The central authority played a very limited role in this process because it was the tribe that always acted as safe harbor for the individual and constructed and maintained the social poetics of the time.[9] With this in mind it would be safe to conclude that the Montenegrin tribesmen of the seventeenth and eighteenth centuries highly valued their tribal alliances and were much more aware of belonging to a particular tribe than they were thinking of themselves in terms of national identity. New national demarcation lines within Montenegro and with respect to its neighbors came into existence only with the advent of the idea of national awakening and national homogenization on a more general level.

The issue of conflicting identities in Montenegro has been, in most cases, interpreted as the tension (informed by politics) between two main concepts: the subordinate concept of the *Montenegrin*, representing the separatist and independentist interpretation of the identity question, and the superordinate concept of the *Serb*, representing ethnic/national/cultural belonging. In a contemporary and a more radical interpretation, those independentist views were portrayed as expressions of anti-Communist, thus anti-Yugoslav, sentiments. In a long article titled "O Etnogenezi Crnogoraca" (On the Ethnogenesis of the Montenegrins), the well-known Serbian ethnologist Špiro Kulišić convincingly argued in favor of separate Montenegrin ethnic identity. The publication of this article provoked strong negative reactions by scholars in both Montenegro and Serbia and resulted in a flurry of articles (mainly political in nature) contesting Kulišić's findings. His opponents advocated the concept of the Serbian origins of the Montenegrins and were supported by the Montenegrin government officials and by the ruling League of Communists of Montenegro. The political pressure exerted upon Kulišić and his publisher was so great that scholarly research on this topic in Montenegro was halted for a prolonged period.[10] The subcategory Serbs from Montenegro was thought to express the notion of territoriality without problematizing the ethnic factor. Thus, many Montenegrins have been perceived as ethnic Serbs living in the geographic region known as Montenegro.

I would argue that such a view represents a simplification of the notion of Montenegrin Serbdom. Contrary to popular belief, the Montenegrins preserved the sense of their political and cultural distinctiveness with regard to other South Slavic groups and continuously reaffirmed it throughout history. The Montenegrin version of Serbdom differs from its manifestations in other areas of the former Yugoslavia, which are populated by peoples of Eastern Orthodox faith. A heroic attitude toward life, the notion of a messianic role in the historical process of the revival of the medieval Serbian empire, and the prolonged armed struggle against the Ottoman invader, as well as the historical continuity of the Montenegrin state, are elements that distinguish the notion of Montenegrin Serbdom from similar notions in Bosnia, Croatia, or Serbia proper. Ultimately, the notion of Serbdom was understood by Montenegrins to be their belonging to the Eastern Orthodox faith and to Christianity in general, as well as to the larger South Slavic context. They incorporated this idea in the building blocks of their national individuality. Because it was understood as the ideology of *constant struggle*, this Montenegrin Serbdom did not stand in opposition to a distinct character of Montenegrin national identity. Rather, it was used as a tool of pragmatic politics in order to achieve the final goal. Montenegrins used the terms *Serbs* and *Serbdom* whenever they referred to South Slavic elements rallied in an anti-Ottoman coalition and around the Christian Cross. Whenever they referred to particular elements of their social structure and their political system, they used the term *Montenegrin*.

What envelops this multilayered character of Montenegrin identity and impedes a more complete understanding of Montenegrin history is, among other things, its tradition of epic poetry, the contents of which are open to various and often conflicting interpretations. To adopt the metaphor of Slavoj Žižek, one could say that epic poetry in Montenegro, unlike the role it plays in other societies, is the stuff *others'* dreams are made of.[11] The political dimension of Montenegrin identities is best illustrated by numerous and contradictory interpretations of the literary achievements of Petar II Petrović Njegoš, the nineteenth-century ruler of Montenegro. His legacy serves as a telling example of how literature, religion, and politics in the Balkans can be interwoven in serving particular political agendas. Njegoš and his poetic endeavors occupy central stage in the South Slavic myth-making factory. His work has been appropriated by both supporters and opponents of a distinct Montenegrin national and cultural identity. Each group managed to find enough evidence in Njegoš's literary work to advance its own political vision of Montenegro. By the end of the nineteenth century, the debate about Njegoš's sense of national identity had developed into a debate about the national and cultural identity of Montenegrins.[12]

Njegoš's magnum opus is his epic poem *The Mountain Wreath*, written in 1846 in Cetinje and published in Vienna in 1847. The poem appeared in print the same year as Vuk Stefanović Karadžić's translation of the New Testament. According to Professor Vasa D. Mihailović, Njegoš "is revered as Montenegro's most illustrious son and the greatest poet in Serbian literature."[13] *The Mountain Wreath* is set in eighteenth-century Montenegro and deals with the attempts of Njegoš's ancestor, the Metropolitan Danilo, to regulate relations among the region's warring tribes. Njegoš constructed his poem around a single event that allegedly took place on a particular Christmas Day in the early 1700s during the Metropolitan Danilo's rule: the mass execution of Montenegrins who had converted to Islam.

The dating of the alleged event is a matter of some controversy. The subtitle of *The Mountain Wreath* tells us that the poem deals with a "Historical Event from the End of the 17th Century" (*Historičesko Sobitie pri Svršetky XVII vieka*). The same dating of the event described in *The Mountain Wreath* appeared in a number of histories of Montenegro published during the nineteenth century, such as those by Simeon Milutinović Sarajlija (Belgrade, 1835) and Dimitrije Milaković. Later studies based their dating of the event on a note allegedly written by the Metropolitan Danilo Petrović himself. It is worth pointing out that Ilarion Ruvarac expressed serious concerns regarding the authenticity of the note, but his concerns were quickly brushed aside by a number of local historians. The aforementioned authors offered three different dates for the "Christmas Day Massacre" (1702, 1704, and 1707), whereas *The Mountain Wreath* positioned the event in the late seventeenth century. It is interesting to note that in his earlier works Njegoš dated the event in 1702. In his poem "Ogledalo Srpsko," Njegoš wrote about the event and positioned it "around the year 1702." A notable exception is Konstantin Jiriček, who, in his *Naučni Slovnik*, stated that the event described in *The Mountain Wreath* never took place.[14]

Regardless of their political agendas, ideological preferences, or religious affiliation, every new generation of South Slav historians and politicians appropriates

Njegoš's work, hoping to find enough quotations to validate their own views. Furthermore, in every English translation of *The Mountain Wreath*, one can detect attempts to remodel the original. The latest English version, by Professor Vasa D. Mihailović, represents yet another attempt to colonize Njegoš's work for the sake of aiding modern political and ideological struggle in the Balkans. For example, Mihailović translated the word *pleme* (tribe) with the English word *nation*, thus ascribing to Njegoš terminology he never used in *The Mountain Wreath*.[15] By using the term *nation* instead of *tribe*, Mihailović attempted to alter the semantics of the poem and alluded to the existence of the direct link between Njegoš's work and the issue of Serb identity. He also implied that characters from Njegoš's poem thought in national terms. In turn, such implications reaffirm a traditional reading of *The Mountain Wreath* that is conditioned by the ideological confines of the Serb national paradigm.

This poem by Njegoš is praised and criticized at the same time. Many Serbian nationalists use it as a historical justification for their attempt to keep alive their dream of Greater Serbia and as the ultimate proof of the Serb identity of Montenegrins.[16] Some Croatian nationalists recognize in Njegoš's poetry the ultimate statement of the oriental nature of South Slavs living east of the Drina River, thus reinforcing the popular notion of a stereotypical *other*.[17] Islamic radicals view *The Mountain Wreath* as a manual for ethnic cleansing and fratricidal murder, a text whose ideas were brought back to life during the most recent nationalistic *danse macabre* in the former Yugoslavia.[18] Montenegrin independentists largely shy away from any interpretation of Njegoš's poetry and only on occasion discuss its literary and linguistic merits.

In spite of the openness of this work to various interpretations (or precisely because of it), one should not forget that what one is reading is a work of literature. I am not suggesting that literature should not be approached as a source for evaluating any given historical period. On the contrary, literature is a litmus test for the deeper understanding of a particular historical period. But its exclusive usage as the primary and sole determining element in the process of historical evaluation across time is a questionable methodological approach.[19]

I would like to propose reading Njegoš's *The Mountain Wreath* as the tale of a long-gone heroic tribal society that was poeticized in order to depict the state of affairs in Njegoš's Montenegro. With this in mind, I believe that his work can be approached as an additional source for assessing the conditions within a particular time frame in Montenegrin history: Njegoš's time, the first half of the nineteenth century. The long-gone Montenegro that Njegoš wrote about had little in common with the Montenegro of his time and has nothing in common with the contemporary Montenegro. However, *The Mountain Wreath* does speak volumes about political, social, cultural, and economic conditions in Montenegro during the early nineteenth century and about Njegoš's efforts to advocate the ideas of pan-Slavism and the Illyrian movement.[20] The early 1840s in Montenegro were years of drought, hunger, and the ever-present threat of Ottoman invasion. For many Montenegrins, converting to Islam meant having access to grain and thus being able to save their extended families from starvation.

Despite the difficulty of proving that an event of such magnitude and in such a manner as described by Njegoš—*the killing of Montenegrins who had converted to Islam*—ever took place in Montenegro, the prevailing attitude is to approach Njegoš's poem as a somewhat poeticized version of a historical event of this kind. A lack of historical sources related to this issue has not prevented the misreading and misuse of Njegoš's poetry.[21] Available sources point out that Njegoš did not base his poem on a historical event.[22] However, he realized the potential significance of a reshaped myth and through poetic license actualized its meanings. The myth of the *slaying of converts* as an act of cleansing and the indication of a fresh start meshed nicely with Njegoš's efforts to turn Montenegro into a modern state.

One also comes across statements that claim intimate knowledge of the metropolitan's private thoughts and that emphasize Njegoš's personal animosity toward Islam: "By unleashing his wrath against the indigenous Slavic Muslims, Njegoš displays his personal hatred of Islam."[23] The fact that the victims in *The Mountain Wreath* are depicted as converts to Islam is not taken as a reflection upon the sociopolitical conditions in Montenegro during Njegoš's time but as an easy explanation for those who believe that a deeply embedded hatred toward Islam exists in Njegoš and in Montenegro. In Njegoš's work it is difficult to find an instance that would indicate his personal hatred toward any group of people or toward any religion. Njegoš did not hate the Turks as a nation or the religion of Islam, and he did not hate individuals in Montenegro who converted to Islam. On the contrary, he managed to find rather sophisticated ways of justifying their conversion to Islam, attributing it to the difficult historical circumstances and harsh living conditions in Montenegro.[24] Of course, one could talk about Njegoš the politician, who fought against Ottoman rule all his life, but this struggle should not be taken as a hatred for Islam. Njegoš's correspondence with neighboring Ottoman officials shows that the metropolitan displayed a surprisingly relaxed attitude toward his political and military enemies.[25]

Based on various misreadings of *The Mountain Wreath*, many scholars have tried to justify their theories about the historical continuity of Montenegrins' violence toward *others*. This "character trait" is then presented as a determining factor in Montenegrin history. The myth of the slaying of infidels in early-eighteenth-century Montenegro is a recurring theme in almost all analyses of the region's history and the mentality of its people. Its usage as the ultimate explanation for the recent historical developments in the region is apparent and particularly troubling. Apart from being a material mistake, the employment of this theme serves the purpose of further restraining Montenegro within the confines of the notions of the so-called "ancient hatred," "irrationalism," and "barbarism." What is being continuously overlooked is the crucial difference between the concept of *being violent* and that of *becoming violent*. Making this distinction might open up new interpretations of Montenegrin history. Such a change in analytical approach constitutes a new discourse that is concerned more with the aspects of the process of *becoming violent* than with a focus on violence and hatred as central features of Montenegrin character.

The contested nature of Montenegrin identities was in the political forefront from 1905 onward and constituted a stumbling block in the relations between Serbia and Montenegro. The issue of identities and loyalties gained prominence due to a number of factors, geography and politics being among the most important. The process of constructing the new geographical boundaries of Montenegro had a profound impact on how interchange took place between local populations and the state authority and on how locals adapted to these new frontiers.[26] The significant change in the country's size, which in turn was closely related to the economic state of affairs on the local level, affected the mechanisms of political and national identification (on an individual level and on the level of a group). Different groups and individuals living in Montenegro at the time had very specific regional and local interests that could not be easily reduced to a universalized "national" character or political unit, and the frontiers delineated by the European powers and by the educational and economic reforms thought to have solidified post-Ottoman identities proved confusing at best. This adaptation was particularly difficult for non-Christians and non-Slavs living in the areas bordering the Old Montenegro, some of whom were later incorporated into the Montenegrin state. Moreover, different groups within a given tribe (family, clan/*familija, bratstvo*) in Montenegro had very specific interests that did not always correspond to the interests of the tribe as a whole. These conflicting needs and aspirations on a microlevel had rendered the process of national homogenization in Montenegro even more difficult and undermined the cohesiveness of the entire undertaking. General perceptions of this process in Montenegro go along the lines of monocausal explanations of ethnic/national identity that is undergoing continuous modification, but in spite of the romanticism of national histories and the persistence of many nationalists, the process of forging a new Montenegrin identity was anything but smooth. Remnants of that old tribal loyalty can still be detected today among the citizens of Montenegro, many of whom display a significant level of attachment and loyalty to their regional, local, and tribal identities. In most cases, the first level of identification is either the region/*nahiya* (Katunjanin, Crmničanin, Lješnjanin, Bjelopavlić, Cuca, Bjelica, Vasojević, Drobnjak, Malisor, Bokelj) or the tribe whose geographic boundaries and name usually correspond with the region (*Vasojevići* tribe, *Drobnjak* tribe, etc.).[27] Only then and only in terms of a more general level of identification, which is at present heavily colored by the ideologies of the day, does one encounter national categories such as Montenegrin, Serb, Serb from Montenegro, Albanian, Muslim, or Croat.

Political conflict during the first decades of the twentieth century also contributed to the formation of national identity. A growing parliamentary opposition characterized the Montenegrin political landscape of the period. The parliament became the arena for a bitter confrontation between the representatives of the so-called people's movement and those representing the government and Prince Nikola (later King Nikola I Petrović). The main political parties were the People's Party (Narodna Stranka), better known as Klubaši (their leader was Šako Petrović), and the True People's Party (Prava Narodna Stranka), known as Pravaši (led by Lazar Mijušković). Supporters of the People's Party not only opposed the policies of Prince Nikola but passionately advocated the unification of Montenegro with Serbia. Most People's Party members regarded Montenegro as a Serbian state and Montenegrins as ethnic Serbs. Consequently, the majority of both party members and supporters identified themselves as ethnic Serbs. The opposing political group consisted of members of the True People's Party, who supported Nikola's policies and the concept of Montenegrin independence and sovereignty. However, no political group in Montenegro at the time represented a uniform entity, particularly when it came to the issue of identity. The Pravaši's demand for independence was heavily influenced by the politics of the time, and most of its members did not dispute the perceived ethnic/national sameness between Montenegrins and Serbs; they considered themselves Serbs from Montenegro. Prince Nikola was one of the principal advocates of such identity politics.[28] In addition, there were also those among the Pravaši who not only advocated Montenegrin independence but thought of themselves as distinctively Montenegrin.

From the turn of the twentieth century onward, relations between Montenegro and Serbia were conditioned by the intensity of the dynastic struggle for prestige among the South Slavs between the Montenegrin dynasty of Petrović-Njegoš and the Serbian dynasties of Obrenović and Karadjordjević. All three dynasties presented themselves as rightful heirs to the ancient crown of the medieval Serbian ruler Stefan Dušan. From as early as the 1870s, developments clearly indicate the main line of confrontation between Cetinje and Belgrade: namely, the struggle for power between these dynasties and the tendency of the Serbian dynasties (especially the Karadjordjević dynasty) to dominate the region and project Serbia as the South Slavic version of Piedmont.[29] This conflict was multifaceted and incorporated the struggle over various contested territories, issues of dynastic prestige, different nationalist visions of the future of the region, and the efforts of elites to exercise absolute control over the political life in the Balkans.[30] Identity politics in Montenegro played a significant role in this process, which began in earnest in the early decades of the twentieth century and has continued with varying intensity and in many forms until the present day.

Bearing in mind the distinct character of Montenegro's traditional culture and the specificities of its historical, political, and economic, as well as cultural development, one is intrigued by the persistent appropriation of Montenegrins by the Serbs and wonders about the reasons for this claim to ownership. New interpretations of these issues, which came to light in recent scholarly literature in Montenegro and supported the claim of Montenegrin cultural, linguistic, and national distinctiveness, indicate the primacy of politics as a discourse in decoding the history of the region and in assessing the nature of relations between Montenegrins and Serbs.[31] The inclusion of Montenegrins in the Serbian national mythos can be identified as a way to establish and preserve the imagined historical/temporal and cultural continuity of the Serbian nation throughout the centuries of Ottoman rule in the region.

For some four hundred years, Serbia proper was ruled by the Ottoman Empire. All aspects of life in the region were subject to regulations and laws imposed by the invader. During the same period, Montenegro existed as a relatively independent polity that displayed a temporal continuity of its own political and historical being. With the advent of the ideology of national homogenization, Serbia sought to establish historical and cultural continuity in the area that was, within the national paradigm, perceived as an integral part of the Serbian medieval state. One way to accomplish this was to appropriate Montenegro. This appropriation happened on many levels and included the positioning of Montenegrins within the Serbian mythos as a symbol of the undying spirit of Serbdom. Only then was the Serbian historical narrative able to bridge the gap of some four centuries of Ottoman rule and establish the temporal continuity needed for the process of national awakening. With this in mind, the Podgorica Assembly not only represented the final stage in the process of annexation of Montenegro by Serbia but also was a highly symbolic act that confirmed the temporal continuity of the Serb presence in the region.

The Writings on the Podgorica Assembly: The Magic Circle of Historiography

The writings in Serbo-Croat on the Podgorica Assembly and the annexation process can be broadly categorized as propaganda, polemics, and memoirs. Of course, there are a number of authors whose work cannot be easily categorized. Only a few decades after the annexation (1940–1950) and onward) one could see the attempts to introduce and employ a proper methodology of research in scholarly works by historians in Serbia and Montenegro. Those writings, however, carried a strong stamp of ideological bias, and impartiality and scientific objectivity were often subordinated to the political dictates of the day. Only very recently have some Serbian and Montenegrin historians indicated a willingness to approach this issue with less ideological baggage.

Among the first to publish an account of the Podgorica Assembly was one of its organizers and a member of the Yugoslav delegation at the Paris Peace Conference,

Janko Spasojević. In 1919, while in Paris for the conference, Spasojević published a brief account of the events of November 1918 titled *Crna Gora i Srbija* (Montenegro and Serbia). The publisher was the Paris branch of the Public Relations Office of the Serbian Ministry of Foreign Affairs. The book was intended for foreign public opinion and policy makers because at that time the new borders of Europe were being determined. Spasojević's writing falls into the category of prounionist propaganda. He interpreted the resolution of the Podgorica Assembly as the expression of the free will of Montenegrins, though he did not present any documents in support of this thesis. Instead, he insistently relied upon the romantic notion of South Slav unity and presented several points that were later used by all those writing in support of unification. First, according to Spasojević, King Nikola I Petrović should be blamed for the capitulation in 1915. Second, Spasojević stressed that the unification with Serbia was something "every Serb in Montenegro was praying for" and that the slogan "unification or death is on the lips of every Serb in Montenegro." Spasojević pointed to the Montenegrin dynasty as the only opponent to this idea and defended the legality of the decisions made in Podgorica in 1918 by referring to the Montenegrin Constitution as reactionary legislation. Without providing any viable source to substantiate his claims, Spasojević maintained that the annexation was the expression of the will of the Montenegrin people. With this in mind, he concluded that the Christmas Uprising of 1919 was a minor side effect, not a popular armed uprising in opposition to the Podgorica Assembly and the annexation of Montenegro.[32]

A similar political point of view can be ascribed to Jovan Ćetković's 1922 account *Omladinski Pokret u Crnoj Gori* (Youth Movement in Montenegro) . Ćetković was an active member of the so-called Youth Brigades, the paramilitary units organized by the Serbian police to fight the rebels in Montenegro. In his work Ćetković repeated the arguments already presented by Spasojević, reinforcing them by quoting various army reports and memoranda. He also employed a new approach to the issue: while emphasizing the importance of South Slav unity, Ćetković for the first time addressed the issue of the future country, stating that "until recently our centuries-old dream was the unification of Serbdom and a free Serb state," and "for the youth the higher ideal is the unification of all South Slavs in one free and democratic state. The youth will not go against nature and common sense and try to make three nations out of one."[33] This statement exemplifies the attitude of unification supporters toward others in the region. What Ćetković implied when talking about "three nations" was the conviction that the Croats, Slovenes, and Serbs were one and the same nation. The Montenegrins were not even mentioned because it was assumed that they were, without a doubt, Serbs. Ćetković's writing can be seen as an early indication of the manipulation and misuse of the idea of Yugoslavia in order to exercise Serbian influence in the region. Ćetković advocated the notion that the future state would be, in essence, a gift from the Serbs to others in the region, thus indicating the desire to see Yugoslavia as Serbia's zone of influence. During the late 1920s and 1930s, such views contributed greatly to Croats' and Slovenes' gradually distancing themselves from the central authorities in Belgrade.

Two years after Ćetković's work appeared in print, another book on the subject was published in Belgrade. The author of *Crna Gora* (Montenegro) was Novica Šaulić, one of the most influential members of the powerful Farmers' Union of Montenegro. This Union was at the time considered to be among the most radical pro-Serbian political organizations in Montenegro. Šaulić lavishes praise on the Podgorica Assembly, referring to it as "a magnificent act," indeed, "so magnificent that it appealed even to those who were earlier acting against the unification."[34] According to Šaulić, the opponents of the unconditional unification were "naïve" and were "deceived by the Italian propaganda and the empty promises by the King Nikola Petrović."[35] This book did not present any new evidence in support of the author's praise of unification; rather, Šaulić's arguments remained within the framework of the romanticized past and the need for South Slav unity.

These three books fall into the category of propaganda advocating the unionist agenda. Even though the authors were active participants in the events they described, they offered few documents to substantiate their claims. All three authors shared the common characteristics of enthusiasm, rhetoric, ideological bias, and inflexibility toward anyone opposed to their policies. They were adamant in their defense of the necessity of unification as the natural outcome of the centuries-old struggle of all South Slavs. These works are primary sources that say much about the character of political life, the attitude toward one's opponent, and the validity of scholarly works of the period in the Kingdom of Serbs, Croats, and Slovenes.

In 1924, Pantelija Jovović, a Belgrade journalist, published *Crnogorski Političari* (Montenegrin Politicians), in which he disputed the official stand toward the events of 1918 in Montenegro. This book was the product of the author's earlier journalistic work. From 1921 onward, Jovović wrote a number of articles about Montenegro for the magazine *Balkan* in which he was critical of the Serbian policy in Montenegro. He disputed the crucial claim of the unionists by arguing that the unification of Montenegro with Serbia was, in essence, forced upon Montenegrins. Before the appearance of *Crnogorski Političari*, the events taking place in Montenegro and the armed uprising against the annexation were not public knowledge in other parts of the Kingdom of Serbs, Croats, and Slovenes. The author placed the blame for the 1919 Christmas Uprising on the unionists and their heavy-handedness in dealing with their political opponents. He also categorically denied the claim that the Montenegrin king had orchestrated the uprising.[36] Jovović's methods deserve credit, despite the journalistic style of his writing. Beside relying on official army reports and documents provided by the civilian authorities in Cetinje, Belgrade, and Podgorica, he conducted a number of interviews with the eyewitnesses of particular events in

Montenegro. Whenever possible, he tried to verify the information by comparing the stories he heard, used sources from both sides of the conflict, and relied heavily on his personal observations.

The end of the 1920s saw the emergence of new books on the subject of annexation, all of which shared a common approach to the Montenegrin Question. That authors who wrote about this issue after 1925 referred to it as the Montenegrin Question might be seen as an indicator of their awareness of the gravity of the problem, as well as of the questionable character and form of the process of unification itself. Such awareness brought a change of attitude toward the issue in terms of methodology, as well as in terms of how many historians entered the debate. Throughout the 1930s and 1940s, with the exception of the work of a few politicians, the majority of books written on the subject were of a scholarly nature. The issue of the unification of Montenegro with Serbia in 1918 and the Podgorica Assembly became the main topic of historical writing in Serbia and Montenegro during this period. The methodology and the treatment of sources became more scholarly, and the arguments became less heated and exclusionist. This is not to say that the debate entered a less emotional phase or that ideology played a less significant role.

The tenth anniversary of the Podgorica Assembly was marked by the appearance of a number of books devoted to the Montenegrin Question. In 1928, Savić Marković Štedimlija published *Gorštačka Krv, Crna Gora 1918–1928* (Highlanders' Blood, Montenegro 1918–1928), an attempt to analyze the political, ideological, and economic reasons behind the unrest in Montenegro and a call for proper political assessment of those events. He strongly opposed the unionist views that were adopted as the official stand in the newly formed kingdom—that is, that the former Montenegrin King Nikola I Petrović was a traitor and the mastermind behind the Christmas Uprising. Štedimlija claimed that the king and his government in exile did not know about the plans for the uprising. To prove his claims, he quoted a letter written by King Nikola to his people at the request of U.S. President Woodrow Wilson on January 22, 1919, during the Paris Peace Conference after the delegates were informed about the events in Montenegro. The letter urged Montenegrins to wait peacefully "for the resolution of Montenegro's future."[37] According to Štedimlija, the letter reached Montenegro too late because the "fighting, burning of homes, looting, killings, and other crimes already became the daily routine for many army units that were showing their might in Montenegro."[38] Although he could only address circumstantial evidence in his book, Štedimlija strongly advocated a conspiracy theory, stating that the unfortunate destiny of the Petrović dynasty, the capitulation of Montenegro in late 1915, and the subsequent departure of the royal family were all parts of a master plan developed in Belgrade. All of it, according to Markovic, led to the final act of the annexation of Montenegro by Serbia.

The importance of *Gorštačka Krv* in the ongoing debate lies in the fact that its author was the first to address the issue of Montenegro's economic sustainability and independence from Serbia. He devoted a number of pages to the economic structure of Montenegro and the potential of its economy, emphasizing export to Italy as the primary source of income for the state. Even though Štedimlija did not offer any viable data to support his claims, he did publicly challenge a crucial unionist tenet: Montenegro's economic instability, insufficiency, and total dependence on Serbia. He also stressed the international aspect of the Montenegrin Question, an issue that had been carefully avoided by earlier writers. According to Štedimlija, the international community had betrayed earlier promises to King Nikola. Štedimlija described how Great Britain maintained its position that, in light of the creation of a new South Slav state, an independent and sovereign Montenegro would be an anachronism.[39] He also bitterly complained about the Great Powers and their treatment of the Montenegrin Question as part of a larger issue of the South Adriatic. As an active participant in this process, Štedimlija maintained that French, British, American, and Italian forces stationed in Montenegro from 1918 onward had a mandate to establish and preserve the rule of law on behalf of King Nikola I Petrović. He interpreted the unexpected pullout of the Allied forces and the complete takeover of Montenegro by the Serbian army as a betrayal of the international forces' original mandate. He went even further, claiming that the Allied commanders in Montenegro acted solely in the interest of Belgrade and supported the unionist agenda. To strengthen his argument, Štedimlija discussed the case of one French General Venell, who was the commander in chief of the Allied Forces stationed in Montenegro. Venell had been relieved of his duties after the Montenegrin government in exile and the king himself complained about the Allied Forces' political actions on the ground and their interference in the conflict on the side of the government in Belgrade. Štedimlija, who saw this incident as the final proof of the Allies' guilt, viewed the Podgorica Assembly as an illegal gathering whose organizers were two Serbian agents—Svetozar Tomić and Petar Kosović, both of whom were members of the Montenegrin Committee for Unification.[40] Štedimlija did not present any proof of his claims, but the available documents clearly point out that Tomić and Kosović were indeed sent to Montenegro by the Serbian authorities to advocate the unionist cause and make arrangements for the upcoming assembly session. Štedimlija also addressed the legal aspects of the assembly: with respect to the Montenegrin Constitution of 1905, he claimed that the meeting in Podgorica was organized contrary to the Montenegrin Constitution and with disregard for the Montenegrin parliament.[41]

The advocates of the unionist approach reacted almost immediately. In 1929, Svetozar Tomić published *Desetogodišnjica Ujedinjenja Srbije i Crne Gore* (The Tenth Anniversary of the Unification of Serbia and Montenegro). This book fits into two of the categories mentioned earlier—propaganda and memoir. The author did not present any new documents but, rather, stayed within the framework of a romanticized unionist agenda. His central thesis can be summed up in the statement that the

Montenegrins were, and always had been, an integral part of the unified Serb nation, thus dismissing all claims of Greens about the distinct ethnic and cultural identity of the Montenegrins. Tomić triumphally stated that in his view, the Montenegrins were grateful to the Serbian army for liberating them and preserving the peace and that the entire population wholeheartedly supported the idea of union with Serbia. Writing about the assembly sessions in Podgorica, Tomić admits that the delegates were chosen according to newly established rules that were not in accordance with the Montenegrin Constitution. Notably he goes on to explain that those rules did not correspond to the Serbian laws of the time because the circumstances were exceptional and the new rules had to differ from the existing legislation in Serbia and Montenegro. By projecting this image of impartiality, Tomić tried to justify and rationalize his view of the election process as free and democratic. The logical implication of his argument is that the Proclamation of the Podgorica Assembly was the expression of the free will of the people and that unification, being outside of the legal framework of both Serbia and Montenegro, was in essence a revolutionary act. Even though Tomić did not specifically ascribe a revolutionary quality to the proclamation, his comments about the armed uprising in 1919 clearly point in that direction: "the supporters of King Nikola and independent Montenegro, assisted by foreign agents, organized a counter-revolution in order to reverse the decisions made by the Great People's Assembly."[42]

Immediately following the publication of Tomić's book, a debate opened on the pages of the Belgrade journal *Zapisi*. The debate was initiated by the editors themselves, who invited submissions on the topic "Crna Gora za Ujedinjenje" (Montenegro for Unification). The first to publish an article was Jovan M. Jovanović, the leader of the Farmers' Union in Serbia, the former Serbian foreign minister, and later the ambassador to Vienna and London. *Zapisi* published excerpts from Jovanović's book *Stvaranje Zajedničke Države Srba, Hrvata i Slovenaca* (The Creation of the Unified State of Serbs, Croats, and Slovenes), in which the author concentrated on purely political issues, including an analysis of the reasons for Montenegro's involvement in World War I. Jovanović claimed that King Nikola was pressured by Montenegrins to become involved in the war because his subjects felt a strong attachment to the Serbian cause and a moral obligation to act together with Serbia and Russia. He also regarded King Nikola as an absolutist who would act only on his own behalf and for his own benefit. Jovanović was frank in pointing out the division in Montenegro between those for and those against unification. He stated that King Nikola, as well as many Montenegrins, was in favor of the union with Serbia, even if it were to take the form of a republic. What Nikola fought against was the rule of the Serbian Karadjordjević dynasty. According to Jovanović, the king favored a union based on equality and mutual respect.

A reaction to Jovanović's article came quickly in an article by Savo Vuletić, a former minister in Nikola's government. Vuletić introduced a new set of questions and attempted to present an impartial approach. Writing about Greens and Whites, Vuletić reminded readers that the division was less about the need to unite and more about the manner in which unification would take place. He appeared confident that everyone in Montenegro would embrace the idea of union with Serbia if it were pursued through the legal apparatus of the Montenegrin state. This, of course, implied the need for the serious consideration of Montenegrin sovereignty and its status in the future unified state. Discussing the issue of Montenegrin capitulation in late December 1915, Vuletić reminded his opponents in the debate that the initiative for this came from the Serbian colonel and, at the time, the chief of staff of the Montenegrin army, Petar Pešić. He quoted Pešić's article in *Pravda* of May 9, 1925:

> I made a suggestion to surrender, being aware of the future implications of such a move. The result of their acceptance of my proposal was that the Montenegrin Army did not fight alongside the Serbian Army at the Thessalonica front. Moreover, King Nikola did not come back to the country together with King Petar [i.e., Serbian King Petar Karadjordjević].[43]

All of the books and articles on the process of annexation/unification that were published up until 1930 shared a common denominator: they all represented and advocated one of the two previously mentioned versions of the Montenegrin future—independence and sovereignty on the one side or union with Serbia for the sake of creating a larger South Slavic state on the other. Despite the attempts by many authors of this period to step out of that magic circle of ideology into the realm of scientific objectivity, their works continued to mark the outer edges of these two political solitudes.

Out of the entire body of literature devoted to the Montenegrin Question and published between World Wars I and II, the work cited most often is *Ujedinitelji Crne Gore i Srbije* (The Unifiers of Montenegro and Serbia) by Jovan Ćetković. It is important to note that this book came out in 1940, one year after the administrative restructuring of the earlier division of the Kingdom of Yugoslavia into *Banovinas* (districts), after the establishment of the District of Croatia (Banovina Hrvatska), and during the hiatus in the decentralization of the Kingdom of Yugoslavia. According to the 1939 Agreement between the prime minister of the Royal Government of Yugoslavia, Dragisa Svetkovic, and the leader of the Croatian Peasant party, Vladko macek, the District of Croatia (Banovina Hrvatska) was established with Zagreb as its capital. The new Banovina Hrvatska included the territories of the earlier Savska and Primorska Banovinas, as well as the following districts: Dubrovnik, Šid, Ilok, Brčko, Gradačac, Derventa, Travnik, and Fojnica. The creation of the Banovina Hrvatska was the first step in what was expected to be the final partition of the Kingdom of Yugoslavia into Croatia and Serbia. The Banovina Srpska (District of Serbia) was soon to be established. According to the draft resolution, the Banovina Srpska

(Srpske Zemlje) would have included the territories of the former Vrbaska, Drinska, Zetska, Dunavska, Moravska, and Vardarska Banovinas, with Skopje as its capital.[44]

Ćetković's book was, at the time, the most detailed account of the events surrounding and following the assembly sessions in Podgorica. It is interesting because of the author's sources; he presented numerous new original documents and also relied on primary sources from both sides of the political and ideological trenches. The main thesis is that the unification represented the popular sentiments of Montenegrins and was the natural outcome of a centuries-old desire of all South Slavs. Ćetković stated that "the idea of the unification of our people is as old as the people itself."[45] Ćetković's view was based on the notion of shared ethnic and religious identity between the Montenegrins and the Serbs, an assumption he never questioned. He stayed within the prounionist political framework, dismissing the notion of Croats and Serbs being two different peoples and saying that "all those new theories about two people are the product of naïve speculations or the lack of understanding of the term *nation*."[46] While writing about the opponents of the union, Ćetković's language stayed within the realm of propaganda ("foreign agents and mercenaries"; "servants"), and King Nikola Petrović was portrayed as a "traitor" and "the traitor of the Serb cause."[47] Ćetković's general view of the conflict between the Whites and the Greens is particularly interesting. He saw this conflict as a revolutionary struggle, but he was unclear as to which was the revolutionary group. He referred to the delegates of the Podgorica Assembly as "the members of the revolutionary government,"[48] whereas somewhat earlier he had written about the "revolutionary activities" in Montenegro under the guidance of King Nikola and with the support of Italy.[49]

Another book that was and still is cited by a number of Montenegrin and Serbian historians is *Crna Gora u Jugoslovenskoj Federaciji* (Montenegro in the Yugoslav Federation) by Živojin Perić. Perić was born in 1868 in the village of Stubline, near the town of Obrenovac, in Serbia. He completed his high-school education in Valjevo and Belgrade and in 1891 earned his university degree at the Faculty of Law in Paris. In 1898 he became a professor at the Belgrade University, where he taught at the Law Faculty until his retirement in 1938. He published numerous books and several hundred scholarly articles in Serbo-Croat, English, and French.

Perić was the first Serbian scholar to address this issue from a legal point of view. His book was an analysis of the political and legal system in Yugoslavia, and he devoted a number of chapters to the constitutional and legal aspects of the unification process. He pointed out that Montenegro had entered the union solely because of the economic and military pressure exerted by Belgrade and because of the international community's lack of support for its independence. Perić stated that this new state was established by force and that the resolution of the Podgorica Assembly was not legally valid and thus was irrelevant. Despite the military achievements of the Montenegrin army during the first two years of World War I and its being a member of the victorious coalition, Montenegro ended up being absorbed by Serbia. Perić described the outcome as "the victory that ended in the disappearance of the victor."[50] He stressed that, even after the formal unification of Montenegro and Serbia, all the state affairs in Montenegro were conducted in accordance with its 1905 Constitution, and he concluded that the resolution of the Podgorica Assembly was in flagrant violation of that Constitution because Montenegro existed in 1918 as an internationally recognized independent and sovereign state. His argument was strengthened by the fact that none of the Great Powers ever formally recognized the resolution of the Podgorica Assembly.

After 1945, Yugoslav historiography continued to concern itself with the issues and events of 1918. The Podgorica Assembly and its resolution were still important but were approached from an entirely different, now Marxist, perspective. Characteristic of this Marxist historiography was the need to emphasize the social component in the events, the influence of Bolshevik ideas on the masses in Montenegro and Serbia, and the role of the Yugoslav Communist Party in finally solving the national question among the South Slavs. The focus was on the importance of the Yugoslav federation as an optimal modus vivendi in that area of the Balkan Peninsula. The Communists claimed their political program rested on the idea of South Slav unity and announced, *urbi et orbi*, that only under their protective ideological and political umbrella could the country finally unite on a solid foundation.

During the 1960s and the early 1970s Yugoslav historians considered the question of Whites and Greens in Montenegro as a conflict between the two reactionary extremes of a political spectrum during World War II. It would seem that from 1941 until 1943 the Greens sided with Italy in the hope that the postwar settlement might result in the renewal of an independent and sovereign Montenegro.[51] In the name of "scientific objectivity," historians in communist Yugoslavia started to build a curious "symmetry" between the two opposites and equally criticized both sides in the conflict. Occasional modification of this discourse, which was typical of historians of the late 1970s, in essence meant a shift in ideology and siding with one of the extremes. This shift indicated the relatively mature phase of the ideological compromise between Communists and nationalists in the former Socialist Federal Republic of Yugoslavia.[52] Vigorous advocacy of the validity of the political credo of either Greens or Whites varied according to the intensity and the nature of the Yugoslav crisis and de facto indicated the preparation for yet another reshaping of Yugoslavia, which occurred in the last decade of the twentieth century. This new historiography claimed to follow and employ the rules of critical examination and evaluation of sources. In this respect, the important work that should be mentioned is that of Dimitrije Dimo Vujović, a greatly respected Montenegrin historian of the period who devoted his life to researching the Montenegrin Question. His most impressive work on this subject is *Ujedinjenje Crne Gore i Srbije* (The Unification of

Montenegro and Serbia), published in 1962. This book is to date the most comprehensive account of events from the period. Even though his analysis was based on the premises of Marxist historiography, his methodology, treatment of sources, and the variety of those sources deserve attention. Vujović was among the first, if not the very first, historian in Yugoslavia to meticulously collect original documents and consult a variety of sources. He was critical of his predecessors' works, their methodological approaches, their lack of flexibility, and their ideological baggage. He was particularly critical of their tendency to simplify matters. In contrast, Vujović pointed out the enormous complexity of the issues.

According to Vujović, unification was an act of historical necessity, and that being the case, its form did not necessarily have to be acceptable to all parties involved. He clearly recognized Montenegro's incorporation into Serbia and not into Yugoslavia. Vujović, however, stressed that the 1918 unification was shaped and carried out by the Serbian bourgeoisie.[53] This distinction made it possible for him to criticize the form and the actions that led to the unification without casting any doubts on the validity of the idea of unification itself. He took a middle ground by criticizing the political attitude of the Serbian elite, whose ideas and activities acquired a radical form in Montenegro in 1918. He was no less sympathetic to King Nikola and to his apparent lack of political pragmatism and flexibility. According to Vujović, both sides in this conflict, each in its own way and for its own reasons, were slowing down and jeopardizing the process of unification. Vujović did not devote much attention to the legal aspects of the debate, and the reasons for this evasion could perhaps be found in the ideological framework within which he was operating. Being a Marxist historian, Vujović saw the legal issue of the Podgorica Assembly as a stage in the evolution of an idea and not as a revolutionary act. He was clearly advocating his party as the only political body able to unite the South Slavs within the legally acceptable framework. In his later writings throughout the 1980s, Vujović moderated his position with regard to the legality of the Podgorica Assembly. His point of departure was the notion that the concept of legitimacy rests with the people and their will to modify and/or change the state structure. He proceeded to argue that the decision of the Podgorica Assembly represented the desire of the majority of Montenegrins at the time, thus rendering it legitimate and legal. Vujović decided neither to engage in elaborating further on the concept of the "will of the people" nor to address the mechanism of a plebiscite as one of its main features. A similar metamorphosis occurred with regard to his assessment of the ideology of the Whites and the Greens. In spite of his criticism of their methods, Vujović portrayed the Whites as progressive because they advocated unification with Serbia and other Yugoslav lands, whereas the Greens were reactionary because they opposed such unification. To put it differently, the conflict between the two groups was, according to Vujović, the conflict between advocates of Greater Serbian nationalism and those harboring separatist tendencies. Such qualifications were aimed at reinforcing the dominant discourse about the Yugoslav Communist Party's decisive role in solving the country's national question.

The issue of the unification/annexation of Montenegro in 1918 and the political and ideological echoes thereof have been addressed by many nonhistorians in Yugoslavia during the last decades of the twentieth century. Economists, politicians, poets, and amateur historians have written on the subject. The debate about the Montenegrin Question has reached a new level in recent years. After the dissolution of the Socialist Federal Republic of Yugoslavia (SFRY), this topic was revived in different geopolitical and ideological circumstances and became a contested issue not only within the scholarly communities in Montenegro and Serbia but also among the general public. In a sense, history entered everyday life, but this time with even more tragic consequences. The ever-present division between Greens and Whites in Montenegro incites the revival of old tribal loyalties and introduces the curious phenomenon of neopatriarchy, proving again that the people of Montenegro are still struggling with both the question of an appropriate state formation and the question of identity.[54]

Notes

1. "The Paris Peace Conference, contrary to what many people have believed since, did not create Yugoslavia—it had already created itself by the time the first diplomats arrived in Paris." Margaret Macmillan, *Paris 1919: Six Months That Changed the World* (London: Random House, 2001), p. 110. Without disputing the fact that the Kingdom of Serbs, Croats, and Slovenes was indeed officiated in Belgrade before the Paris Peace Conference started, and without questioning the will of many South Slavs to unite in one state, I would contest Macmillan's view. First, it unjustly marginalizes the role of the Great Powers in the process of creating the first South Slav state. In fact, if it had not been for the outside pressure exerted by R.W. Seton-Watson and his colleagues in mediating between the Serbian government and the representatives of the Yugoslav Committee for Unification (based in London), we might have seen more than one South Slav state appearing on the map. Sources related to such mediation clearly show significant differences between the two sides. Moreover, Macmillan's statement fails to recognize the existence of many unresolved issues among the South Slavs and reflects the deeply embedded generalization that all South Slavs supported the manner in which the new state was created. The troubled history of the Kingdom of Yugoslavia provides ample evidence of contesting visions of the common state.
2. Ivo Banac, *The National Question in Yugoslavia: Origins, History, Politics* (Ithaca, N.Y.: Cornell University Press, 1984), p. 138.
3. See Barbara Jelavich, *History of the Balkans: Twentieth Century*, vol. 2 (New York: Cambridge University Press, 1983); R.W. Seton-Watson, *The Rise of Nationality in the Balkans* (London: Constable, 1917); L.S. Stavrianos, *The Balkans, 1815–1914* (New York: Holt, Rinehart & Winston, 1963); Stephen Clissold, ed., *A History of Yugoslavia from Early Times to 1966* (Cambridge: Cambridge University Press, 1966); H.W.V. Temperley, *History of Serbia* (New York: Fertig, 1969); Dimitrije Djordjević and Stephen Fischer-Galati, eds., *The Creation of Yugoslavia, 1914–1918* (Santa Barbara, Calif.: Clio Books, 1980); Ivo Lederer, *Yugoslavia at the Paris Peace Conference: A Study in Frontier Making* (New Haven, Conn.: Yale University Press, 1963).

4. "From the tenth to the twentieth century, the Zeta area preserves a nucleus of Serbian culture and nationalism at a time when Serbia was overrun by Bulgars or Ottomans." Christopher Boehm, *Montenegrin Social Organization and Values: Political Ethnography of a Refugee Area Tribal Adaptation* (New York: AMS Press, 1983), p. 9. Barbara Jelavich wrote about Montenegro as "the second Serbian state." *History of the Balkans*, vol. 2, p. 247.
5. Adrian Hastings, *The Construction of Nationhood: Ethnicity, Religion, and Nationalism* (Cambridge: Cambridge University Press, 1997), p. 142. Also see Jozo Tomašević, *Peasants, Politics, and Economic Change in Yugoslavia* (Palo Alto: Stanford University Press, 1955), p. 126n.
6. Joseph S. Roucek, *Balkan Politics: International Relations in No Man's Land* (Westport, Conn.: Greenwood, 1948), p. 3.
7. "Montenegro was divided into two parts: Montenegro and Brda. The first was Old Montenegro with some additions on the Herzegovinian side; the second, the mountain mass that borders on Albania." Mary Edith Durham, *Some Tribal Origins, Laws, and Customs of the Balkans* (London: George Allen & Unwin, 1928), p. 34.
8. Nahija was the smallest administrative unit in the Ottoman state. Katunska Nahija was the core of Old Montenegro.
9. Svetlana Boym views social poetics as the basis for cultural identity and as "cultural intimacy that provides a glue in everyday life. . . . Such identity involves everyday games of hide-and-seek that only 'natives' play, unwritten rules of behavior, jokes understood from half a word, a sense of complicity. State propaganda and official national memory build on this cultural intimacy, but there is also a discrepancy and tension between the two." Svetlana Boym, *The Future of Nostalgia* (New York: Basic Books, 2001), pp. 42–43. Also see Michael Herzfeld, *Cultural Intimacy: Social Poetics in the Nation State* (New York: Routledge, 1997), pp. 13–14.
10. See Špiro Kulišić, "O Etnogenezi Crnogoraca" (Titograd: NIO Pobjeda, 1980).
11. This expression is borrowed from the title of Slavoj Žižek's guest lecture "Yugoslavia: The Burden of Being the stuff OTHERS' Dreams Are Made Of," at the Conference on Construction, Deconstruction, Reconstruction of South Slavic Architecture, Hollis Auditorium, Cornell University, New York (March 27, 2001).
12. On Njegoš and the appropriation of his work, see Milan Bogdanović, "Vratimo Njegoša Literaturi," *Srpski Književni Glasnik* 2, no. 16.7 (1925), pp. 577–579. Also see Jaša M. Prodanović, "Gorski Vijenac kao Vaspitno Delo," *Srpski Književni Glasnik* 2, no. 16.7 (1925), pp. 558–562; Nikola Škerović, "Njegoš i Jugoslovenstvo," *Nova Evropa* 2.1 (1925), pp. 1–8; Ljubomir Durković-Jakšić, *Njegoš i Lovćen* (Beograd, 1971); Savić Marković Štedimlija, "Sto Godina Narodne Poezije," *Nova Evropa* 28, nos. 4–5 (1935), pp. 120–129; Srdja Pavlović, "Poetry or the Blueprint for Genocide," *Spaces of Identity OnLine* 1, no. 1 (January 2001), available at: http://www.spacesofidentity.net.
13. P.P. Njegoš, *The Mountain Wreath*, trans. Vasa D. Mihailović, translator's introduction (Belgrade: Serbian Europe Publishing, 1997), pp. 5-6.
14. P.P. Njegoš, *The Mountain Wreath* (Vienna, 1847), title page. Also see Njegoš, *Ogledalo Srpsko* (1845).
15. Njegoš *The Mountain Wreath*, trans. Mihailović, p. 38, verses 652–656.
16. "It epitomizes the spirit of the Serbian people kept alive for centuries; indeed, there is no other literary work with which the Serbs identify more." Mihailović, translator's introduction to Njegoš, *The Mountain Wreath*, p. 38. Also see Ivo Banac, *National Question*, p. 272.
17. Branimir Anžulović, *Heavenly Serbia: From Myth to Genocide* (New York: New York University Press, 1999), pp. 61–67.

18. B. Anžulović, ibid., pp. 61–76, and also Ivo Žanić, *Prevarena Povijest: Guslarska Estrada, Kult Hajduka i Rat u Hrvatskoj i Bosni i Hercegovini, 1990–1995. Godine* (Zagreb: Duriex, 1998), pp. 271–303.
19. Božena Jelušić, "Otvoreni za Njegoša," *Matica* 2, no. 6 (Summer 2001), pp. 97–106.
20. See Njegoš's letter written May 2, 1848, to the Serbian minister of the interior, Ilija Garašanin, the author of *Načertanije*. P.P. Njegoš, *Izabrana Pisma* (Beograd: Prosveta, 1967), p. 166. Also see Njegoš to Josip Jelačić, Cetinje, December 20, 1848, in Njegoš, ibid., pp. 173–174.
21. "*The Mountain Wreath* represents a synthesis in another sense as well. It is based on historical facts, thus it can be called a historical play." Mihailović, introduction to Njegoš, *The Mountain Wreath*, p. 38. Also see Ivo Banac, *National Question*, p. 272.
22. A comprehensive analysis of the alleged killing of converts is provided in the monograph by Vojislav P. Nikčević, *Istraga Poturica u Njegoševom Gorskom Vijencu* (Cetinje, 1990). Also see Vojislav P. Nikčević, "Istrage Poturica Nije ni Bilo," *Ovdje*, no. 189 (Titograd, 1985), pp. 8–10.
23. Alexander Greenawalt, "Kosovo Myth: Karadžić, Njegoš, and the Transformation of Serb Identity," in *spacesofidentity.net* 1, iss. 3, October 2001. Available at http://www.spacesofidentity.net.
24. "It may not be the turncoat's fault as much / the infidel enticed them with falsehood, / and entangled them in the devil's net. / But what is man? In truth, a weak creature!" Njegoš, *The Mountain Wreath*, trans. Mihailović, p. 42, verses 760–763.
25. "Huseinu-Begu Gradaščeviću," Cetinje, February 4, 1832. In Petar Petrović Njegoš, *Izabrana Pisma* (Beograd: Prosveta, 1967), p. 33; also see "Mehmed-Spahiji Lekiću," ibid., p. 79, and "Osman-Paši Skopljaku," ibid., p. 133.
26. During the reign of Prince (later king) Nikola I Petrović, Montenegro quadrupled its territory. As Ivo Banac points out, after the Balkan wars and for the first time, "Montenegrins ruled not only over a large body of hostile Muslims, many of them Albanians, but also over highland tribes with a tradition of strong ties to Serbia." Banac, *The National Question*, p. 275.
27. *Katunjanin* is a person from *Katunska* Nahija.
28. Ivo Banac pointed out: "The tradition of Montenegrin self-centeredness did not, however, prevent reciprocity with the Serbians, though on the basis of a veritable worship of Montenegro. On the contrary, the Serb tradition percolated down to the consciousness of most ordinary herdsmen by a system of mnemonic devices by which the church continually admonished the Montenegrins to remember the glories of the Nemanjić state. Time and again, Montenegrin rulers took the lead in attempting to restore the medieval Serbian empire." *The National Question*, p. 247.
29. "The comparison between Serbia and Piedmont regularly pressed in these years was fundamentally flawed because Piedmont was far too provincial a part of Italy to dominate and alienate the rest of a once united country. Serbia, on the other hand, was a country already gripped by an obsessive nationalism, basically of a Germanic sort, bent on the 'ethnic cleansing' of a 'Greater Serbia' long before the 1990s. Ethnic cleansing had been written into Serb nationalism from the early nineteenth century." Hastings, *The Construction of Nationhood*, p. 143. Domination over the unwanted "other" and the eventual "cleansing" of desired territory are common features in every case of expansionist nationalism throughout the world, and the case of Serbia should be seen as the rule rather than an exception. Even though my own views on this matter differ considerably from those of Hastings, I believe that his assessment of the nature of Serbian nationalism carries certain validity. Also see

Mirko Grmek, Marc Gjidana, and Neven Šimac, *Le Nettoyage Ethnique: Documents Historiques sur une Ideologie Serbe* (Paris: Fayard, 1993). In spite of its one-sided approach to the issue of nationalism in Yugoslavia, this volume provides essential documentation covering both the nineteenth and the twentieth centuries.

30. "Serbia wants to liberate and unite the Yugoslavs and does not want to drown in the sea of some kind of Yugoslavia. Serbia does not want to drown in Yugoslavia, but to have Yugoslavia drown in her." Letter from Serbian prime minister Nikola Pašić to Jovan M. Jovanović-Pižon in London, October15, 1918, in Dragovan Šepić, *Italija, Saveznici i Jugoslavensko Pitanje, 1914–1918* (Zagreb: Skolska Knjiga, 1970), p. 358. Also see Djordje Dj. Stanković, *Nikola Pašić i Jugoslovensko Pitanje*, vols. 1–2 (Beograd: BIGZ, 1985), and Charles Jelavich, "Nikola Pašić: Greater Serbia or Yugoslavia?" *Journal of Central European Affairs* 11 (July 1951), pp. 14–28.
31. See Senka Babović, "Kulturna Politika u Zetskoj Banovini" (Ph.D. diss., University of Montenegro, 1997). Also see Vojislav Nikčević, *O Postanku Etnonima Dukljani, Zećani, Crnogorci* (Podgorica, 1987); V. Nikčević, *Crnogorski Jezik* (Cetinje, 1993); and V. Nikčević, *Pravopis Crnogorskog Jezika* (Podgorica: Montenegrin PEN Center, 1997); as well as Dragoje Živković, *Istorija Crnogorskog Naroda* (Cetinje, 1989), and Šerbo Rastoder, *Skrivana Strana Istorije: Crnogorska Buna i Odmetnički Pokret, 1918–1929. Dokumenti*, vols. 1–4 (Bar: Nidamentym Montenegro, 1997).
32. Janko Spasojević, *Crna Gora i Srbija* (Paris: Informativna Služba Ministarstva Inostranih Dela, 1919), p. 62. Unless indicated otherwise, all translations in English are mine.
33. Jovan Ćetković, *Omladinski Pokret u Crnoj Gori* (Podgorica, 1922), p. 13.
34. Novica Šaulić, *Crna Gora* (Beograd: Narodna Misao, 1924), p. 42.
35. Šaulić, ibid., p. 42.
36. Pantelija Jovović, *Crnogorski Političari* (Beograd, 1924), p. 74.
37. Šerbo Rastoder, "Crna Gora i Konferencija Mira u Parizu," *Vijesti*, no. 267 (Podgorica, 1998).
38. Savić Marković Štedimlija, *Gorštačka Krv, Crna Gora, 1918–1928* (Beograd, 1928), p. 132.
39. Štedimlija, ibid., p. 136.
40. Štedimlija, ibid., p. 157.
41. Štedimlija, ibid., p. 172.
42. Svetozar Tomić, *Desetogodišnjica Ujedinjenja Srbije i Crne Gore* (Beograd, 1929), p. 84.
43. Šerbo Rastoder, *Skrivana Strana Istorije: Crnogorska Buna i Odmetnički Pokret, 1918–1929*, vol. 1 (Bar: Nidamentym Montenegro, 1997), p. 26.
44. See Anto Valenta, "Podjela Bosne i Borba za Cjelovitost," *Dom i Svijet*, no. 288 (Zagreb, 2000). Available at: http://www.hic.hr/dom.
45. Jovan Ćetković, *Ujedinitelji Crne Gore i Srbije* (Dubrovnik, 1940), p. 135.
46. Ćetkovic, ibid., p. 317.
47. Ćetkovic, ibid., p. 317.
48. Ćetkovic, ibid., p. 381.
49. Ćetkovic, ibid., 331.
50. Rastoder, *Skrivana Strana*, vol. 1, p. 36.
51. Valuable documents related to the collaboration of Whites with the Serbian Chetnik movement and with the occupying forces in Montenegro are available in Vlado Marković and Radoje Pajović, *Saradnja Četnika sa Okupatorom u Crnoj Gori: Dokumenti, 1941–1945* (Podgorica and Cetinje: Republički Odbor SUBNOR-a Crne Gore, 1996). Robert Lee Wolf rightly noted that the Greens rebelled against the Italian occupation when it became clear that Italy's intentions were to turn Montenegro into a puppet state. See Robert

Lee Wolff, *The Balkans in Our Time* (Cambridge, Mass.: Harvard University Press, 1956), pp. 214–215.

52. Srdja Pavlović, "Understanding Balkan Nationalism: The Wrong People, in the Wrong Place, at the Wrong Time," *Southeast European Politics on Line* 1, no. 2, December 2000, Central European University, Budapest, Hungary, available at http://www.seep.ceu.hu.

53. Dimitrije Dimo Vujović, *Ujedinjenje Crne Gore i Srbije* (Titograd: Istorijski Institut Crne Gore, 1962), p. 325.

54. In light of Traian Stojanovich's work on the theory of neopartiarchal societies, I have used the term *neopatriarchy* within the context of contemporary Montenegrin politics to explain the abrupt and vehement resurrection of old Montenegrin "tribes" and "clans" on the political scene. During late 1997 and early 1998, and in the midst of political confrontation between Montenegrin President Milo Djukanović and Slobodan Milošević, almost forgotten Montenegrin clans and their self-proclaimed leaders reappeared and began taking sides with Slobodan Milošević and his Montenegrin supporters. Far from coming into existence and acting spontaneously, as their leaders prefer to present it, these clans and tribes had been largely fabricated and maintained by Slobodan Milošević's political regime. One of the most telling characteristics of their second coming in Montenegro was their one-party membership. They consisted almost exclusively of members of the Socialist Peoples Party (SNP), which was the main pro-Milošević party in Montenegro.

CHAPTER ONE

Historical Background

◆ Poets and Warriors ◆

For scholars interested in Montenegro's past, writing about its history means probing through layers of mythologized yesteryears and trying to shed more light on the question of the origins of Montenegrins. When was Montenegro first mentioned, and in what sense? Who are Montenegrins? Are they Serbs populating the area known as Montenegro, thus adopting the toponym as their ethnic name? Are they a South Slavic people with their own distinct identity that incorporates certain (cultural, social) elements of the pre-Slavic inhabitants of the Balkan Peninsula? Are they an integral part of a broader Serbian ethnic body of evidence ("the best of the Serbs") that ended up isolated from the nation's nucleus due to unfortunate historical circumstance? Is it possible to establish and defend an argument about the historical continuity of Montenegro's statehood and sovereignty independent of an all-inclusive Serbian paradigm?

The available historical sources do not provide any clear answers to these questions. The initial contact and later mixing and intermarrying of Slavs with the indigenous population in the Balkans entirely blur the lines of ethnic distinction. Montenegrins show many characteristics that were thought common to the indigenous population of the Balkans (Illyrians, Docleans, Tracheans), but the Slavic elements of their character and social structure are predominant. However, it is possible to make a distinction between Montenegrins and Serbs in terms of their traditions, customs, moral codes, and elements that best define the social cultures of their respective societies. The issue of the contested identity of Montenegrins represents the starting point in every debate that revolves around the question of political relations between Montenegro and Serbia. From the Serbian perspective, Montenegrins were and still are ethnic Serbs living in Montenegro, and their state is regarded as proof of the continuity of a Serb presence in the region from medieval times to the present.

Because of this, it seems appropriate to provide a historical background for this tiny principality, beginning with the first times it was mentioned in written documents.

The name of Montenegro, as part of the province of Zeta, was first mentioned at the end of the thirteenth century in a document written around 1296 by King Milutin. This document refers to the property and workforce provided to the monastery of Vranjina and states the following: "I have also included from Montenegro, from Arbanas, Vasilj with his children so that he too works for Saint Nicholas." The village of Arbanas was located in the Montenegrin county of Ceklin.[1] Another source dated at around 1183 also mentions Montenegro as part of the former Roman province of Prevalitanis (also known as Doclea, and later called Zeta/Zentae), the region north of Lake Scutari (Shkoder/Skadar). In the twelfth century (around 1183), an unknown Doclean Benedictine priest (Pop Dukljanin) wrote a chronicle titled "Regnum Sclavorum," also known as Ljetopis Popa Dukljanina or Barski Rodoslov. This chronicle talks about "usque ad planitiem Zentae." The literature in Serbo-Croat devoted to this chronicle is immense.[2]

Documents of the Venetian Senate related to peace negotiations between the Republic and Djuradj Branković in 1435 mention Montenegro on four occasions and in different variants, such as "Monte Zernagora" and "Černagora."[3] In numerous fifteenth- and sixteenth-century documents in the archives in Kotor, the term *Montenegro* appears more often than *Černagora* or *Čarnagora*, and it seems that the

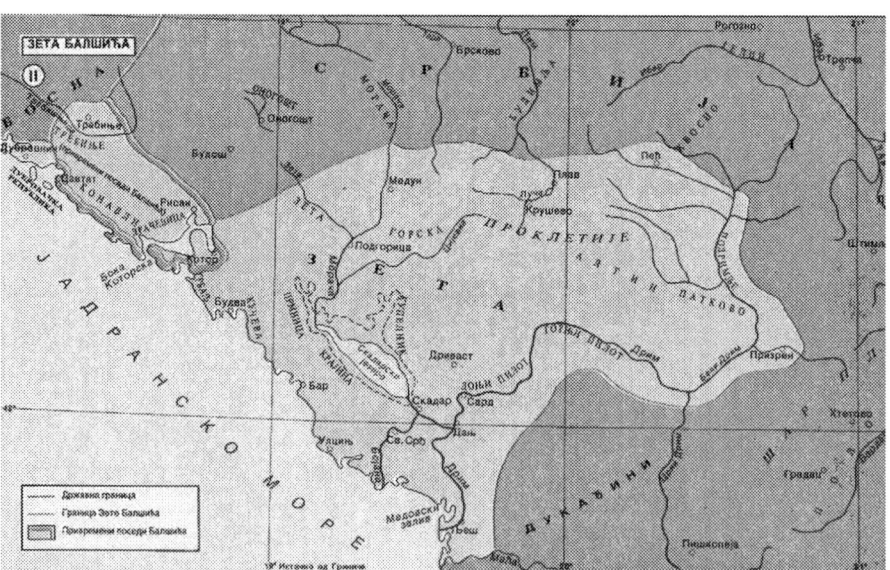

Figure 1. Zeta during the Balšić dynasty

term *Montenegro* has only been used instead of the older name, *Zeta*, to describe this state and its territory since the fifteenth century.[4]

From 1465 to 1490 Ivan Crnojević ruled the region from his see in the small castle of Žabljak on the banks of Lake Scutari. The fort of Žabljak ("castello de Zabiach") was first mentioned in 1460 as the see of Ivan Crnojević, the "ruler of Zeta," or "gospodar zetski" (dominus, hospodar). Ivan was granted the title of grand duke and the rank of captain in the Venetian Republic.[5] Soon after ascending to power, Ivan realized that the expansion of the Ottoman Empire represented a danger to his tiny principality, and he managed to strengthen the alliance with Venice. As noted in the Venetian chronicles, Ivan's soldiers fought alongside Venetians in defending the town of Scutari (Shkoder/Skadar) from the army of Sultan Mehmed II.[6] In 1474 the defenders of Scutari were victorious, only to be forced to surrender the city five years later. Fearing Ottoman retaliation for siding with Venice, Ivan Crnojević decided in 1482 to move his capital from the town of Žabljak farther north to the village of Dolac (later named Cetinje), on the slopes of Mount Lovćen. Two years later, in 1484, next to his court Ivan built a monastery that became the residency of the Montenegrin Orthodox metropolitans in the following year (1485) and the see of a bishop. When Ivan died in 1490, it was as the monk Jovan Crnojević.[7]

Ivan's oldest son, Djuradj, succeeded him and ruled Montenegro from 1490 to 1496. Being unable to resist growing pressure from the Ottomans, Djuradj left

Figure 2. Ivan Crnojević's coat of arms

Montenegro and settled in Venice in 1496. Despite ruling for only six years, Djuradj Crnojević left behind an important legacy—the establishment of the first Cyrillic printing press among the South Slavs.[8] He was succeeded by his brother Stefan, who nominally ruled Montenegro until 1499, when the region became part of the newly established Ottoman administrative unit, the Sanjak of Scutari.

Meanwhile, Ivan's youngest son, Staniša, disillusioned by the impossibility of succeeding his father, went to Istanbul and converted to Islam. As a loyal servant of the Ottoman sultan, Staniša Crnojević (who adopted the name Skender after his conversion to Islam) was appointed in 1513 as the Sanjak-Bey in charge of Montenegro and neighboring Albanian tribes.[9] The following year (1514), Sultan Bayezid II designated Montenegro as a separate region (*Sanjak*). Staniša (now known as Skender-Bey) Crnojević nominally ruled the region until 1528 but failed to subject Montenegrin tribes to his authority.[10] In spite of protracted efforts by Ottoman authorities to impose their rule in the region known as Stara Crna Gora (Old Montenegro), its tribes managed to preserve their autonomy and self-government.

From 1519 onward, the tribes of Old Montenegro were ruled by their religious leaders, who had the title of *vladika* (metropolitan/prince-bishop).[11] In the beginning, *vladikas* came from different families, such as Boljević, Borilović, and Kaludjeričić, and were elected by popular vote at the assemblies of tribal leaders. Pavel Apolonovich Rovinsky, a nineteenth-century Russian ethnographer, described their function as follows:

> the vladikas were the true spiritual and popular leaders of the Montenegrin people. The vladika was a guardian of the spiritual strength of the people, and a figure that embodied a notion of identity that was based on faith and the tradition of heroism and glorious ancestors . . . the vladikas governed not by brute force but purely by their moral influence, through persuasion and prayers. And they all recognized the supreme authority of the Faith and the Church, in which the vladikas and the people were one. It was a special kind of spiritual brotherhood.[12]

This is, of course, a romanticized image of the role the vladikas played in Montenegro. One should not forget that for centuries Montenegrin tribesmen refused to acknowledge any type of authority whatsoever. The protracted efforts of their vladikas were thus concentrated on establishing some form of central authority, and they were not always successful in accomplishing this task. Local chieftains and regional leaders were, in most cases, only titular leaders, without any real power. Joseph Kermpotich, the Austrian envoy to Montenegro, wrote in 1788 that Montenegrins

> have a bishop, serdars, gubernador, and voyvodas. But these are mere names. People obey only as long as they gain by so doing. . . . We even heard a common man tell the vladika to his face: "Holy bishop, you lie like a dog! I will cut

out your heart with the point of my knife." Except that they fast, they have no religion whatsoever.[13]

In 1697, at the tribal assembly (Plemenska Skupština, or Zbor) in Cetinje, Bishop Danilo Petrović (Šćepčević) was elected leader of the Montenegrin tribes (as Danilo I Petrović) with the significant novelty of being allowed to appoint his successor. Although Orthodox clergy in general are permitted to be married, bishops are required to stay celibate. Vladika Danilo I Petrović passed his office to his nephew, thus creating the Petrović dynasty, whose rule over Montenegro (as religious and secular leaders) lasted until 1918, except for two short reigns of an impostor known as Šćepan Mali (Stephen the Small, 1767–1773) and later the Vladika Arsenije Plamenac (1781–1784).[14] In 1700, Danilo I Petrović chose to receive the title of vladika from the Serbian patriarch in exile, Arsenije III Čarnojević; his religious authority extended over Old Montenegro and the surrounding mountainous region (Brda) as well as over several towns on the Adriatic coast.[15]

Danilo's reign (1697–1735) was marked by the gradual deceleration of Ottoman expansion in Europe. Moreover, Montenegro strengthened its ties with Russia and began relying upon its assistance more than ever before. The replacement of Venetian with Russian patronage had significant consequences. After Vladika Danilo I visited Peter the Great in 1715, Montenegro began enjoying financial aid from Russia, including 2,700 ducats and 13,400 rubles for the reconstruction of various churches and monasteries. In addition, Peter promised that Russia would provide Montenegro with 500 rubles of financial assistance to be paid triennially. This was followed by Russia's benevolent attitude toward Montenegro's modest territorial expansion. Russia also played an important role in the process of the formal recognition of Montenegro (then ruled by Vladika Petar I Petrović Njegoš) by the Ottoman State in 1789.

Danilo's successor, Vladika Sava Petrović Njegoš, was a less than memorable figure in Montenegrin history. During his rule, the country became an arena of constant and bitter tribal rivalries and struggles for power among numerous clan leaders. During Vladika Sava's prolonged stay in Russia (1742–1744), his nephew Vladika Vasilije Petrović gained a considerable influence among the tribesmen and managed to take over the affairs of state from his uncle. Vladika Vasilije Petrović was a forceful proponent of military confrontation with the Ottomans and advocated Montenegro's total reliance upon Russia. He planned to organize and coordinate an uprising of the Balkan Slavs against the Ottoman Empire and traveled to Russia in the hope of rallying support for his political concept of Montenegrin statehood and sovereignty by portraying Montenegro as an ideally placed exponent of Russian political interests in the Balkans.

During his stay in St. Petersburg (1752–1754), Vladika Vasilije wrote the first history of Montenegro (*Istorija o Černoj Gori*), which was published in 1754, hoping

Figure 3. Metropolitan Danilo Petrović – Šćepčević

that the work might aid his political agenda. He later undertook two more trips to Russia to seek assistance for Montenegro. It is interesting to note that Vladika Vasilije did not travel to Russia alone. On his second trip to St. Petersburg (1758) he took twelve young Montenegrins with him and was planning to enroll them in Russian schools. This effort by Vladika Vasilije represented the first attempt to organize schooling abroad for Montenegrin youth. Vladika Vasilije undertook yet another trip to Russia in 1765, hoping to rally further political support for his tiny country and to obtain long-promised financial assistance from St. Petersburg. In 1766, however, he died of pneumonia in St. Petersburg and was buried there.[16]

After the death of Vladika Vasilije Petrović, the country entered thirty years of political instability, marked by the protracted efforts of members of the well-known Radonjić family to forge an alliance with Austria and distance Montenegro from Russia. This political turn was paired with tribal conflicts, a power struggle between rival families, and the constant military threat of the Ottoman armies in the region.

This was the time (around 1766) when an unknown man, an alleged healer, appeared in the village of Maine. Stories about his healing powers started to spread across Montenegro while his unknown origins and unclear life-history initiated interesting rumors. His name was Šćepan Mali (Stephen the Small). While staying in Maine, Šćepan resided with Marko Tanović, the local captain. It was Tanović who began spreading stories about his guest's "real" identity and tried to convince people that the healer was in fact the Russian Tsar Peter III, who was reported to have been murdered by the lover and supporters of Catherine II in 1762. At the time, Montenegrins believed that Peter III was not dead but had somehow managed to escape his assassins. The news about the Russian tsar's finding refuge in Montenegro spread like wildfire, and even tribal leaders appeared to be convinced that the ruler of "mother Russia" was among them. The tribal assembly in Cetinje decided to formally acknowledge the tsar's "real" identity and proclaimed him the ruler of Montenegro. A delegation of sixty people was dispatched to Maine to inform Šćepan of the assembly's decision.[17] In order to leave a good impression upon his new "subjects,"

Šćepan refused to accept the honor of ruling Montenegro until the tribal chiefs solemnly declared that they would stop tribal infighting. His demands and the manner in which they were delivered seemed to convince every skeptic in Montenegro that Šćepan was indeed the Russian tsar.

Šćepan's rule in Montenegro was stern. He had some of the prestige of the Russian tsar he impersonated, and he also presented himself as a man on a mission from God. Furthermore, because he practiced the profession of herbalist, he also possessed the charisma associated with the supernatural powers Montenegrins attributed to healers. One can say that Šćepan's powers over Montenegrins of the period were chiefly psychological.[18] He was particularly keen on rooting out blood feuds among Montenegrins and resorted to capital punishment in order to accomplish this goal.[19] His eighteen-member bodyguard unit executed his orders. Measures introduced by Šćepan the Small resulted in a significant decline in cases of theft and blood-feud-related murders in Montenegro and the establishment of its first permanent court in 1771. Twelve highly respected tribal leaders were chosen to act as councilors and judges, and the ruler directed their activities. This supratribal court was empowered to settle blood feuds in the traditional manner and to punish as murderers men who committed homicide while feuding. Such a political mechanism depended upon a liberal dose of coercive force originating from the political center, that is, from the ability and willingness of Šćepan the Small to resort to harsh measures in implementing his orders. Šćepan was also responsible for initiating the first census in Montenegro in 1773. The more his power grew in Montenegro, the more the Ottomans hated him. On January 23, 1774, the self-proclaimed Russian tsar and ruler of Montenegro was assassinated by his barber, Stanko Palikarda, who had been paid to kill him by the Pasha of Scutari.[20] His blood-feud courts became ineffectual, and the other reforms he had implemented disappeared overnight.

The decade that followed the assassination of Šćepan the Small was a time of bitter intertribal conflicts, repeated Ottoman military assaults, and jockeying for positions of power in Montenegro.[21] During this period, the *guvernadur* (governor), Jovan Radonjić, tried to gain greater influence with the tribal leaders and to side with Austria but was successful in neither.

From 1784 until 1830, the newly appointed Montenegrin ruler, Vladika Petar I Petrović Njegoš, worked to stabilize the country and to establish the essential elements and mechanisms of the future state apparatus. He managed to preserve a tenuous tribal confederacy bound more by atavistic appeals to loyalty and the force of oaths than by common institutions. His appeals to a common ancestry were often capable of ending clannish conflicts among Montenegrins, who were susceptible to the nostalgia of lineage.[22]

In October 1796, Montenegrin tribal leaders under the supervision of Vladika Petar I adopted the first official legal document drafted in Montenegro, known as

Zakonik Opšti Crnogorski i Brdski (General Law of Montenegro and Brda). Tribal chiefs solemnly swore that they would uphold the law of the land:

> Calling God to our aid, we confirm these gifts composed by us on the day of the Transfiguration, 1796. We denounce any traitor, curse him forever, and declare him dishonored and expelled from the tribe.[23]

This legal code had sixteen articles regulating issues of criminal and family law, as well as providing various procedural guidelines.[24] However, because this law made provisions for the population to be taxed, many tribal leaders avoided implementing it. In 1803, Vladika Petar I summoned tribal chiefs to Stanjevići Monastery to reaffirm their allegiance to him and again to adopt the same law. During this tribal assembly, Montenegrins established the first law court in the country (*Praviteljstvo Suda Crnogorskog i Brdskog*), known as *Kuluk*. The main duty of this legal body was to mediate between families pursuing the old tribal practice of blood feud. The assembly also modified article 20, which dealt with taxation, and declared that every household would pay "60 para per year in taxes."[25] This tax legislation, however, was unenforceable. The reign of Vladika Petar I Petrović in Montenegro was marked by his efforts to establish a state apparatus and consolidate mechanisms of a power structure. Even though this process was on occasion marked by the enforced submission of various tribes to the vladika's will, it nevertheless paved the way for the establishment of the future Montenegrin state. Vladika Petar I Petrović died in 1830 at the age of eighty-three.

His successor, Rade Tomov Petrović, entered the priesthood on October 31, 1830, and, as Petar II Petrović Njegoš, was proclaimed the new ruler of Montenegro. Two years later, with the assistance of Count Vujić, Rade Tomov managed to persuade Montenegrin tribal leaders to establish a senate under his presidency. Twelve of the most prominent leaders were elected members of this newly formed body and provided an annual salary of 40 talirs.[26] The senate had legislative, judiciary, and executive powers and was the first state institution in Montenegro. Its decisions were enforced by the military unit called the *Gvardija*; the senate also functioned as the government of Montenegro. The Gvardija was an army unit initially comprised of 150 soldiers. Later, their number rose to 420. Its duties included enforcing the decisions and proclamations made by the senate, mediating in various civic disputes, and acting as a police force.[27] A separate paramilitary unit called the *Perjanici* was also formed; it served as Petar's personal guard, as well as a police force.

In March 1833 Rade Tomov Petrović went to St. Petersburg to be ordained as vladika. He was given considerable financial aid (18,000 rubles) by Tsar Nicholas I, in addition to the 10,000 rubles that had been promised to Montenegro some years back.[28] Nicholas I was rather generous toward the young vladika and gave him an additional 8,000 rubles to strengthen state institutions in Montenegro. Furthermore, the Russian synod promised to regularly provide all the necessary equipment and much-needed funds for maintaining religious services in Montenegro. Regarding the political aspects of the vladika's visit to St. Petersburg, he was given assurances that Russia would always act on behalf of Montenegro as if it were one of its own gubernias.[29] Shortly after his return from Russia in 1833, Vladika Petar II opened the first two elementary schools in Montenegro (one was in Cetinje and the other in Dobrsko Selo).[30] The following year he brought a new printing press from Venice. This printing press worked until 1852, when, during Omer Pasha Latas's military assault on Montenegro, Prince Danilo Petrović ordered all its letters to be melted and turned into bullets.[31] Vladika Petar II also opened two small factories to produce gunpowder in Rijeka Crnojevića and built roads and four artesian wells in Crmnička and Katunska Nahijas.[32] He sent sixteen young Montenegrins to be educated in Serbia, seven of whom returned after completing school; they were among the few literate people in Montenegro.

In addition to establishing a central authority and attempting to create an infrastructure in Montenegro, in 1833 Petar II Petrović Njegoš introduced a new tax policy. Some tribes reacted defiantly, claiming that Montenegrins had always refused to pay taxes to the Ottomans and challenging Vladika Petar II to come and collect the tax himself. Knowing that a modern state could not function without a properly administered tax system, Njegoš acted promptly and somewhat ruthlessly in dealing with tax evaders.

Petar II Petrović Njegoš has been widely regarded as the most competent and forward-looking Montenegrin leader. Apart from having laid down the foundation of the modern Montenegrin state and the subsequent Kingdom of Montenegro, he was also one of the most highly acclaimed South Slav poets of his time. His most famous works include *Gorski Vijenac* (The Mountain Wreath), *Luča Mikrokozma* (The Ray of the Microcosm), *Lazni Car Šćepan Mali* (The False Tsar Stephen the Small), and *Pustinjak Cetinjski* (The Hermit of Cetinje). His most famous work, *The Mountain Wreath,* written in the Montenegrin vernacular, synthesized much of the popular wisdom of the time and became a key

Figure 4. Metropolitan Petar II Petrović –Njegoš

literary symbol in the process of nation-building. There is hardly a Montenegrin who cannot quote a proverb or passage from *The Mountain Wreath*. Petar II Petrović Njegoš died on October 31, 1851. He was thirty-nine years old.

Petar II Petrović Njegoš was succeeded by his first cousin, Danilo I Petrović Njegoš. In March 1852, Danilo I Petrović Njegoš decided to abandon his assigned religious role and establish secular rule in the principality. It seems that Danilo's love for Darinka Kvekić (a woman whom he wanted to marry; she was not of noble origin) was the main reason behind this decision, even though some historians claim that on Danilo's trip to Russia in the same year he had been able to secure the Russian tsar's support.[33] The news about St. Petersburg's endorsement spread fast, and while Danilo was still in Russia, the Montenegrin senate passed a proclamation on the secularization of the state. The decree stated, among other things, that

1. Montenegro is a secular state with a hereditary government headed by the prince.
2. Danilo Petrović Njegoš is called upon to take up his position as prince; after his death, this title will forever stay with his male descendants according to the principle of *primo genitor*.
3. The bishop or archbishop, who will rule over religious matters, will be elected and appointed by the government and will be a member of the famous Petrović family or of some other well-respected Montenegrin family.
4. Laws, legislations, and customs that were in effect and were obeyed in the past will stay in effect. The only exceptions to this rule are the reforms introduced by this decree.[34]

Five years later, during his stay in Paris in 1857, Prince Danilo was offered the protection of France and some financial assistance but was asked in return to distance his state from Russia as much as possible. Aware of the negative consequences the Crimean War was having on Russia, Prince Danilo was hoping that France could and would exercise its political and economic influence over the sultan and that his temporary and rather superficial siding with France would secure Montenegro's independence and international recognition.[35] This policy shift put Danilo in a difficult position both in Montenegro and vis-à-vis St. Petersburg. His political opponents in Montenegro repeatedly invoked the traditional Montenegrin ties with Russia and interpreted Danilo's political maneuvering as treason. It also took him some time to convince Russian diplomats that Montenegro had never really sided with anyone but Russia.

As the result of Danilo's successful military campaigns against the Ottoman armies and his victory over Husein Pasha's army at Grahovo in 1858 in particular, the Great Powers decided to settle the issue of Montenegro's borders with the Ottoman state. During a November 1858 conference in Istanbul, they set up a commission to delineate these boundaries. The official protocol acknowledging Montenegro's new borders with the Ottoman state in the west (toward Herzegovina) and in the southeast (toward Scutari/Skadar) was signed in April 1860.[36] Montenegro enlarged its territory by approximately 1,500 square kilometers.[37] Many scholars interpret this border delineation with the Ottoman state and its international recognition as de facto international recognition of Montenegrin independence and sovereignty.

Central issues in Danilo's domestic policy were establishing a proper army and eliminating separatist tendencies among various Montenegrin tribes. He ordered that able-bodied men from all tribes should be listed as members of a Montenegrin standing army known as the Cross-Bearing Army (*Krstonosna Vojska*).[38] In order to prevent further separatist moves by any of the tribal leaders, Prince Danilo reorganized the senate by bringing in individuals loyal to him. He also reorganized local authorities, strengthening their ties with the senate and with him personally, and worked on dismantling the earlier institutions of local princes (*Knez*) and introducing captains (*Kapetan*) as new local leaders. In 1855 Danilo promulgated a more elaborate legal code. This legislation marked the transition from a system of equal tribes to a system of central government in Montenegro.

Figure 5. Prince Danilo Petrović – Njegoš

After ruling Montenegro for nine years, Prince Danilo I Petrović Njegoš was assassinated in the Austro-Hungarian coastal city of Kotor on August 1, 1860.[39] The motives for the assassination and the political affiliation of the assassin, Todor Kadić, are a matter of some controversy. Official accounts tell us that Kadić was acting in revenge because Danilo had had an affair with his wife; the entire issue was presented at the time as the case of a jealous husband resorting to extreme measures to protect his honor. Other sources indicate that Kadić was affiliated with the Austrian authorities and point to a different set of motives. Some scholars claim that Prince Danilo's closeness to Russia and the issue of the new Montenegrin borders were adequate motives for Austria to encourage his assassins. Jagoš Jovanović, for example, tells us that in 1859, the Austrians plotted to assassinate the prince, his older brother Grand

Duke Mirko Petrović, and several senators during their stay in Rijeka Crnojevića. The plan never materialized, but Todor Kadić was one of the conspirators.⁴⁰

The day after the assassination, Danilo's nephew Nikola Petrović Njegoš was appointed ruler of Montenegro and given the title of prince. Under the political guidance of his authoritative father, Mirko, Prince Nikola I Petrović continued to influence neighboring tribes in Herzegovina, fanning the flames of their dissatisfaction with the Ottomans in the hope that Montenegro might benefit from an armed rebellion. But the circumstances had changed, and neither Russia nor France was inclined to turn a blind eye to Nikola's expansionist policies. They were concerned that the ideas of Garibaldi might find fertile ground among the Balkan Slavs and ignite national revolutions. However, Prince Nikola I and his father continued to engage in local rebellions in Bosnia and Herzegovina despite the objections of the Great Powers. The Ottomans responded in 1862 with a massive attack on Montenegro led by Omer-Pasha Latas.⁴¹ Montenegro suffered a humiliating military and political defeat, and representatives of the Great Powers had to intervene to prevent the occupation of Cetinje. The peace agreement that followed forced Montenegro to accept Ottoman jurisdiction over some parts of its territory. Moreover, the consequences of this defeat had an impact on the future political strategy of the Montenegrin ruling dynasty and the perception of the future Montenegrin state.

Once the assault on Montenegro by Omer-Pasha Latas ended, Serbian Prince Mihailo Obrenović dispatched his representative, Milan Piroćanac, to Cetinje to propose signing an agreement between the two states to secure future cooperation between Serbia and Montenegro in any armed conflict with the Ottomans. Both Prince Nikola I Petrović and his father, Grand Duke Mirko, were open to this offer but wanted a full military treaty with Serbia to be implemented immediately, whereas the Serbian side favored signing a general agreement that would help coordinate common future defense policies. This reluctance on the part of Serbia was caused by their fear of

Figure 6. King Nikola I Petrović – Njegoš

possible Austrian intervention. However, despite the grand duke's strong objections, the proposed general treaty was signed on September 23, 1866.

The two countries agreed to work diligently toward achieving the liberation and unification of the Serbian people. In order to accomplish this goal, both Montenegro and Serbia agreed to organize an armed insurrection in the bordering Ottoman territories. Furthermore, the agreement stated that the Montenegrin prince would incorporate his country into Serbia and recognize the Serbian Prince Mihailo as supreme ruler. The Montenegrin ruler would remain second in line for succession of the throne and would be given a civilian salary of 20,000 dinars. The Montenegrin people would enjoy equal rights with the people of Serbia. Moreover, Montenegro was obliged neither to act against the Ottoman interests in any way nor to engage in any negotiations with the Ottoman state without Serbia's consent. The agreement also stated that in wartime everything would be done according to Serbian military plans.[42]

Serbian envoy Milan Piroćanac described this agreement as "the first step on the road to achieving closer relations between two Serbian states." Piroćanac also stated, with evident satisfaction, that Prince Nikola had told him that he was "ready to abdicate in favor of Prince Mihailo."[43] Establishing "closer relations between two Serbian states" had been part of the political program of every Serbian government since 1807, when Serbian rebel leaders had defined their war aim to be the freeing of all Serbs from Ottoman oppression and then uniting them. In practical terms, this meant the liberation of Bosnia and Herzegovina and unification with Montenegro.[44] A less revolutionary version of this political concept was outlined in 1844 in Serbian Minister of the Interior Ilija Garašanin's document "Načertanije," which outlined Serbia's expansionist policies. But despite Milan Piroćanac's enthusiasm, neither side ever fully complied with the signed agreement because, for both the Petrovićes and Obrenovićes, dynastic interests were paramount. This unwillingness to comply with the signed document resulted in latent and prolonged hostility between the two dynasties and the two governments.[45]

Ten years later, in June 1876, Montenegro and Serbia jointly declared war on the Ottoman state. This war was the consequence of prolonged armed conflict between the Slav Orthodox population and the Ottoman authorities in Bosnia and Herzegovina, which was politically encouraged and financially and militarily aided by both Prince Nikola I Petrović and his Serbian counterpart. Both the Montenegrin and Serbian governments were convinced that their war efforts would be victorious and that they would enjoy some territorial gains.[46] This war, which ended with the signing of a peace treaty in San Stefano in February 1878, proved to be of great significance for Montenegro. The Ottomans agreed to recognize the independence of Montenegro, which it formally did in the summer of 1878 during the Berlin Congress. According to the Treaty of Berlin, Montenegro doubled in size, to some 8,655 square kilometers, and acquired the towns of Podgorica, Nikšić, Spuž,

Žabljak, Kolašin, Bar, and Ulcinj. However, Montenegro was forced to accept the so-called Protocol X and Article 29, both of which granted Austria-Hungary the right to monitor the Montenegrin port of Bar. The logic behind Article 29 was rationalized as the "need to protect the Montenegrin merchant fleet."[47]

On April 2, 1879, Prince Nikola summoned the tribal assembly in Cetinje in order to introduce new reforms in state administration.[48] The assembly decided to dismantle the senate and to establish a state council, various ministries, and a supreme court instead. Prince Nikola's cousin, Duke (Vojvoda) Božo Petrović, was appointed the first president of both the State Council and the Supreme Court. Several ministries were also formed, such as the Ministry of Foreign Affairs, the Ministry of the Interior, the Ministry of Justice, the Ministry of Finance, and the Ministry of Defense. Before the introduction of these reforms, Montenegro had only had 103 bureaucrats employed by the state administration. Furthermore, Prince Nikola and the members of the tribal assembly decided to divide the territory of Montenegro into new administrative units, thus acknowledging the new territorial arrangement. The enlarged territory of Montenegro was divided into ten *nahijas*. Katunska, Riječka, Crmnička, Lješanska, Primorska, Brdska, Nikšićka, Zetska, Moračka, and Vasojevićka.[49]

The following decades were marked by a trend toward upward social mobility in Montenegro and the development of much-needed infrastructure, such as roads, elementary and secondary schools, a postal service (est. 1871), a banking service (Prva Nikšićka Štedionica, est. 1901), telephone service (est. 1907), as well as the establishment of the first tobacco monopoly, in 1903.[50] These first steps in the development of the Montenegrin economy and the restructuring of its state apparatus had some negative consequences. While Prince Nikola was working on strengthening the central authority and elevating his own role in the country's affairs, some tribal leaders felt increasingly marginalized and saw their authority diminished. Nikola's departure from the traditional way of conducting politics (i.e., consulting with tribal leaders) was seen as not only the abandonment of the "old ways" but also as the first step in dissolving the traditional values of Montenegrin society. Tribal leaders, such as Marko Miljanov Popović, Jole Piletić, Peko Pavlović, Mašo Vrbica, and others, began rebelling against the prince's autocratic methods and his strengthening of the central authority.[51] Another effect of the country's development was the establishment of workers' organizations. The first Radnički Savez (Workers' Alliance) was established in Bar in 1903, and its first president was Jovan Hajduković.[52]

Being acutely aware of the potential strength of the opposition and aiming at lessening the political influence of his opponents, Prince Nikola decided in 1905 to grant a Constitution. On December 19, 1905, the Constitutional Assembly, known as Nikoljdanska Skupština (the St. Nicholas Day Assembly), proclaimed the first Montenegrin Constitution. According to the new law of the land, Montenegro was a constitutional but not a parliamentary monarchy. The profile of future governments depended exclusively on the prince's will, and the assembly did not have any say in the matter.[53] What followed was a series of short-term political alliances, a succession of more or less inefficient governments, and the development of serious political rivalries. Growing parliamentary opposition characterized the Montenegrin political landscape of the period. The parliament became the arena of a bitter confrontation between the representatives of the so-called people's movement and those representing the government and Prince Nikola. The main political parties were the People's Party (Narodna Stranka), better known as Klubaši (their leader was Šako Petrović), and the True People's Party (Prava Narodna Stranka), known as Pravaši (led by Lazar Mijušković). The political credo of Klubaši was the unification of Montenegro and Serbia and the dethroning of Prince Nikola.[54] Being a rather pragmatic politician, Prince Nikola managed to weather this stormy domestic political scene. He also took full advantage of the crisis that erupted after the annexation of Bosnia and Herzegovina and acted as if he were the undisputed leader of all South Slavs. After fifty successful years of ruling in Montenegro, he decided to proclaim the Montenegrin Kingdom in 1910.

From the turn of the twentieth century onward, the political climate in both Montenegro and Serbia underwent many significant changes. The nature of these changes was defined by the intensity of the dynastic struggle between the Montenegrin dynasty of Petrović-Njegoš and the Serbian dynasty of Karadjordjević and by the game of power politics played between Belgrade and Cetinje. These events, in turn, set the tone for the political processes that came about a few decades later. In spite of all the diplomatic lip-service that was exchanged between Montenegro and Serbia in the decades that followed, the main lines of the policies implemented in Cetinje and in Belgrade from as early as the 1870s clearly indicate that political developments in the region were dominated by the struggle for power between the two dynasties and the tendency of the Serbian dynasty and the political elite in Belgrade to dominate in the region. Because this tendency was easily detectable in many policy decisions made by the Serbian government, a frequently cited slogan of the time, "the Balkans to the people of the Balkans," seemed to have been only a tool of political rhetoric aimed at obscuring real agendas: problems of various contested territories, issues of dynastic prestige, different nationalistic visions of the region's future, and an urge on the part of the elites in power to achieve absolute control over the political landscape in the Balkans. The ruling elite in Serbia of the period felt so uneasy about the strengthening of state power in Montenegro that they were even against Prince Danilo's secularization of the state. For the elites in Serbia, this event (and many others that followed) signified the establishment of a rival dynasty and the strengthening of a state that could challenge Serbia's primacy among the South Slavs and diminish its role in the South Slavic Piedmont.[55]

The key year 1910 was characterized in Montenegro by two main government activities. The first concerned the tightening of security measures in the country amid fear of possible terrorist attacks initiated from Serbia. The political leaders in Montenegro made an effort to monitor the activities of Montenegrin emigrants in Serbia and Macedonia, as well as to follow closely the activities undertaken by members of the opposition parties in Montenegro itself. Borders were closely monitored, and the army units stationed in the area bordering Serbia and Austria-Hungary were put on alert. These security measures were introduced during preparations for the celebration of the fiftieth anniversary of Prince Nikola's rule in Montenegro and were motivated primarily by rumors that the government of Serbia and its military leaders were plotting to dethrone and assassinate him.[56]

The second major political activity of the Montenegrin government in 1910 was the preparation for Prince Nikola's coronation. During 1909 Prince Nikola initiated a broad range of diplomatic activities aimed at making the Montenegrin Question an issue in international politics. The French, Italian, and Austro-Hungarian fleets were invited to visit the Montenegrin port of Bar. Several of the naval officers from these fleets also visited Cetinje and held several meetings with the prince. All of them left Montenegro with the impression that his coronation, which was planned as the culmination of the celebrations, would certainly take place and that Montenegro would soon become a kingdom. They all presumed that the fiftieth-anniversary celebration was the perfect occasion for such an important event. Prince Nikola and the Montenegrin government's intention to proclaim a Kingdom of Montenegro was the main topic in the Serbian and Montenegrin media early in 1910.[57] Speculations were encouraged by the prince himself, who in his New Year's address mentioned the coronation as a possibility. Encouraged by this, the New Year's issue of *Glas Crnogorca* in Cetinje published an editorial suggesting that the coronation of Prince Nikola Petrović would be an appropriate gesture in light of all of his earlier achievements.

In the editorial, titled "Recapitulating the Year That Passed," the significance of the annexation of Bosnia and Herzegovina and the negative impact it had on the political processes among the Serbs were stressed, suggesting that the coronation would be a remedy for strained relations with Serbia. The article also mentioned some of the successful diplomatic activities of the Montenegrin government, such as the easing of restrictions on trade and on the movement of military units along the Montenegrin coast, which had been imposed at the Congress of Berlin, and the visit of Crown Prince Danilo to St. Petersburg. The editorial also mentions the uncovering and successful resolution of an antigovernment plot in Vasojevići (a region in northern Montenegro bordering Serbia and Austria-Hungary), as well as the visit of the French navy fleet to the Montenegrin port of Bar.[58] The editorial concludes by emphasizing the importance of the forthcoming jubilee:

We entered this New Year with such a joyful event. This is the year in which Montenegro celebrates the fiftieth anniversary of the rule of its resurrector and the true Father of the Nation. His achievements and victories during the past years will be best awarded with the satisfaction of his soul, when he looks back to all his successes: the well-being of his beloved people and the respect Montenegro enjoys around the world.[59]

However, despite frequent references to the future celebration in the press, the government waited for some time before releasing an official statement. The announcement came only four months before the event took place. An organizing committee was formed, headed by the Montenegrin metropolitan, Mitrofan Ban. The committee issued an official statement on April 2, 1910, stating that the celebration would take place in Cetinje between August 28 and 30.[60] Local authorities also formed organizing committees, the membership of which, significantly, was open to leaders of the opposition parties in Montenegro.[61] In portraying himself as the ruler of all Montenegrins regardless of their political affiliation, Prince Nikola showed a certain level of political pragmatism by including his political opponents in the process of organizing the celebration. Such a move, while perhaps only an expression of utmost cynicism on his part, helped him to stabilize the domestic political scene, at least for a brief time.

Judging by the headlines in numerous Serbian newspapers, it seems that the view in Serbia of Nikola's coronation was predominantly negative. As soon as the celebration was officially announced, the Serbian media, as well as the media in other parts of the Balkans, began to speculate on whether Serbian King Petar Karadjordjević would attend the ceremony in Cetinje. This question dominated discussion in Serbia; it was the main focal point in numerous editorials and commentaries that appeared in the Serbian press.[62] All of the available documents indicate that this was also uppermost in Prince Nikola's mind. For him, as well as for the Montenegrin government, its people, and foreign diplomats in Cetinje, the attendance of King Petar Karadjordjević would be a clear sign that Serbia approved of all intended political and structural changes in Montenegro.

Many newspapers and journals attacked Prince Nikola Petrović's decision and demanded that King Petar Karadjordjević not travel to Cetinje under any circumstances. The Belgrade newspaper *Štampa* asked in an editorial: "What do they want in Cetinje and why does Prince Nikola need a crown?" The same editorial pointed out that it should be enough if Crown Prince Aleksandar attended the ceremony, which "without any real reason and need, and without their own money, they want to organize in Cetinje."[63]

In contrast to the manner in which the Serbian media treated the issue, the reactions of the government in Belgrade were diplomatically well measured. But despite a velvet-gloved approach to the question, Serbian politicians found it difficult to fully suppress their disapproval of the political developments in Montenegro. On many occasions, politicians from Serbia appeared eager to voice their discontent and express their worries for the future of Serbdom. The reaction of the leader of the Serbian Radical Party, Nikola Pašić, was particularly negative. For him this was

> a new bad political occurrence among the Slavs because it confronts two dynasties, the Petrović-Njegošes and the Karadjordjevićes. A possible conflict between the two dynasties means a conflict between their states, and such a thing could lead to the division of Serbdom into two antagonistic camps.[64]

Pašić also voiced his disagreement with the manner in which Prince Nikola greeted guests from Bulgaria, wishing them a warm welcome "in the name of the Serbian people."[65]

On the day before the celebration, a delegation from Belgrade arrived in Cetinje. It was led by Crown Prince Aleksandar Karadjordjević. Other members of the delegation were Minister of Defense Stepa Stepanović, a commander of the IX Division of infantry named after Prince Nikola Petrović, King Petar's chief of staff, and four army officers. There were no political leaders from Serbia. The only other member of the Serbian royal family to arrive in Cetinje was Princess Jelena. However, she was not there in her official capacity but as a private person.[66] Several journalists from Serbia also attended the ceremony. It is important to note that some newspapers from Belgrade had encouraged people to travel to Cetinje. However, according to press reports, only some fifty private citizens from Belgrade attended the ceremony.[67]

On August 28, 1910, the members of the Montenegrin People's Assembly voted unanimously to accept legislation affirming Nikola's coronation and the elevation of Montenegro to the rank of kingdom. That same day, assembly president Marko Drljević, together with all members of the assembly, went to Prince Nikola to ask him to accept the crown. In response to a speech delivered by Marko Dožić, the vice president of the assembly, King Nikola I Petrović, declared that he had been for some time "aware of the glorious role of this land of ours in the history of the Serb nation" and accepted the crown. He kept his earlier title of ruler (*gospodar*), which can be understood as a distant reference to Ivan Crnojević and a sign that the feudal tradition was still rather strong among Montenegrins.[68]

Nikola's coronation represented an effort to strengthen his own weak political position at home as well as to internationalize the question of Montenegro. Supporters of his decision claimed the historical right of Montenegro to act as a leading force among the Serb states in the Balkans. For them, the coronation was a continuation of the tradition of Montenegrin independence and an important step forward in the process of completely renewing the ancient Kingdom of Zeta, which had existed since 1077. The Petrović-Njegoš dynasty, they claimed, were the descendents of ancient dynasties such as Vojislavljević, Nemanjić, Balšić, and Crnojević. While emphasizing their attachment to the Serbian nation, King Nikola I and his supporters pointed out the importance of Montenegrin independence and sovereignty, effectively distancing themselves from Serbia and dividing Montenegro into two hostile political camps.

In 1912 Russia instructed the Bulgarian prime minister to initiate the establishment of a Balkan Alliance against the Ottoman state. What followed was a series of alliance treaties between Bulgaria, Serbia, Greece, and Montenegro.[69] On September 24, 1912, Montenegro declared war on the Ottoman state, thus igniting the First Balkan War. After the conclusion of hostilities in the First Balkan War, Serbia attempted to annex regions in Albania in order to gain access to the Adriatic. This move was opposed by Austria-Hungary and Italy, not to mention by the Albanians, who had proclaimed their independence. Dissatisfied with the outcome of the London Conference in May 1913, Serbia demanded that Bulgaria make significant territorial concessions in Macedonia. Bulgaria refused to accommodate Serbia's demands and on June 29, 1913, initiated military operations against its former ally. Montenegro sided with Serbia, Romania, and Greece, hoping that prolonged hostilities against Bulgaria would result in Montenegrin annexation of the besieged town of Scutari. As a result of the Second Balkan War, most of Bulgaria's earlier territorial gains melted away.

At the outset of the First Balkan War, the Montenegrin army was divided into three army groups totaling just over 35,000 soldiers. King Nikola I Petrović was the commander in chief, and the chief of staff was Commander Jovan Bećir. The Montenegrin army concentrated its efforts on occupying the towns of Scutari and Prizren and the surrounding areas. Only one-third of the Montenegrin forces (the Fourth Division, under the command of Janko Vukotić and numbering 10,000 soldiers) were positioned toward the Sandžak region. The division under the command of Crown Prince Danilo, Zetska Divizija, was entrusted with the most important task—the capture of Scutari.[70] During the Balkan Wars in 1912 and 1913 Montenegro's aim was to enlarge its territory, and by the end of the First Balkan War its territory encompassed 14,443 square kilometers, including the fertile region of Metohia (in present-day northeastern Kosovo). Montenegro gained new territories east of Podgorica and in the region of Sandžak. It annexed the towns of Mojkovac, Bijelo Polje, Pljevlja, Berane, Plav, Gusinje, Rožaje, Peć, Djakovica, and Tuzi. However, in spite of this initial military success and the capture of Scutari on April 23, 1913, King Nikola I was forced by the Great Powers to abandon the city and to "submit to the will of Europe."[71] On May 14, 1913, international troops marched into the city. As John Treadway rightly points out, the web of uncertain political alliances and unpredictable military treaties prior to and during the Balkan Wars, as well as the Scutari crisis, represented a "dress rehearsal for the prelude to war the following summer."[72]

Regarding the internal political landscape of Montenegro, this was the period when the political option of unification with Serbia gained in prominence. The newly elected parliament fully supported close ties with Serbia, and the foreign policy of

Janko Vukotić's new government was tailored toward full collaboration with Serbia. The government's program stated:

> We are in favor of the unity of Serbs and Croats, and following the tradition of Montenegro and its rulers we will work honestly to establish Yugoslav solidarity and union.[73]

Nikola's kingdom proved to be a transitory accomplishment because, at the end of World War I, Montenegro lost its independence and sovereignty and first found itself part of Serbia and later part of the Kingdom of the Serbs, Croats, and Slovenes.

Independent Montenegro: The History of an Idea

Despite the Ottoman administration's persistent efforts over the course of centuries to conquer Montenegro, all of the Montenegrin tribes maintained a relatively high level of independence. In addition to designating a converted Slav as the administrator of the region, Ottoman authorities granted a number of economic privileges to Montenegrins and recognized certain forms of local autonomy. However, during periods of internal crisis in the Ottoman state, these privileges had often been revoked, resulting in numerous rebellions by the Montenegrin tribes. These early conflicts between Montenegrins and the Ottoman authorities revolved around the protection of economic privileges and did not have the character of a broad-based freedom movement. Only in the second half of the seventeenth century did Montenegrin armed resistance display the elements of an organized liberation movement. However, the idea of liberation from Ottoman oppression should not be immediately equated with the concept of establishing an independent and sovereign Montenegrin state. During the seventeenth century such a concept was not a part of the Montenegrin political consciousness. What they were aiming for was the replacement of the Ottoman threat with the patronage of Venice, Russia, or both. The idea of Venetian patronage slowly faded and was replaced by the strong presence of Russia in the state-building plans of every Montenegrin ruler.

Vladika Danilo's initial benevolence toward potential Venetian patronage of Montenegro rested on the fact that despite all potential problems, the Republic was Montenegro's ally and, moreover, was a Christian state whose powerful army was able to confront their common enemy, the Ottomans.[74] However, a number of unsuccessful military engagements by Venice in Montenegro (its failed defense of Cetinje during the assault by Suleiman Pasha in 1692 in particular) tipped the scale in favor of Russia.

In soliciting Russia's assistance, the Montenegrin struggle for the preservation of its independence acquired an ally that was becoming much more powerful than Venice. At the beginning of the eighteenth century this struggle modified in character, becoming a fight for national liberation. Russia treated Montenegro as a unified political structure and viewed Vladika Danilo I as the undisputed leader of Montenegro's militant tribesmen. Russia's attitude represented the first international acknowledgment of the validity of Montenegro's claims to independence, while their armed resistance against the Ottomans and their state-building project were elevated from a local issue to the level of the so-called Balkan Question.

Russia's policy shift regarding Montenegro represented a crucial moment in the process of establishing future power relations in the region. The eventual liberation of Montenegro and its establishing itself as an independent state was something the Ottoman authorities proved incapable of preventing. Furthermore, by attaching international significance to the Montenegrin Question, Russia tried to strengthen its position and increase its presence in the Balkans and, in turn, significantly influence the internal policies of the Ottoman state. Similar tactics were employed in other regions ruled by the Ottoman Empire and populated by Orthodox Christians, and by 1774 Russia had forced the Ottoman authorities to officially acknowledge its role as protector of all Christians living under Ottoman rule.

Vladika Danilo I Petrović's historical consciousness was based on the notion of the Crnojevićes as the last rulers (*gospodari*) of Montenegro and the personification of the Montenegrin tradition of statehood. He perceived the office of the metropolitan in Cetinje to be the only institution of that former state to have survived Ottoman conquest. Following this logic, it can be said that Danilo I Petrović understood the Montenegrin vladikas/metropolitans (himself included) to be the legitimate successors of the Crnojevićes.[75] Furthermore, Danilo was the first Montenegrin metropolitan to show territorial aspirations toward parts of present-day Albania and some regions along the Adriatic coast. He thought that Montenegro had a historical right to these regions. From his time onward, the issue of historical right represented the main point of departure for every ruler of Montenegro.

The importance of the Russian factor in realizing the concept of Montenegrin statehood was fully acknowledged during the rule of Vladika Vasilije Petrović. His vision of a future Montenegrin state was based upon Russian support, and he did everything he could to acquire that support, traveling to Russia three times and staying there for more than three years in total.

Even though he was familiar with the history of the medieval Serbian Nemanjić dynasty and with the myth of Kosovo, and even though he thought of Montenegro as the only free part of the former Serbian empire, Vasilije's model for a future Montenegrin state was the idea of renewing the old Crnojević state (known as Ivanbegovina).[76] He thought that Montenegro should be an independent secular state (the "Montenegrin principality"), ruled by a dynasty that had the Crnojevićes' historical right of succession. He also had a clear idea of the territorial boundaries of this new independent state; according to Vasilije, it should include all the territories that had comprised the former Crnojević principality. It is interesting to note that the vladika's vision of the future Montenegrin state's boundaries is almost identical to Montenegro's twentieth-century borders. Vasilije's "Montenegrin Principality" encompassed the following territories: Katunska, Riječka, Lješanska, and Crmnička Nahija; then regions of Zeta, Šestani, Bjelopavlići; tribal lands of the so-called Brda, such as Piperi, Rovca, Pješivci, Kuči, Bratonožići; and the territories of the Albanian tribes of Klimenti, Hoti, and Kastrati; as well as the coastal regions of Spič, Šušanj, Paštrovići, and Grbalj. Finally, he envisaged parts of Herzegovina as being integral to his state.[77] For Vladika Vasilije, this was the ultimate goal and the essence of Montenegrin statehood and the basis of his antagonism against the Ottomans. Such a framework was significantly different from the eighteenth-century popular political model in the Balkans: the model of renewing an empire.[78]

Neither Vladika Petar I Petrović Njegoš nor his successor, Vladika Petar II Petrović Njegoš, entirely shared Vladika Vasilije's vision of Montenegrin statehood. Both of these rulers played significant roles, however, in establishing and strengthening the state apparatus in Montenegro and in enlarging its territory. Vladika Petar II Petrović Njegoš established permanent state institutions (the senate, the Gvardija, and the Perjanici) and made sure that these institutions functioned properly. Both vladikas saw the territorial expansion of Montenegro as vital for its survival and worked tirelessly to unite the tribes in Montenegro with those in the neighboring mountainous regions (Brda). Unlike their predecessor, both vladikas also envisioned the resolution of the Montenegrin Question within the larger context of first defeating the Ottoman state and then establishing a Christian empire in the Balkans. This empire was to be either Slav, Serbian, or Russian.[79] Within this cognitive framework, their ideas about Montenegrin statehood rested upon the following assumptions:

1. The Montenegrin Question could not be fully addressed through its gaining international recognition, independence, and new territories according to the principle of "historical right," but rather it had to be part of a more general solution to the "Eastern Question."

2. The issue needed to be solved together with "questions" of other Balkan Christians.

3. Once it was solved, Montenegrin independence and state sovereignty would become irrelevant and obsolete because Montenegro would become part of a larger empire (either Christian, Slavic, or Serbian).

Neither of these two vladikas believed that the state sovereignty and independence of Montenegro represented a permanent form of its historical existence because they did not envisage the establishment of separate state individualities in the Balkans. Their vision was of one large, unified political structure that, with the assistance of the Great Powers, would replace the Ottoman state in the Balkans. Moreover, they did not believe in the idea of the evolution of statehood in the region because they thought of the disappearance of the Ottoman state not as a process but as a consequence of a general Christian uprising that would force settlement through an international peace conference. Both of them believed that it was necessary to wait for this "great moment."

The visions that Vladikas Petar I and Petar II held of the Montenegrin future were also influenced and shaped by their historical consciousness. Both of them saw Montenegro as a historical part of the Serbian empire and as having gained its independence unwillingly and due to the unfortunate historical circumstance of the Ottoman conquest of the region. Changing these circumstances should logically result in Montenegro's going back to its earlier historical position as an integral part of a large Serbian empire. This concept rested on the inevitability of Montenegro's surrendering elements of statehood and independence for a greater good and meant the loss of its historical identity. For Petar II Petrović Njegoš, the historical role of the Montenegrin state served to preserve the Christian Orthodox population in the region until the Ottoman state collapsed. In essence, both rulers situated the idea of Montenegrin statehood in a political and historical context that guaranteed its negation. A free and enlarged Montenegro was not their final goal but only a means for reaching the desired solution: the creation of a new, or the reestablishment of an old, empire. Regardless of the various justifications and rationalizations of their goal, it is safe to say that its only basis was in a mythologized historical consciousness. Insisting on such a concept meant that these Montenegrin rulers abandoned the earlier idea of Montenegrin statehood advocated by their predecessor Vladika Vasilije.

By juxtaposing these two conflicting political visions, one can recognize the crucial problems of Montenegrin historical and political identity. In general terms, these problems can be summed up by the following questions. Should Montenegro be an independent state, or was its independence only a functional element of a different and larger political process? Was the authentic form of Montenegro's historical identity an independent state or part of a larger empire? When would the Montenegrin Question cease to exist as such: when Montenegrins established their own state and enlarged its territory or when other "Slav brothers" managed to do the same? Vladika Vasilije Petrović provided very different answers to these questions than had his successors, with the exception of Prince Danilo I Petrović Njegoš. And Montenegrins and their rulers and presidents have continued to give different answers to these same questions ever since. These conflicting visions of Montenegro's future status and position in the Balkans reflect the problematic nature of Montenegrin identity.

Regarding Prince Danilo I Petrović's vision for a future Montenegrin state, he embraced the concept advocated by his predecessor Vladika Vasilije: the revival of the old Crnojević state. Establishing an independent Montenegrin state within the boundaries of the old principality of Ivan Crnojević was the final aim of Danilo's policy and was presented as the ultimate goal of Montenegro's struggle for liberation.[80] Contrary to Vladika Petar II, Prince Danilo did not use history to construct political goals but relied upon it as a means of legitimizing his aspirations based on the political pragmatism of the time. Danilo's concept rested upon the ideological premise of Montenegro's "historical right." This meant that Montenegrins sought to repossess only those territories that were thought to be rightfully theirs because they had been a part of the earlier Crnojević principality. With this in mind, the concept of a new Montenegrin state was presented as a case of reclaiming the historical continuity of statehood and territory.

During the first few years of his rule, Prince Nikola I Petrović embraced the idea of Montenegrin statehood as advocated by his immediate predecessor, but after the military debacle in 1862, he abandoned Prince Danilo's policies and began embracing the concept of Montenegrin statehood advocated earlier by Vladika Petar II Petrović Njegoš. Never again would Nikola I attempt to solve the Montenegrin Question outside of the larger political and diplomatic context. It seems that he had realized his own limitations and stopped believing in the possibility of accomplishing Prince Danilo's ideas about an independent Montenegro. Nikola I became a firm believer that the Montenegrin Question could be successfully resolved only by the liberation and unification of the entire Serbian people. The fact that this historical vista presupposes the disappearance of the Montenegrin state did not seem unusual to him. Prince Nikola had two reasons for adhering to such a vision. One was political in nature, and the other was historical.

The political landscape of nineteenth-century Europe was marked by the affirmation of the idea of national integration and homogenization advanced by Napoleon III. Because he was elected to power via a plebiscite, it seems to have been a matter of pragmatic domestic and foreign policy for Napoleon III to embrace the strategy of respecting "popular will" and present it as the guiding political principle of his reign. Having been educated in Paris, Nikola I Petrović adopted this political concept tailored to the mid-nineteenth-century French idea of national integration and based upon the proclaimed principle of one nation, one state. Once the practical application of this slogan had proved its value, as in the case of Austria in 1859, people in the Balkans firmly believed that it could also work in their struggle against the Ottoman state. Prince Nikola I envisaged the development of national policies in the Balkans as a repetition of the so-called Italian model. In practical terms that meant fighting for the one-nation, one-state principle in the Balkans.

Prince Nikola's historical consciousness was also clearly shaped by the literary achievements of his predecessor, Vladika Petar II Petrović Njegoš. Accordingly, he thought of Montenegrins as a free segment of the Serbian people and viewed Montenegro as a part of the medieval Serbian empire that had never been conquered. Nikola's historical consciousness was heavily influenced by the mythologized tradition of Tsar Stefan Dušan's medieval Serbian state. Even though such a historical vision of Montenegro might have been less than factually accurate, Nikola I firmly believed in its validity until the last several years of his rule. Nikola I believed that new nation-states in the Balkans would replace Ottoman rule and that the territories of these future states would correspond to historical models from the Middle Ages. This was the concept of reviving long-lost state formations, whose national territories were to be integrated according to the principles of historical right and ethnic homogeneity. In Nikola's mind Montenegro had always remained a part of the Serbian state, so it was only natural that it should also be a part of this revived empire, together with Serbia, Bosnia, Herzegovina, and parts of Dalmatia, Old Serbia (present-day Kosovo), and Macedonia.

Until the early 1900s, Nikola viewed the Montenegrin state as anything but the product of unfavorable historical conditions and did not think about Montenegro in terms of the historical continuity of its statehood. For the time being his political pragmatism brushed aside those facts that did not correspond to his political vision. He was aware that the concept of the historical continuity of the Montenegrin state did not fit comfortably into the mythologized all-inclusive grand narrative of a medieval Serbian empire and that it was in direct opposition to his political agenda and to his portrait of his dynasty as the rightful heir to the medieval throne. In the early years of his rule, Nikola I maintained that the medieval state of Doclea had never existed as such, insisting that the history of Montenegro began with the Balšić dynasty. His version of the one-nation, one-state principle meant one Serbian state and one Serbian nation. Nikola I was hoping to succeed in strengthening his position as the self-styled supreme leader of the South Slavs. Adherence to the notion of Serbdom and projection of the image of Montenegro as its pinnacle seemed to him suitable vehicles for confirming his central role in the process. He constantly praised the heroism of the Montenegrins and wrote about their persistent struggle to defend Serbdom and Eastern Orthodoxy as being the everlasting norm in the life of a traditional Montenegrin community and the ideal model for constructing their reality and worldview. The romanticized image of Montenegro as the last remaining heroic society in Europe and the perception of the cultlike status of its highlanders were also shared by many South Slavs and foreigners. Writers such as Simo Matavulj and Marko Car viewed Montenegro as the "proverbial Balkan Piedmont" and its ruler as someone "resembling Richard the Lion Heart."[81] Under the umbrella of such common denominators (Eastern Orthodoxy, Serbdom, and belonging to the South Slavic world), the conflicting concepts of Montenegrin historical distinctiveness and political individuality on one hand and the all-inclusive notion of being an integral part of Serbdom on the other did not collide but seemed somehow connected. Montenegrins of the period saw themselves as fearless warriors and as people who guarded the past glories of Serbdom by being true to their Eastern Orthodox beliefs and by remaining within the confines of the patriarchal social organization. They were deeply attached to their world of heroism and patriarchal order, a world in which the laws of the modern civic society were worthless. Their perception of themselves and their immediate environment was an idyllic image of a paradise lost and an island where the notion of Serbdom was preserved in its purest form.

Such sentiments were nourished in particular through the Montenegrin school system. What becomes apparent in any analysis of the social and cultural climate in Montenegro in the late nineteenth century is the aggressive Serbianization of its society and its cultural space. During Nikola's rule the number of foreigners working in the state apparatus in Montenegro grew considerably. Prominent writers, teachers, and political activists from Serbia, Vojvodina, and Croatia found their way to Cetinje. The period between 1871 and 1900 in Montenegro was devoted to promoting ideas and concepts advocated by an organization called the United Serbian Youth (USY). The USY was established in Vojvodina in 1866 with the aim "to work on national awakening and spiritual unification of Serbs, regardless of state boundaries" and was headed by Vasa Pelagić. Even though its official role was of a scholarly and literary character, the USY displayed strong characteristics of a militant patriotic league. In the early 1870s they concentrated their efforts on Montenegro, and many prominent members of the organization moved to Cetinje. During the late nineteenth century the USY played a dominant role in shaping the national consciousness in Montenegro.[82] Former members of the USY controlled the cultural life in Montenegro in its entirety. Intellectuals such as Jovan Sundečić, Milan Kostić, and its president, Vasa Pelagić, were instrumental in establishing the literary association the Montenegrin Warrior in February 1872. Even though the Montenegrin Warrior officially claimed to be a literary association, its main goal proved to be the education of Montenegrin youth according to the pan-Serbian program. Even Prince Nikola looked benevolently on their activities, and his poem "Onamo 'namo" became the unofficial anthem of this organization.[83] The first Montenegrin newspaper, *Crnogorac*, was an unofficial newsletter of the USY, and its editorial policy was tailored toward "interpreting feelings and desires of the entire Serbdom." The *Glas Crnogorca* had a similar editorial policy. Until 1891 its editors were Simo Popović, Stevo Čuturilo, Jovan Pavlović, Boža Novaković, and Lazar Tomanović, all of whom were former members of the USY and prominent "outsiders" (as citizens of Serbia) who shaped the cultural landscape in Montenegro.[84] One of the most prominent "outsiders" in

Montenegro was Jovan Pavlović. He worked as editor for various newspapers and journals in Montenegro and as the principal of the Cetinje Gymnasium and later was appointed the Montenegrin minister of education. In his writing, Pavlović displayed absolute adoration for Montenegro and its central role in the process of liberating and uniting Serbdom. In one of his articles he went so far as to state that "whoever does not want to remedy Serbdom through Montenegrinity desires Serbdom to be the laughing stock of the world." At one point the Serbian media accused him of being a Montenegrin separatist.[85]

During the school year 1909–1910 there were eighteen new teachers working in various schools in Montenegro, and only two of them were Montenegrin-born.[86] With the gradual improvement of economic conditions and as a result of the reforms of the state apparatus in the first decades of the twentieth century, the issue of children's education gained prominence in Montenegro. When the number of books brought in from Serbia proved to be insufficient, Prince Nikola established the School Commission in 1892 to oversee the publication of textbooks in Montenegro. The commission found that a number of submitted manuscripts were of poor quality and of questionable content. One of the commission members, Savo Vuletić, expressed his frustration in an article, complaining that "we do not have a simple textbook on the geography of Montenegro from which our school children could learn about their fatherland."[87] The commission nevertheless gave permission for a number of new textbooks to be published. Through late 1916, more than 130 primers and textbooks had been published for use in elementary schools in Montenegro. Of a total of 23 authors, 11 were so-called outsiders, people not born in Montenegro. In 1907 Prince Nikola issued a new law regulating the system of public schools in Montenegro.[88] A number of new schools opened between 1903 and 1910, and in the year Montenegro became a kingdom, some 44 percent of all children were attending elementary schools. In the same year the Montenegrin National Theatre was established in Cetinje.

In 1898 the commission approved the publication of the *History of the Serbian People for the Third and Fourth Year of the Elementary Schools*. This textbook was coauthored by Mile Kovačević and Lazar Perović. The minimal competence of the authors is evident in the first paragraph of the introductory section. In their introductory comments about the prehistoric periods, these two authors stated, "The first land where people lived was Asia. If we would want to look for that land, we would have to turn toward the east and then walk into that direction for a very long time, until we arrive at that land." As far as the history of the Slavs was concerned, the authors again displayed their attachment to the traditional Greater Serbian nationalist worldview:

> Our ancestors began their journey from their homeland in Asia, and after following the trail marked by other peoples they finally reached the land called

> Europe. Learned men from those times told us that our ancestors were called Serbs, meaning "cousins" . . . and that the Serbs were the most numerous people of the period. After their numbers grew even further, they started dividing into tribes. Each tribe used its own (tribal) name, while later all of them began calling themselves Slavs: It was only we, from Lužice, who kept our old ethnic name, the Serb.[89]

This text exemplifies the most radical version of the Greater Serbian nationalistic perception of history and identity. According to the authors, the Slavs were the segment of a much greater ethnic stock, the Serbs, rather than the other way around. Moreover, the true meaning of the word Serb, *cousins* (*rodjaci*), implies the existence of a close and possibly blood relation among all the Slavs. It was due to demographic changes, we are told, that the tribal differentiations took place. Finally, the Lužicani (who somehow ended up in the Balkans) were the only ones who remained true to their roots by preserving the "old ethnic name, the Serb." The story of the preservation of the old ethnic name meshed nicely with the ideological construction that presented the Serbs as the only true guardians of the Slavic tradition and values. The references to possible blood relations and tribal differentiation corresponded to ideas of the unification of all South Slavs and the role of Serbia in the process. Presenting themselves as the only true guardians of the ancestral spirit, the Serbs assumed the right to play the central role in the process of unification. Such a self-image and the notion of the messianic role among the South Slavs later gave birth to even more radical theories of the origins of the Serbs and their culture.[90]

The *Reader for the Fourth Year of the Elementary School* had five sections and an appendix and addressed subjects as varied as geography, identity, and history. The author, Djuro Popović, with the imagination of a medieval explorer, created his own geography. He described the Adriatic Sea in the following way: "The Adriatic Sea has been the Serbian sea from the old times, and during the times of the glorious Serbian tsars and emperors it was surrounding the Serbian state." The identity of the Montenegrins was presented as an issue of geography because, according to the author, Montenegrins adopted the toponym as their name, even though they were without doubt "of the Serbian nationality." To prove such a claim, Popović remarked that the Montenegrin knows "about the Serbian glory and the Serbian empire, about Nemanjićes and Kosovo, as all Serbs do." As for the origins of the Montenegrins, he claimed that they came from Kosovo.[91] The section on history is entirely devoted to praise of the three Serbian rulers from the medieval times, Stefan Nemanja, Stefan Dušan, and Prince Lazar Hrebeljanović. They were described as "the three particularly important rulers who wisely ruled over their people." This fact, according to the author, brought recognition to the Serbian people from far and wide. "The mentioning of these people (rulers) will never cease. . . . It could be said that Prince Lazar lives to this day among our people as if he had disappeared yesterday. . . . Is there a young Serb whose parents did not sing about the emperor Lazar?"[92] This section ended with a long poem by V.J. Jovanović about all the joys of being a Serb. To illustrate the theme of the poem and its "educational" character, it suffices to quote only a few lines.

> I am the young little Serb, Serbdom is waiting for me.
> I will remain the Serb, o God, for the rest of my life . . .
> I will live according to the Serb way, I will rule according to the Serb way, and I am always ready to sacrifice myself for it. . . .[93]

The Montenegrin youth had to learn this and other similar songs by heart and repeat them on a regular basis. Considering the nature of those pledges of allegiance, it is not surprising that many young Montenegrins thought of themselves as Serbs.

Another textbook, titled *History of Montenegro*, was written by Ž. Dragović and published in 1910 in Cetinje. It offers a particularly interesting insight into the period of the early South Slav states in the Balkans.

> One of the regions that the Serbs conquered after they arrived on the Balkan Peninsula during the first half of the twelfth century was Zeta. Nemanja himself favored Zeta among other Serbian regions and thought of it as being very important, and with a particular kind of love and respect called it his ancestral land.[94]

Dragović described Cetinje as the center of both religious and secular authorities, while he saw Montenegro as the eternal guardian of Serbian freedom and the Serbian state idea. A year later, in 1911, the new *Geography of the Kingdom of Montenegro for the Third Year of the Elementary Schools* was even more explicit when it came to the national and cultural identity of people living in Montenegro.[95]

> In Montenegro live pure and true Serbs who speak the Serbian language and their number is around 300,000. The majority of them are of the Eastern Orthodox faith, whereas there are small numbers of them that are of the Roman Catholic and the Mohammedan faith . . . it is important to know, however, that all of us are of Serbian origin and Serbian ethnicity.[96]

Time and again the authors of those textbooks resorted to appropriation in order to prove the primacy and continuity of the Serbian presence in the region. By constructing the image of the ancestral land that needs to be reclaimed and by positioning the Serbs as its supreme guardians while simultaneously referring to Montenegrins as the best of all Serbs, the educators worked tirelessly on the Serbianization of Montenegrin youth.

It is, however, important to remember that the content of all of the textbooks used in the elementary schools in Montenegro until late 1915 was evaluated and approved by the school commission. This fact confirms that many Montenegrins thought of themselves as Serbs and did not necessarily regard the trend as an imposition by the dominant Serbian culture. The efforts to reshape the cultural model in Montenegro and to reinforce the notion of the Serbian identity of its people found fertile ground both among the ruling elites and in the general population. But it was an imposition nonetheless because it prevented the development of the mechanism for defining and expressing the distinctiveness of the cultural patterns in Montenegro. The Montenegrin tradition and its system of values were the product of contacts and exchanges between various different ethnic and religious groups. The Serbianization of the Montenegrin education system was by definition exclusionist and drastically reduced the room for recognizing and acknowledging the distinct and multilayered character of the social and cultural fabric in Montenegro.

Nikola's dream of becoming the liberator and the unifier of the Serbs and all South Slavs, and the manner in which he went about projecting it, clearly demonstrate his illusions of grandeur. He failed to recognize that the Montenegrin state institutions he helped create functioned on anachronistic models. In the Europe of the period, many people were reading Dostoyevsky and Baudelaire while Cezanne and van Gogh painted their *Card Players* and *Sunflowers*. In Cetinje, on the other hand, the effort to strengthen the Greater Serbian militant ideology was underway. Thoughts of revenge for Kosovo were nourished through epic poems, and the poorly educated population of Montenegro was confined within the boundaries of a military camp. Given their self-image at the time, it was not so difficult to convince Montenegrins that one can defend one's state only by acting as a hero (in accordance with traditional rules) and by shedding one's own or someone else's blood. Self-sacrifice was presented as the ultimate virtue and as the only human effort worth writing poems about. At the turn of the twentieth century it was the Greater Serbian state for which they were asked to sacrifice. Many Montenegrins were happy to oblige. Nikola's urge to protect and preserve the Petrović dynasty, his sense of patriotism and enthusiasm toward pan-Serbian ideas, and his dreams of empire would come back to haunt him during the last decade of his rule.

Russia was another important factor in strengthening Nikola's belief in the one-nation, one-state principle. He was discreetly reminded that Russia would favor a political scenario featuring the revival of a large and uniform Slavic state in the Balkans, and that it saw the Montenegrin prince as the rightful successor of Stefan Dušan's crown. Counting on Nikola's vanity, Russia was, in fact, trying to turn Montenegro into a stepping stone for its domination in the region and to change Serbia's pro-Austrian foreign policy. The fact that officials in St. Petersburg regarded not Montenegro but Serbia as their real ally and potential prize political possession became clear to Prince Nikola I in 1866, when Serbia's ruler, Prince Mihailo Obrenović, abandoned earlier pro-Austrian policies and Russia pressured Montenegro to enter into an agreement with Serbia according to which the Montenegrin prince would relinquish his title in favor of the Serbian Obrenović dynasty and recognize the political primacy of Serbia over Montenegro.[97] This agreement, in addition to those that the Serbian prince signed with Greece (1867) and Romania (1868), made Serbia "the center of revolutionary and national activity in the Balkans."[98]

Nikola I Petrović Njegoš had an acute sense of dynasty, and at the close of the nineteenth century, he focused on political actions that would secure the dynastic prestige of the Petrović family among the South Slavs. He was aware that any future unification of South Slav lands into one state would place the dynastic issue at the political forefront and would result in a conflict between his family ruling in Montenegro and the family ruling in Serbia. Prince Nikola I moderated Montenegrin state policies in accordance with his wish that the Petrović family occupy the throne of such a "revived" empire, and from then on tried to do everything in his power to prove his rightful claim to the ancient crown. His actions were aimed in two directions: establishing a unified Serbian state and eliminating the rival dynasty. For Nikola I, to sit on the throne of "his ancestors" was not only a matter of pride and historical right but also a matter of the very survival of his dynasty.

Notes

1. Stojan Novaković, *Zakonski Spomenici Srpskih Država Srednjega Veka* (Beograd: Srpska Akademija Nauka, 1912), p. 580.
2. Slavko Mijušković, *Ljetopis Popa Dukljanina* (Titograd, 1967), p. 154. See Ferdo Šišić, *Ljetopis Popa Dukljanina* (Posebna Izdanja SKA, 1928), no. LVIII, and N. Radojčić, *O Najstarijem Odeljku Barskog Rodoslova* (Cetinje: Naučno Društvo NR Crne Gore, Istorijski Institut, 1951). Also see Ivan Bozic, *Istorija Crne Gore* (Titograd: CANU, 1967), vol. 1, pp. 294–338, and Andrija Jovićević, "Zeta i Lješkopolje," *Srpski Etnografski Zbornik* 38 (1926), p. 456.
3. Ivan Božic, "Katuni Crne Gore," *Zbornik Filozofskog Fakulteta u Beogradu*, vol. 10 (Beograd, 1968), p. 245 and p. 247.
4. Ivan Bozic. *Istorija Crne Gore*, vol. 1 (Titograd: CANU, 1967), pp. 94, 307.
5. Risto Kovijanić, *Pomeni Crnogorskih Plemena u Kotorskim Spomenicima XIV–XVI Vijek*, vol. 2 (Titograd: Istorijski Institut Crne Gore, 1974), p. 49. For a more detailed analysis of Ivan Crnojević's title and his position of power in Zeta (Montenegro), see Rade Mihaljčić, "Gospodar—Vladarska Titula Ivana Crnojevića," *Istorijski Zapisi* 72, nos. 3–4 (Winter 1999), pp. 7–15.
6. "1474. Giovanni Cernovicchio Duca di Sabiaco Signor di Forcone, e di Montenegro, un lungo tratto di Paese nell' Albania fu figliuolo do Stefano, et assisti la Republica Veneta in varie importanti Imprese contro Turchi e particolarmente nell'assedio di Scutari." In "Genealogija Crnojevica" (Cavtat, Arhiv Valtazara Bogišića, Sekcija 2-Naucni Arhiv, *Rukopisi Bogišićevog Arhiva*, File 15, No. 19).
7. F. Radičević, *Starine*, vol. 7 (Cetinje: Prosvjeta, 1896), p. 384. Also see Božidar Šekularac, *Dukljansko-Crnogorski Istorijski Obzori* (Cetinje: CNB, 2000), p. 38.
8. Šekularac, *Dukljansko-Crnogorski Istorijski Obzori*, p. 38. B. Kovačević, "Djuradj Crnojević i Njegov Značaj," *Bibliografski Vjesnik*, vols.1–2 (Cetinje: Muzeji i Galerije, 1990). Djuradj's printing press produced only five books: *Oktoih Prvoglasnik, Oktoih Petoglasnik, Psaltir s*

CHAPTER ONE

Posledovanjem, Trebnik (Molitvenik), and *Četvorojevandjelje. Oktoih Prvoglasnik* (according to its first page) was printed on January 4, 1494. See Jagoš Jovanović, *Istorija Crne Gore,* 2nd ed. (Cetinje/Podgorica, 1995), p. 52.
9. Dragoje Živković, *Istorija Crnogorskog Naroda* (Cetinje, 1989), p. 367. Barbara Jelavich tells us that "the Balkan Peninsula, which was regarded as a single administrative unit, was divided into sections that were called at various times *eyalets, vilayets,* or *pashaliks*; these in turn had subordinate jurisdictions known as *sanjak* or *livas,* which were further subdivided into *kazas,* then into *nahijas.*" Barbara Jelavich, *History of the Balkans: Eighteenth and Nineteenth Centuries* (New York: Cambridge University Press, 1983), p. 57.
10. The last mention of Staniša Crnojević (Skender-Bey Crnojević) is in a document he wrote in 1527, confirming the property rights to the monastery of Vranjina (the document is known as "Vranjinska Povelja"). Božidar Šekularac, *Vranjinske Povelje* (Titograd: CANU, 1984), p. 127.
11. Jagoš Jovanović, *Stvaranje Crnogorske Države i Razvoj Crnogorske Nacionalnosti* (Cetinje: Obod, 1948), pp. 54–55.
12. Pavel Apolonovich Rovinsky, *Crna Gora u Prošlosti i Sadašnjosti* (Cetinje, 1993), pp. 352–353.
13. Quoted in Mary Edith Durham, *Some Tribal Origins, Laws, and Customs of the Balkans* (London: George Allen & Unwin, 1928), p. 77.
14. Jovanović, *Stvaranje Crnogorske Države,* p. 56.
15. Vladika Danilo's religious authority extended over the Grbalj regions (the area between the coastal towns of Kotor and Budva) and Paštrovići (the modern-day municipality of Budva), as well as over the towns of Bar (Antivari), Ulcinj (Dulcigno), Skadar (Shkodra/Scutari), and Podgorica. Jovanović, *Istorija Crne Gore,* p. 89.
16. Živko M. Andrijašević, ed., *Kratka Istorija Crne Gore, 1496–1918* (Bar: Conteco, 2000), pp. 70–71. Also see Jovanović, *Istorija Crne Gore,* pp. 123–128.
17. Jovanović, *Istorija Crne Gore,* p. 129.
18. For a more detailed analysis of Šćepan's rule in Montenegro, see Gligor Stanojević, *Šćepan Mali* (Beograd: Srpska Akademija Nauka i Umetnosti, 1957).
19. For an interesting analysis of blood feuds, see Andrei Simić, "The Blood Feud in Montenegro," in William G. Lockwood, ed., *Essays in Balkan Ethnology,* special publications no. 1 (1967), pp. 83–94.
20. Jovanović, *Istorija Crne Gore,* pp. 138–140.
21. In 1775 the army of Mahmout Bushatlija, Pasha of Scutari, attacked the tribe of Kuči hoping to subdue them and split up the Montenegrin tribal confederation. His first attempt ended in disaster, and his second military campaign in 1776 was also a defeat for the Ottomans. Jovanović, *Istorija Crne Gore,* p. 143.
22. Jovanović, ibid., pp. 149–150.
23. This passage is from the solemn oath taken by the tribal leaders present when this legal code was adopted. Quoted in Mary Edith Durham, *Some Tribal Origins,* p. 78.
24. On October 18, 1798, the Tribal Assembly in Cetinje reconfirmed this law and voted to add seventeen new articles to the existing code. Jovanović, *Istorija Crne Gore,* p. 158. See also Andrijašević, *Kratka Istorija,* p. 86.
25. Jovanović, *Istorija Crne Gore,* p. 159. Andrijašević, *Kratka Istorija,* pp. 86–87. Also see Jelavich, *History of the Balkans,* vol. 2, pp. 248–249.
26. Niko S. Martinović, ed., *Rovinski o Njegošu,* trans. from Russian by Radisav Paunović (Cetinje, 1967), p. 68. Original publication: St. Petersburg, 1889.
27. Jovanović, *Istorija Crne Gore,* p. 199. Martinović, *Rovinski o Njegošu,* p. 69.
28. J. Jovanović, *Stvaranje Crnogorske Države* (Cetinje: Obod, 1947), p. 73.
29. Jovanović, *Istorija Crne Gore,* p. 202.

30. The first teacher in Cetinje was Petar Ćirkovic from Kotor. In order to attract more students, Vladika Petar II Petrović Njegoš established a type of scholarship that included free room and board for those in attendance. The students were mostly grown men. They were taught to read and write; arithmetic was studied less intensively. M. Kostić, *Škole u Crnoj Gori* (Pančevo, 1876), p. 13.
31. Jovanović, *Istorija Crne Gore*, p. 203.
32. *Nahija* were administrative units in Montenegro; their borders closely corresponded to the boundaries of tribal lands.
33. Jovanovic, *Stvaranje Crnogorske Države*, p. 238. Also see Durham, *Some Tribal Origins*, p. 58.
34. Gabriel Frile and Jovan Vlahović, *Savremena Crna Gora*, trans. from French by Rosanda Vlahović (Podgorica: CID, 2001), pp. 65–66. Originally published as *Le Montenegro Contemporain, par G. Frilley, officer de la Legion d'honneur et Jovan Wlahovitj, captain au service de la Serbie* (Paris, 1876).
35. France promised to pay an annual sum of 200,000 francs in return for Danilo's cutting off political and financial ties with Russia. Jovanovic, *Istorija Crne Gore*, p. 262.
36. Andrijašević, *Kratka Istorija*, p. 120.
37. The newly acquired territories were: Grahovo, Rudine, Nikšićka Župa, areas in Drobnjak, Tušina, Uskoci, Lipovo, and Gornji Vasojevići. Montenegro also got parts of the Kuči region. Jovanović, *Istorija Crne Gore*, p. 272.
38. This first standing army in Montenegro was 9,777 soldiers strong. Jovanović, *Istorija Crne Gore*, p. 241.
39. Jovanović, ibid., p. 273.
40. Jovanović, ibid.
41. Jelavich, *History of the Balkans*, vol. 2, p. 252. Omer-Pasha Latas was an Islamicized Serb from Bosnia. Born Mico Latas in the village of Janja Gora, he was taken away at an early age by Ottoman soldiers. The taking away of Christian Orthodox boys and their conversion to Islam was known in Bosnia as *Danak u Krvi* (blood tax, or Devsirme). A number of these converts managed to occupy high administrative posts in the sultan's power structure. One of the most famous was Mehmed-Pasha Sokolović (Sokoly), who reached the position of grand vizier.
42. The first publication of this agreement was by M. Mijuškovic in *Politika*, Daily, Beograd, July 7, 1932. Also see Dimitrije Dimo Vujović, *Ujedinjenje Crne Gore i Srbije* (Titograd: Istorijski Institut Narodne Republike Crne Gore, 1962), p. 26.
43. Jovanović, *Istorija Crne Gore*, p. 281.
44. Vasa Čubrilović, *Istorija Političke Misli u Srbiji XIX Veka* (Beograd, 1958), pp. 87–89.
45. Čubrilović, *Istorija Političke Misli*, pp. 241–246.
46. "As their objectives, the governments hoped that the war would result in the annexation of Hercegovina by Montenegro and Bosnia by Serbia. Although the Montenegrin operations were to be successful, the Serbian action soon became a military disaster." Charles Jelavich and Barbara Jelavich, *The Establishment of the Balkan National States, 1804–1912* (Seattle: University of Washington Press, 1977), p. 145.
47. Jelavich and Jelavich, *Establishment*, pp. 153–157. Jovanović, *Istorija Crne Gore*, pp. 304–305.
48. This was the last meeting of the Tribal Assembly, and it marked the beginning of a new phase in the development of state institutions in Montenegro.
49. Jovanović, *Istorija Crne Gore*, pp. 308–309.
50. The first tobacco monopoly was established as a kind of joint venture company, together with an Italian partner, the so-called Anonymous Society. The Italian partner invested 2.5

million liras and had a majority vote in the company. Jovanović, *Istorija Crne Gore*, pp. 327–328.
51. Vojvoda (Duke) Jole Piletić and Vojvoda Peko Pavlović were exiled to Serbia. Vojvoda Marko Miljanov Popović was getting ready to leave his birthplace of Medun for Serbia, accompanied by numerous families of the Kuči tribe, but at the last moment Prince Nikola persuaded him to remain in Montenegro.
52. Jovan Hajduković worked in Belgrade and Kragujevac between 1895 and 1901. The first Radnički Savez in Bar had only 243 members, but Hajduković was soon able to establish branches in Podgorica, Nikšić, Cetinje, and Danilovgrad. Jovanović, *Istorija Crne Gore*, p. 336.
53. The first Montenegrin Constitution was drafted jointly by Prince Nikola and his legal adviser, a journalist from Belgrade named Stevan Ćurčić. The text of this document greatly resembled that of the Serbian Constitution of 1869. Jovanović, *Istorija Crne Gore*, pp. 337–338.
54. See Jovan Djonović, *Ustavne i Političke Borbe u Crnoj Gori, 1905–1910* (Beograd, 1939).
55. S. Popović, *Memoari: Crna Gora i Srbija*, Arhiv Istorijskog Instituta Crne Gore (hereafter AIICG), File 137/II.
56. Novica Rakočević, *Politički Odnosi Crne Gore i Srbije, 1903–1918* (Cetinje: Obod, 1981), p. 113.
57. See Rakočević, *Politicki Odnosi*, p. 114. Also see *Glas Crnogorca* (January 2, 1910) and *Cetinjski Vjesnik* (January 2, 1910).
58. *Glas Crnogorca* (January 15, 1910).
59. *Glas Crnogorca*, ibid.
60. *Glas Crnogorca* (March 3, 1910).
61. The vice president of the local organizing committee in Kolašin (in northern Montenegro) was Janko Tošković, a former member of the Montenegrin People's Assembly and leader of Narodna Partija (the People's Party) that had been banned some years before. He was also the editor of the party's journal *Narodna Misao*.
62. See *Štampa* (July 8, 1910, and July 31, 1910). Also see *Radničke Novine* (January 12, 1910, and July 10, 1910), and *Samouprava* (July 21, 1910). Also see Djonović, *Ustavne i Političke Borbe*, pp. 321, 287.
63. *Štampa* (June 21, 1910). The same editorial continues: "Cetinje has been overtaken by a contagious madness and megalomania. Such an acute phase of this disease has yet to be recorded in medical literature. Now we can see how the illness has grown larger and larger with the shrinking of the state territory. . . . These lunatics will try anything they can think of and will always hold grudges against all those who try to reason with them." It is believed that the author of this editorial was Milutin Tomić, an émigré from Montenegro. See Rakočević, *Politički Odnosi*, p. 117.
64. Rakočević, *Politički Odnosi*, p. 120.
65. Rakočević, ibid.
66. *Glas Crnogorca* (March 18, 1910).
67. *Cetinjski Vjesnik* (September 1, 1910).
68. *Glas Crnogorca* (August 20, 1910).
69. Serbia formed an alliance with Bulgaria on March 13, 1912, and signed a military agreement on July 2, 1912. King Nikola I Petrović made a verbal agreement with the Bulgarian king regarding joint military action against the Ottoman state. By the end of June 1912, Montenegro had signed a military agreement with Greece, and on September 14, 1912, it entered into an alliance with Serbia. According to the agreement with Serbia, Montenegro was obliged to declare war on the Ottomans before Serbia did. Jovanović, *Istorija Crne Gore*,

pp. 384–391. Also see John D. Treadway, *The Falcon and the Eagle: Montenegro and Austria-Hungary, 1908–1914* (West Lafayette, Ind.: Purdue University Press, 1983), pp. 105–108.
70. Jovanović, *Istorija Crne Gore*, pp. 387–392.
71. In his note to the British representative in Montenegro, Count de Salis, King Nikola stated: "My dignity and that of my people not permitting me to submit to isolated demands, I leave the fate of the town of Scutari in the hands of the Powers." Quoted in Treadway, *The Falcon and the Eagle*, p. 151.
72. Treadway, ibid., p. 157.
73. *Stenografske Bilješke Crnogorske Narodne Skupštine za 1914* (Cetinje, 1915), p. 47.
74. In order to appease Venice, Danilo I Petrović allowed the establishment of the post of guvernadur, a civilian governor whose main role was to protect Venetian interests in Montenegro.
75. It seems that for the same reason Danilo I Petrović adopted the two-headed eagle from Ivan Crnojević's coat of arms as the central symbol of the Montenegrin coat of arms.
76. Živko M. Andrijašević, "O Crnogorskoj Državnoj Ideji," *Matica Časopis za Društvena Pitanja Nauku i Kulturu* 1, no. 2 (2000), p. 118.
77. *Cetinjski Ljetopis* (Cetinje, 1962). Reprint by the Montenegrin National Library.
78. Ideas about the renewal of the Serbian medieval empire of Stefan Dušan and later of the Byzantine empire under a Russian protectorate enjoyed particularly strong support among the Orthodox clergy.
79. Andrijašević, "O Crnogorskoj Državnoj Ideji," pp. 120–121.
80. Andrijašević, *Kratka Istorija*, p. 113.
81. Vido Latković, *Simo Matavulj u Crnoj Gori* (Skopje: Južna Srbija, 1940), p. 9.
82. On the structure and aims of the USY, see Slobodan Jovanović, *Sabrana Dela: Vlada Milana Obrenovića*, vol. 4 (Beograd, 1990).
83. "Over there, o'er there, beyond those hills, / Where the heavens bend the blue sky, / Towards Serb fields, towards martial fields, / Over there, brothers, let's prepare to go! // Over there, o'er there, beyond those hills, / One can find, they say, Miloš's tomb! . . . / Over there! . . . My soul will receive its rest / When the Serb no longer will be a slave" ("Onamo, 'namo, za brda ona, / Gdje nebo plavi savija svod, / Na srpska polja, na polja bojna, / Onamo braćo, spremajmo hod! // Onamo, 'namo, za brda ona, / Milošev, kažu, prebiva grob! . . . / Onamo! . . . Pokoj dobiću duši/Kad Srbin više ne bude rob"). Nikola I Petrović Njegoš, *Pjesme* (Cetinje: Obod, 1969), pp. 45–46. I have borrowed the English translation of this poem from Banac, *The National Question*, pp. 247–257.
84. *Zbornik Povodom Pola Milenijuma Crnogorskog Štamparstva* (Cetinje: Matica Crnogorska, 1995), p. 13.
85. *Zbornik*, p. 14. For a detailed description of the activities of Jovan Pavlović in Montenegro, see Dušan Martinović and Radivoje Šuković, *Jovan Pavlović: Život i Djelo* (Novi Sad, 1988).
86. Perko Vojinović, *Crnogorska Inteligencija od Polovine 18 Vijeka do 1918. Godine* (Nikšić: Istorijski Institut SR Crne Gore and NIO Univerzitetska Riječ, 1989), p. 132.
87. *Književni List* (1902).
88. "Zakon o Narodnijem Školama u Knj. Crnoj Gori," *Glas Crnogorca*, February 2, 1907.
89. Mile Kovačević and Lazar Perović, *Istorija Srpskog Naroda za Treći i Četvrti Razred Osnovnih Škola* (Cetinje: Školska Komisija za Rukopis, 1898), pp. 19–27.
90. Some modern-day Serbian theorists claim that India was the old ancestral land of the Serbs and that the Serbian culture is much older than the one whose remnants were discovered at the Greek island of Crete.
91. Djuro Popović, *Čitanka za Četvrti Razred Osnovne Škole*, Šesto Izdanje (Cetinje, 1909), p. 195.

92. Popović, ibid., p. 164.
93. Popović, ibid.
94. Ž. Dragović, *Istorija Crne Gore* (Cetinje: KC Ministrastva Vojnog, 1910), p. 24.
95. Djuro Popović and Jovan Roganović, *Geografija Kraljevine Crne Gore za Treći Razred Osnovnih Škola* (Cetinje: Školska Komisija, 1911).
96. Popović and Roganović, ibid., p. 3.
97. Živko M. Andrijašević, "Crnogorska Državna Ideja u Vrijeme Nikole I Petrovića Njegoša," *Matica* 1, no. 3 (2000), p. 152.
98. Jelavich, *History of the Balkans*, vol. 2, p. 246.

CHAPTER TWO

Montenegro during World War I

❖ Saving the Dynasty or Saving Serbdom? ❖

On Sunday, June 28, 1914, Archduke Franz Ferdinand, heir to the Habsburg throne and inspector general of the Armed Forces of the Habsburg Empire, visited Sarajevo. It was St. Vitus Day (Vidovdan), the 525th anniversary of the Battle of Kosovo, and therefore the most sacred day in the mythologically saturated calendar of Serb nationalism. Following the itinerary that had been published the previous day in the *Bosnische Post*, the archduke's convoy of limousines drove past no fewer than six Young Bosnian (Mlada Bosna) assassins armed with bombs and pistols. Five failed to act, but Gavrilo Princip managed to fire two fatal shots, killing the archduke and his wife, the Duchess of Hohenberg. The reaction in Vienna was anger, and the immediate concern there was finding as much evidence as possible about the involvement of the Serbian government in the plot. Many Bosnians made up their minds very quickly about who was to blame. On the evening of June 28, 1914, there were anti-Serb demonstrations and riots in Sarajevo, during which many Serb-owned shops and houses were destroyed.[1] As Friedrich von Wiesner specified in his report, there was only circumstantial evidence that the Serbian government had been directly involved in the plot. It has been said that the Serbian prime minister at the time, Nikola Pašić, learned about the conspiracy sometime in May but was in no position to do anything about it. He instructed the Serbian envoy in Vienna to warn the administration about potential problems and to suggest the cancellation of the archduke's visit to Bosnia. Different theories about the identity of those who planned the assassination included the Russian secret police Okhrana, a Hungarian connection, Istvan Tisza, British and French Masonic organizations, and even pan-German and anti-Habsburg circles in Germany; nonetheless, all available sources point to the Serbian secret organization Union or Death (Ujedinjenje ili Smrt) as the main instigator. The officials in Vienna, nevertheless, decided to issue an ultimatum to Belgrade on July 23, 1914. The ultimatum emphasized that the Serbian government had "tolerated the machinations of various societies and associations directed against the monarchy, allowed unrestrained language on the part of the press and glorification of the perpetrators of outrageous acts, and participation of officers and officials in subversive agitation."[2] The Serbian government accepted all but two of the ultimatum's demands, but Vienna was not satisfied with their level of compliance, and on July 28, Austria-Hungary declared war on Serbia.

Montenegro suddenly became the focal point of Austro-Hungarian diplomatic activities in the region as representatives from Vienna revived their contacts with Montenegrin officials. Their aim was to persuade Montenegro to stay neutral. The Central Powers appeared willing to significantly compensate Montenegrin military abstention.[3] It seems that General Franz Conrad von Hotzendorff, the chief of the Austro-Hungarian general staff, was in favor of an independent Montenegrin state; he advocated numerous incentives for Montenegro, including supporting King Nikola and the Petrović dynasty in their bid to dominate the political scene in the region. He was also in favor of providing financial and economic assistance to Montenegro and of supporting its policies in the international arena.[4] King Nikola was aware that engaging in a new armed conflict so soon after the two Balkan wars would harm his country's economy and its army. On the other hand, he was conscious of the significant pro-Serbian popular sentiment in Montenegro. His ambitions to strengthen the position of his dynasty at home and to enlarge the state's territory partly corresponded to Central Power efforts to distance Montenegro from Serbia. The territorial expansion of Montenegro played a crucial part in Nikola's political strategy because he thought that enlarging his country's territory would lessen his dependence on Serbia. Moreover, the regions that Nikola desired for Montenegro were contested—Serbia claimed the historical right to the same territories. It seems that Nikola understood very early on that Serbia presented the greatest threat to Montenegro's future and the future of his dynasty. By proposing to enlarge the territory of Montenegro and increase its population, which in turn would broaden and secure the country's economic base, Nikola evidently was hoping to prove that his tiny kingdom could survive without Serbia. Montenegrin politicians and the king himself argued in favor of occupying the town of Scutari and the surrounding areas because, according to them, Montenegro was in desperate need of the fertile plains in the region. At one point they even debated draining parts of Lake Scutari so that Montenegro could gain much-needed arable land. A number of Montenegrin politicians seriously considered the idea of neutrality for the same reasons.[5] These sentiments remained long after Montenegro entered the war on the side of Serbia and the Allies. In December 1914, the main topic of conversation in Cetinje was whether Montenegro should remain neutral and preserve its sovereignty so that it could reap the benefits of territorial expansion after the war. Officials talked openly about the future incorporation into Montenegro of the Boka region (the Bay of Kotor) and the coastal area all the way to Dubrovnik. Nikola's territorial aspirations increased considerably once Italy entered the war on the side of the Allies in the spring of 1915. His idea was that once the war was over and Italian forces withdrew from parts of the Adriatic coast, Montenegro and not Serbia would occupy areas of southern Dalmatia. In early 1915 King Nikola spoke about incorporating into Montenegro territories such as Albania all the way to the Mat River, including the town of Scutari, the whole of Herzegovina, and the Boka region all the way to the Neretva River.[6]

Such rhetorical and diplomatic activities on the part of the Montenegrin envoy to St. Petersburg, Mitar Martinović, were interpreted by Belgrade as an attempt to weaken Serbia's position in the region. The Serbian officers and diplomats stationed in Montenegro expressed concern about Montenegro's unilateral diplomatic actions and portrayed Nikola and his government as a less than loyal ally of Serbia.[7] Russian officials also expressed concern about Nikola's aspirations to dominate the region's politics. In early 1915 the Russian foreign minister, Sergei Sazonov, tried to assure his Serbian counterpart of Russia's support for Belgrade by stating that "the question of the unification of Serbdom does not depend on the Montenegrin king" and that "Italy cannot influence future border delineation between Serbia and Montenegro."[8] According to Serbian sources, the Russian foreign minister instructed Martinović that "Montenegro had to remain in full cooperation with Serbia and must not do anything without its consent."[9] These instructions marked the failure of Montenegrin attempts to rally Russian support in distancing itself from Serbia.

Other important factors influencing Montenegrin policy with regard to its participation in the war were public opinion and the obligations that the Montenegrin government had accepted by signing a military treaty with Serbia. Pro-Serbian sentiment was high among many Montenegrin citizens, and Nikola and his government had to take it into account. A pro-Serbian rally was held in front of the Austrian embassy in Cetinje, and the day after Vienna issued its ultimatum to Serbia, the Montenegrin government sent a letter to its Serbian counterpart. The Montenegrin representative in Belgrade was instructed to convey the message: "It is not easy to decide how to reply to Austria. In any case, convince Pašić that we are with Serbia, and that we will share with Serbia all good as well as all bad things."[10] On August 1, 1914, the Montenegrin parliament met in an extraordinary session and unanimously voted in favor of declaring war on Austria-Hungary. The members of parliament urged the government to respond to Austria-Hungary with an immediate declaration of war so that "brothers could engage in a holy war hand in hand." The members of parliament also stated that this war would be fought not only for the preservation of Serbian and Montenegrin independence but also for the liberation and unification of the Serbian people.[11] A week later, on August 6, 1914, the Austro-Hungarian representatives left Cetinje, and Montenegro declared war on Austria-Hungary.[12]

The Montenegrin Treaty with Serbia: Generals without an Army

Montenegro's declaration of war was in accordance with the pre–World War I military treaty that it signed with Serbia on August 4, 1914, and resulted in a unified command structure of the two armies. The Montenegrin government consented at the outset of the war that the Serbian High Command would be in charge of all the operations of both Serbian and Montenegrin armies. The Montenegrin government also agreed to provide the Serbian army with two-thirds of its total military capabilities for the purpose of a joint action with the Serbian Užice Army Group.[13] On August 6, 1914, the commander in chief of the Serbian forces, Radomir Putnik, designed a "Plan for the Joint Action of the Serbian and the Montenegrin Armies in the War against Austria-Hungary." The Montenegrin forces were to be positioned in the region of Pljevlja (in northeastern Montenegro) so that they could take part in the military operations of the Serbian army aimed at advancing into Bosnia and eventually taking Sarajevo. The remainders of the Montenegrin forces were to defend Montenegro's borders with Herzegovina to the east and with Albania to the west and to defend the southern front line on Mount Lovćen Mountain. The timing of Putnik's plan is a matter of some controversy, and many historians have argued that it was devised at a later date (August 17, 1914). I would argue that the plan was designed and delivered to Montenegro on August 6, 1914, because its content and its arguments clearly indicate that it was written before the Austro-Hungarian offensive in the Drina River region, which started on August 12, 1914. Moreover, on August 3, 1914, the Montenegrin government instructed its representative to the Serbian High Command, Brigadier General Jovan Bećir, to request the text of the plan. Furthermore, on August 5, 1914, the Serbian government was informed about the upcoming Montenegrin declaration of war (issued on August 6, 1914), and it is logical that the Montenegrin government and its High Command had received the plan just before the declaration of war was passed.[14] General Božidar Janković was appointed the Serbian representative to the Montenegrin headquarters and the commander in chief of the Montenegrin army, and his staff included Colonels Petar Pešić, Borivoje Nešić, Dragoljub Mihailović, and Djordje Paligorić. They arrived in Montenegro on August 21 and were met in Andrijevica (a town in northern Montenegro) by the king's representative, Miro Božović. The Serbian envoys arrived in Cetinje on the same day and had an audience with the king two days later.[15] The Montenegrin High Command appointed Brigadier General Jovan Bećir as its representative to the Serbian army headquarters, but he resigned his post on October 13,

1914, in protest over the strong prounionist sentiment among the Serbian officers.[16] He also returned the medal awarded to him by the Serbian High Command. The case of Jovan Bećir illustrates that a level of political propaganda in favor of future unification was present at the time among Serbian troops and officers.[17] According to Bećir's complaint to Nikola Pašić, the Serbian army openly discussed the issue of Serbia's annexing Montenegro. Particularly vocal were officers who were members of the organization known as the Black Hand (Crna Ruka). Bećir complained that these officers talked to him about the liquidation of the Montenegrin dynasty and tried to solicit his help. Furthermore, he stated that it was thanks to Russian benevolence that such an anti-Montenegrin attitude was widespread in the Serbian army.[18] The Serbian government tried to minimize the negative impact of Bećir's resignation and instructed its representative in Cetinje to convince King Nikola that the general's dissatisfaction had been caused by inappropriate remarks of individuals whose opinions did not reflect official Serbian policy. Even though it seemed that the king accepted the explanation from Belgrade, he did not appoint a Montenegrin officer as Bećir's replacement but, rather, decided to name Serbian General Bozidar Janković as his representative to the Serbian High Command. Until his resignation over the Scutari crisis, General Janković was responsible for several posts, and his duties often conflicted. He was the commander in chief of the Montenegrin High Command and the representative of the Montenegrin High Command with the Serbian military authorities as well as the representative of the Serbian High Command to Montenegro. It would seem that Bećir's accusations were not unfounded. The captain of the Montenegrin army, Radivoje Milošević, who was attached to the Serbian High Command, wrote that in early 1915 he had been approached by Apis to assassinate Nikola. Apis, a high-ranking intelligence officer in the Serbian army, was the alleged leader of the secret organization known as the Black Hand, which was believed to have organized the assassination of Franz Ferdinand. His response to Apis was that an organization already in place in Montenegro was working toward unification and that the goal would be achieved without spilling anyone's blood.[19]

In spite of the fact that King Nikola remained the nominal supreme commander of the Montenegrin army, the bulk of his forces were under the command of Serbian officers. Moreover, it was Serbia and not Montenegro that had control over the disbursement and spending of Allied financial support, as well as food rations and equipment donations, all of which were originally designated to Montenegro. All this indicates that Montenegro was entirely under Serb control. The Montenegrin government attempted to organize regular supplies to its army independent of Serbia, and in early 1915 two envoys were dispatched, one to England and France and one to Corfu. Later that year the Montenegrin government sent Andrija Radović to France as its representative in charge of purchasing food and supplies. The Serbian government paid close attention to everything Radović did in France, and the

Serbian prime minister issued an order to his representatives in Paris and London to monitor Radović's every move.[20]

The French, English, and Russian representatives in Cetinje also pressured Montenegro to abandon the idea of defining separate war aims and confirmed that the funds granted to Montenegro for the purchase of arms and military equipment must be used only when the Serbian High Command had decided their purpose. They also favored the unified command structure because they were suspicious of Nikola's plans to advance into the Boka region. Furthermore, the Serbian Ministry of Foreign Affairs ordered its representatives in Cetinje, London, and other European capitals to pay close attention to the kinds of materials purchased for Montenegro and to monitor the money spent.[21]

> Montenegrin representatives Colonel Banaševic and Director Nikezić are allowed to receive the material designated to Montenegro that is being shipped from Russia through Prahovo. The chief of the general staff has ordered that they are to be closely monitored and followed, and that they can be allowed to remain in Prahovo only while the material is being unloaded. . . . Crossing into Romania is strictly forbidden.[22]

The strength of Serbia's position (domestic and international) became clear after its government decided to unilaterally define its war aims at a meeting in Niš on December 7, 1914. This document became known as the Niš Declaration, and its main point was the proclaimed need for the postwar unification of Serbs, Croats, and Slovenes. Montenegro was slowly pushed to the margins of the ongoing state-building process in the region, and this move on the part of Serbia was supported by France, Britain, and Russia.[23]

In spite of the obvious primacy of Serbian military aims over those of King Nikola, Montenegrin officials tried to act outside of the designated framework and to send as many army units as they could to advance their own military goals of territorial expansion in Albania and Macedonia at the expense of Serbia. Army commanders exchanged numerous letters and argued over contested territories in Macedonia. One of the Montenegrin commanders, General Radomir Vešović, complained to the Serbian commander of the so-called New Territories (Macedonia and Kosovo) about the Serbian troops occupying territories in northern Albania in June 1915. According to General Vešović, these territories belonged to Montenegro because "Ljubižda was occupied by the Montenegrin army in November 1913 when the Serbian army evacuated the Nahija of Djakovica . . . and since then we have had authority over the area . . . and I plead with you to order your units to withdraw from Ljubižda because there is no need to argue over it at this time."[24] The Serbian commander, General D. Popović, replied that the area was within the Serbian zone of influence and refused to accommodate Vešović's request.[25] The Serbian High Command ordered its representative in Montenegro to act decisively against any unilateral action by Montenegrin army units:

> Prevent any downsizing of the number of soldiers that Montenegro has to put under our command, since it is obvious that they are moving their troops toward the Drim River . . . and are occupying more and more territory. Their political goal is to capture Scutari and St. Giovanni di Medua. . . . You have to let them know that by doing this they only jeopardize common interests.[26]

King Nikola was particularly keen on advancing deep into Albanian territory and capturing the town of Scutari (thus replicating the achievement of 1913), and this military engagement by the Montenegrin army proved to be the incident that finally discredited the Montenegrin king among his war allies. A couple of days before the fall of Scutari, General Janković reported the Montenegrin army's operation to his High Command. He stated that this movement of forces had been ordered by the Montenegrin minister of war and was supported by the entire Montenegrin government against the wishes of the Unified Serbian-Montenegrin High Command and without its knowledge. Janković informed his High Command that he would resign his post and transfer his duties to his second-in-command, Colonel Petar Pešić. He also reported that King Nikola had told him that he did not know that the government had ordered this movement of troops and pleaded with Janković to trust him, but the general politely refused to do so.[27] When the Montenegrin army captured the town of Scutari in June 1915, Janković resigned his post in protest. "Because Montenegro occupied Scutari and because it did so without the consent of General Janković, the commander in chief, it is clear that General Janković can no longer remain in Cetinje as the representative of the Serbian government and as the commander in chief."[28] His decision was supported by the Serbian foreign minister, and shortly thereafter he was replaced by Colonel Petar Pešić.

After the capture of Scutari, the relations between Serbia and Montenegro entered a new phase, marked by open animosity between the two commanding structures and by repeated attempts by the Serbian government to discredit its Montenegrin counterpart. Serbian accusations that the Montenegrins had engaged in secret negotiations with the Austro-Hungarian government were particularly harmful for the Montenegrin government and the Petrović dynasty. Even before World War I the Serbian government had made similar accusations. In 1907 historian Radovan Perović-Tunguz produced a document titled "The Secret Agreement between Montenegro and Austria." This document, allegedly written in Vienna and dated June 12, 1907, carried the signatures of Emperor Franz Joseph and Prince Nikola Petrović. This forgery had been reprinted on several occasions and often used as the ultimate proof of King Nikola's treachery.[29] The foreign representatives in Montenegro also connected the capture of Scutari with this alleged agreement. It was rumored that

Prince Petar (Nikola's son) had made a pact with an Austrian agent in Cetinje on June 11, 1915, and the Russian representative in Belgrade reported that this agreement was directly connected with the Scutari issue:

> Austrians are allowing Montenegrins to take Scutari and are agreeing to cease the bombardment of Montenegrin territory so that Montenegro can freely transport necessary goods and supplies. For their part, Montenegrins will cease their military activities against Austria.[30]

The meeting between Prince Petar and the Austrian agent in Cetinje was not a secret. It occurred as the result of an official invitation extended by the Montenegrin authorities to one Major Hubka, a member of the Austro-Hungarian legation in Montenegro, to discuss the issue of civilian casualties in Montenegro: the Montenegrin government wanted the Austro-Hungarian military authorities to stop bombing civilian targets. Even though the main topic of conversation was public knowledge, it still remains uncertain what other issues (if any) were discussed. Hubka's report indicates that the prince expressed a desire to establish friendly relations between the two countries once the war ended. He also expressed concern for the fate of the Petrović dynasty after the war and stated that "King Nikola was very much inclined to avoid war against the Monarchy, but he could not resist the pressure put on him by various parties." Official Montenegro was very critical of the assassination of the archduke in Sarajevo, and all celebrations with regard to St. Vitus Day in Montenegro were cancelled. The government-controlled *Glas Crnogorca* reported in its editorial on the Sarajevo crime that the archduke had been the victim of a gang of "horrible assassins."[31]

The Allies were also opposed to the taking of the town of Scutari and further territorial enlargement of Montenegro. In March 1915 the Italian foreign minister, Sidney Sonnino, informed his ambassador in London that Serbia should be given Dubrovnik and San Giovanni di Medua, as well as Kotor and the port city of Bar, "if and when Serbia unites with Montenegro." A few days later Sonnino added that Serbia should also be given Bosnia and the mountainous region (Herzegovina) should be divided between Serbia and Montenegro.[32] It seems that Sonnino was certain the two countries would unite after the war. The Montenegrin representative to Britain was told openly by the Foreign Office that the capture of Scutari was the reason why Britain was reluctant to send any aid to Montenegro.[33]

The Role of the Serbian Envoy in Montenegro

The Serbian envoy in Montenegro, Colonel Petar Pešić, was attempting to secure the future cooperation of King Nikola. After the resignation of General Janković, it was Pešić who took over the command of the Montenegrin troops. Aside from being Serbia's political representative in Montenegro, he now had some 30,000 Montenegrin soldiers under his control. Pešić's reports to the Serbian High Command indicated a healthy dose of skepticism with regard to King Nikola. At one point he even suggested a plan for breaking off all relations with Montenegro. In one of his reports, Pešić confirmed that Nikola had promised him that he would not interfere in military operations any longer and that he would communicate with the army solely through Pešić. Furthermore, he cited several clauses from an agreement regarding Scutari that had allegedly been signed in 1911 between Montenegro and Austria and reported that the British and the Italian military representatives in Cetinje had confirmed the allegations about this secret treaty. According to Pešić's report to the Serbian minister of war, Petar Bojović, and the commander in chief of the Serbian army, Radomir Putnik, the clauses of the alleged agreement included the following territorial concessions to Montenegro: Austria would give Scutari and the areas toward the Drim River to Montenegro whereas the rest of Albania would remain as an autonomous state under the sovereignty of King Nikola. Having in mind the negative reactions of the Great Powers to the Montenegrin capture of Scutari, Pešić suggested that it would be an opportune moment to break off relations with Montenegro. He further pointed out that the official reason for doing so should not be the issue of Scutari because the Montenegrin general public approved of the occupation of the town. Instead, Pešić suggested that it would be better to wait until Nikola again started intervening in military matters; Pešić would then resign in protest and the Serbian Mission in Montenegro could take over. In the closing paragraph of his report, Pešić stated: "our interests demand that we put Montenegro in a desperate position," and asked that these plans be kept secret.[34] A few days later, Pešić suggested to his superiors that extraordinary measures be taken to control King Nikola:

> Considering the king's character and the fact that he is very restless, it is indeed necessary and in our best interest to have one of our officers with him at all times to keep track of the king's actions.[35]

The Serbian representative in Montenegro sought other ways of pressuring Nikola into submission and influencing public opinion in Montenegro. One of the tools he used was the distribution of food supplies provided by the Allies. In a report to the Serbian High Command, Pešić pointed out the motives for such an approach:

> The allies were adamant in refusing to provide safe passage across the sea for food convoys to Montenegro and are creating many difficulties for the Montenegrin government because of the occupation of Scutari and the alleged alliance with Austria. Aid coming from Serbia is viewed as great help; people think that if it were not for Serbia's assistance in providing food supplies, ammunition and money, Montenegro would have been ruined a long time ago. This is a

particularly good strategy and we should accommodate all future requests, and also find a way for civilians and soldiers in Montenegro to learn that this aid is coming from Serbia and not from Russia as presented by the court officials and the government.[36]

During 1914 and 1915, the Serbian representative in Montenegro worked hard to advocate the future unification of the two states among the soldiers and the civilian population in Montenegro. The Serbian government provided its envoy in Cetinje and newspaper editors across Montenegro with various publications favoring the option of a unitary South Slav state.[37] The principal advocates of such a form for the future state were the Serbian officers stationed in Montenegro. The Montenegrin government took some steps in trying to lessen the damage of prounionist propaganda. A number of Serbian soldiers stationed in Montenegro were accused of attempting to organize a coup and on May 20, 1915, were tried for treason. All of the accused were found innocent and released.[38] There were also a number of Montenegrins who opposed King Nikola's policies and worked diligently to persuade the population to opt for a future union of the two states. The responsibility for coordinating their actions was assigned to the Serbian representative in Montenegro. Pešić was in constant contact with Montenegrin prounionists such as Todor Božović. In January 1915 Božović addressed a gathering in Podgorica and spoke passionately about postwar Serbia and Montenegro. The Montenegrin government reacted immediately and dismissed the regional administrator, Janko Spasojević, blaming him for not having prevented Božović's speech. Spasojević tried to explain that his inaction was the product of the political reality in the region where, according to him, people were in favor of union with Serbia.[39] Shortly after his Podgorica speech, Bozović pleaded with the Serbian government to help him leave Montenegro for the United States. He invoked an earlier agreement with Nikola Pašić that at some point he (Božović) would travel to the United States to do propaganda work in favor of a unitary state. The Serbian government responded that the time was not right for Božović to travel to the United States, but that he could come to Niš, where the Serbian government had offices. It also instructed its representatives in Cetinje to assist Božović in leaving Montenegro but to do it in a discrete manner.[40] Soon after his arrival in Niš, Božović was dispatched to the United States, where he worked with Jovan Djonović on advocating the idea of unification among Montenegrins living there. In September 1915, Montenegrin officials intercepted a letter written by a Montenegrin man to Serbian officers discussing an upcoming coup that would aid the prounionist agenda. Three individuals were arrested in connection with this letter. Colonel Petar Pešić informed his superiors in Niš about the incident and stated that the time was not right to address the issue of unification:

> I suggest that an order be issued to our officers forbidding them from engaging in these discussions because it could bring more harm than good to us, especially

at a time when our standing among Montenegrin people who want unification with Serbia is very high.⁴¹

In order not to compromise its work on the annexation of Montenegro, the Serbian government and its High Command ordered Serbian officers not to discuss the issue and not to engage in political debate. In a letter to the Serbian minister of foreign affairs, Nikola Pašić suggested that soldiers be advised not to participate in any political discussions "because these issues do not fall within the realm of officers' activities and discussions."⁴²

The Capitulation of Montenegro

At the outset of the war, the Montenegrin army had 30,000 old Russian and 8,000 Mauser rifles that had been confiscated during the Balkan Wars. In addition, they had 9,000 single bullet rifles. The only supply of arms that Montenegro ever received from the Allies was a few batteries of old cannon and 36 automatic rifles. From August 1914 until January 1916 Montenegro received some 9,000 tons of supplies for the army and the general population from the Allies. These contingents consisted mainly of flour, corn, rice, and gasoline, as well as some clothes and boots.⁴³ Firefighter units from Paris provided some 9,000 incomplete uniforms for the soldiers. At the time, the Montenegrin army needed approximately 15,000 tons of flour per year and 47,000 army coats for its soldiers. It should be noted that in 1914–1915 Montenegro also had to provide food for some 40,000 refugees from Bosnia and Herzegovina.⁴⁴ Due to the constant engagement of numerous Montenegrin army units on frontlines designated by the Serbian High Command and the lack of food and equipment needed to successfully fight a war, Montenegro quickly found itself in a desperate situation, and its government pleaded with the Allies for assistance in obtaining food and war matériel. Because Montenegro honored the clauses of its pre–World War I military agreement with Serbia and put at Serbia's disposal some 30,000 of its soldiers for operations in Bosnia and in Sandžak, Montenegro's southwestern, western, and southern borders were defended by just over 10,000 soldiers. Army supplies were running so low and the situation was so dramatic that on August 7, 1915, the Montenegrin minister Petar Plamenac wrote to Andrija Radović, the Montenegrin representative in Marseilles, that

> if supplies do not reach us on time, the Montenegrin army will have to be sent back to their homes because of a lack of food. The army has enough food until 10 August. Send a steamer with food to Gallipoli as soon as possible.⁴⁵

On October 22, 1915, the Austro-Hungarian forces began a new offensive against the Montenegrin army along the 500 kilometer-long front line. The Montenegrin army numbered only 53,320 soldiers, two-thirds of whom were allocated to fight on the front lines outside of Montenegro. Equipment was scarce and food lacking.[46] By the end of November the Serbian army was retreating through Montenegro and Albania toward the Adriatic coast, and the bulk of the Montenegrin forces were trying to secure safe passage. While the Serbian army and many Serbian civilians were slowly retreating toward Durazzo (Drač, Durres) in Albania and farther toward Thessalonica, the Montenegrin units tried to protect their flanks along the front line, Lever Tara-Mojkovac-Turjak-Čakor, in northern and northeastern Montenegro.[47] During the initial phase of this operation, the role of the Montenegrin army was to protect the right flank of the retreating Serbian forces and civilians, but it quickly acquired the much larger mission of protecting the retreat of the entire Serbian army toward Scutari and Durazzo. Bitter fighting between Austro-Hungarian and Montenegrin forces occurred around Mojkovac from December 17 to December 23, 1915.[48] Meanwhile, the Austro-Hungarian army concentrated its efforts on the southern borders of Montenegro and advanced steadily toward the Lovćen mountain range. The Montenegrin army could barely hold on, and as the fighting continued there were repeated attempts at mutiny among the soldiers. The Serbian representatives in Montenegro reported to their high command that the situation was critical and that the Montenegrin soldiers were refusing to fight:

> All attempts by the officers and personal pleas by Prince Mirko and Prince Petar to the soldiers proved in vain; soldiers from almost all the battalions in the Lovćen Brigade stated that they will not fight any longer and that they will leave the frontlines and return to their homes. They said that they will do this because they have not received any bread rations for the past four days and because they cannot fight without proper clothing and boots in such cold weather. The government suggested to the king that he should seek a ceasefire and, if necessary, that he should proceed with negotiating the terms for the complete secession of hostilities with the Austrians. The king rejected this proposal and ordered that the army should fight for as long as it can. The government offered its resignation, but the king refused to accept it.[49]

On December 29, 1915, all foreign representatives and embassies were evacuated from Cetinje and moved to Podgorica. Some state institutions were also moved to Podgorica while King Nikola went to the front line at Lovćen to urge the soldiers to fight.[50] The ever-suspicious Petar Pešić reported to his superiors that the king's trip to the Lovćen front line would prove to be an effort in vain and that all of this might be yet another maneuver on Nikola's part to convince foreign representatives that he was ready and willing to fight the war to its bitter end. Pešić stated that Nikola had to seek peace with Austria-Hungary because of the widespread hunger in Montenegro. Furthermore, he reported that the cold weather, lack of food, and constant heavy shelling by the Austro-Hungarian army indicated that soldiers on the slopes of Mount Lovćen might not be able to resist the pressure for longer than a day or two.[51] Pešić's gloomy prognosis proved correct; that same day Montenegrin authorities decided to seek a ceasefire. General Boža Janković reported to the Serbian High Command that at 3:00 p.m. the Royal Government of Montenegro had dispatched two officers to Njeguši to negotiate with the enemy commander a ceasefire for the Njeguši-Lovćen front line with the aim of arranging a six-day cessation of hostilities. Simultaneously, these parliamentarians were instructed to request the appointment of delegations for both parties to meet at Njeguši and negotiate a peace settlement between Montenegro and Austria-Hungary.[52] In a letter dated December 29, 1915, Colonel Petar Pešić suggested to the Montenegrin minister of war that the government and the court, together with the foreign representatives and the army staff, should leave Montenegro. On December 29 at midnight before the Montenegrin parliamentarians returned from their mission, the king and his family left Cetinje and headed for Podgorica. The government joined them. The king seems to have been in agreement with Pešić's proposal, but the government insisted that he should remain in the country and seek peace with Austria-Hungary. Nikola refused to do so, and the government resigned, but again the king would not accept its resignation.[53] The representatives of the Serbian High Command left Cetinje the next day because it was believed that the enemy would enter the city in a matter of hours.[54] Once in Podgorica, Nikola received the following answer from the Austro-Hungarian High Command:

> The Austro-Hungarian High Command will cease the hostilities only if and when the entire Montenegrin army lays down its arms unconditionally and without any negotiation, and when all Serbian troops stationed on Montenegrin territory surrender to Austria-Hungary. Therefore, until these conditions are fully met Austria-Hungary will continue its operations.[55]

At first, King Nikola refused to accept the Austro-Hungarian terms of surrender and urged his commanders to continue fighting. The Montenegrin government, in contrast, was in favor of accepting the proposed terms, but Nikola refused to discuss the issue. The situation was desperate, and on January 12, 1916, the government persuaded the king to seek peace with Austria-Hungary. On that day the Austro-Hungarian forces took Lovćen. On January 13, 1916, they entered Cetinje, and the Montenegrin government issued an official memorandum to Vienna proposing a peace settlement. On the same day the king telegraphed Emperor Franz Joseph, pleading with him for an honorable peace settlement:

> Sir, your troops have occupied my capital once again, and the Montenegrin government is forced to ask your royal government for a ceasefire and peace between my country and the country of your royal highness. The conditions imposed by a happy victor might be harsh. I am writing to your royal highness in hope that you will mediate so that a just and honorable peace settlement is reached. I am hopeful that your benevolent and brave heart will not allow my people to suffer any undeserved humiliation.[56]

The Montenegrin government hoped that a peace agreement would soon be reached and wrote four versions of its final proposal. All four versions included a paragraph requesting the preservation of Montenegrin sovereignty and independence and the keeping of territory not already occupied by the Austro-Hungarian forces. It also requested the inclusion of Cetinje, even though the city was already occupied. The fourth version differed somewhat because in it the Montenegrin government agreed to the occupation of the country under the condition that the army and the civilian population remain as they were and suffer no consequences. This version also agreed that the king would leave the country.[57]

The Austro-Hungarians' response came on January 16, and its content was the same as that of their earlier response on December 29, 1915: it demanded the unconditional surrender of the Montenegrin army and the surrender of all Serbian troops in Montenegro. After Emperor Franz Joseph, the Austro-Hungarian government, and its High Command rejected King Nikola's plea, the Montenegrin government was forced to accept the imposed conditions but stated that there were no Serbian troops in Montenegro and that all of them were already in Albania. It would seem that Nikola's rhetoric of a fight to the end was perceived by many as his true desire to confront all the challenges that lay ahead. It is interesting to note that some prominent unionists believed that the king was betrayed by his ministers. While praising King Nikola for his determination to fight to the very end, Marko Daković castigated the Montenegrin government and in particular Prime Minister Lazar Mijušković and Ministers Marko Radulović, Risto Popović, and General Radomir Vešović for surrendering. According to Daković, the government was "in the final phase of moral depression" and at the end it "finally capitulated."[58] Privately, the king told General Janković that Montenegro would not conclude any peace agreement with Austria-Hungary before every Serbian soldier and officer had been sent safely to Scutari.[59] King Nikola and almost all of his government ministers left Montenegro for Scutari on January 19, 1916. In spite of his promise to return to Podgorica the next day, Nikola proceeded farther to Lješ in Albania and then to San Giovanni di Medua.[60] Several of Nikola's ministers; his second son, Prince Mirko; and the new Montenegrin commander in chief, Janko Vukotić, remained in Montenegro. It is still unclear why Prince Mirko stayed behind. Some have speculated that he decided to remain in Cetinje because of illness, whereas others thought that Nikola left his son behind in the hope that his constant presence in Montenegro might facilitate the future return of the Petrović dynasty.

Immediately upon his arrival in Italy, Nikola issued an order to General Janko Vukotić demanding that the army continue to fight and that any eventual retreat must be aimed at connecting with the remaining Serbian army in the region. He also ordered that no person could under any circumstances enter into peace negotiations with Austria-Hungary without the consent of the king and that Prince Mirko and the remaining government ministers must retreat with the army.[61] Contrary to

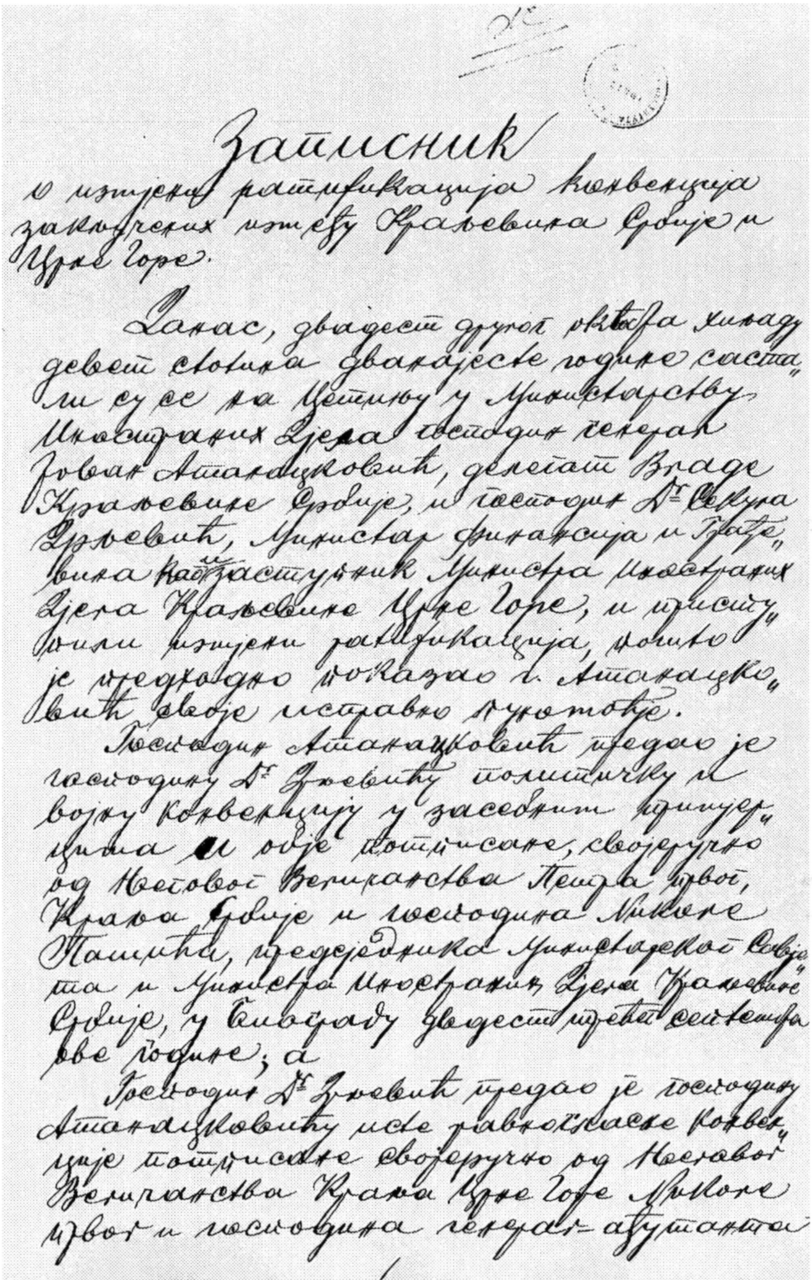

Записник
о измјени ратификација конвенција
закључених између Краљевина Србије и
Црне Горе.
Данас, двадесет другог октобра хиљаду
девет стотина дванаесте године соста-
ли су се на Цетињу у Министарству
Иностраних Дјела господин генерал
Јован Атанацковић, делегат Владе
Краљевине Србије, и господин Dr Секула
Дрљевић, Министар финансија и прав-
вде и заступник Министра Иностраних
Дјела Краљевине Црне Горе, и изврши-
ли измјену ратификација, пошто
је предходно показао г. Атанацковић своје исправно пуномоћје.
Господин Атанацковић предао је
господину Dr Дрљевићу политичку и
војну конвенцију у засебним примјер-
цима и обје потписане, својеручно
од Његовог Величанства Петра првог,
Краља Србије и господина Николе
Пашића, предсједника Министарског Савје-
та и Министра Иностраних Дјела Краљевине
Србије, у Београду двадесет првога септембра
ове године; а
Господин Dr Дрљевић предао је господину
Атанацковићу исте равногласне конвен-
ције потписане својеручно од Његовог
Величанства Краља Црне Горе Николе
првог и господина генерал-ађутанта

Figure 7. Cover page of the *Annex to the Military Agreement between Serbia and Montenegro*, 1912 the king's orders, the ministers who remained in Montenegro proclaimed themselves the new government and, in accordance with Austro-Hungarian demands, issued a proclamation to the Montenegrin armed forces to surrender all weapons. The process of disarmament began in early January 1916 under the watchful eye of the Austro-Hungarian officers in Podgorica, Nikšić, Kolašin, Šavnik, Andrijevica, and other towns. The Montenegrin ministers who remained in the country also entered into further peace negotiations with Vienna. These activities of the ministers prompted the king and his government in exile to characterize their work as illegal and as collaboration with the occupying force.[62] The government in Podgorica found itself in an awkward position because the Austro-Hungarian authorities also contested its legality and its mandate to carry forward any political negotiations. In an attempt to shield themselves from Nikola's accusations, the three ministers who remained in Podgorica decided on February 17, 1916, to issue a memorandum signed by Marko Radulović, Risto Popović and Radomir Vešović as well as by Prince Mirko Petrović and by General Janko Vukotić. The memo dismissed all accusations, claiming that the king had left Montenegro without the knowledge of the government and that the government had not had an opportunity to formally transfer power to those who remained in the country. This was interpreted as a breach of Article 16 of the Montenegrin Constitution. Moreover, the ministers in Podgorica claimed that the king's departure had had a devastating effect on the army and the general population and resulted in chaos and the danger of an internal conflict. It was necessary to provide some stability in the country and make sure that the population remained calm. They stated that the aforementioned reasons motivated the three ministers' decision to continue functioning as the legal representatives of his majesty's government, and denied that they had ever received any written orders from the king that would indicate otherwise. Furthermore, the ministers requested written authorization from King Nikola that would enable them to fully engage in the process of peace negotiations and resolve the misunderstanding.[63] In order to safeguard their position and to protect themselves from Nikola's eventual refusal to appoint them his representatives in the country, the three ministers asked the Austro-Hungarian government about its support for a change in the country's leadership. They were eager to find out if Austria-Hungary would approve of Prince Mirko's being proclaimed king.[64] The government in Vienna and its military representatives in Montenegro were dissatisfied with the speed with which the disarmament of the Montenegrin army was proceeding and blamed the three ministers for failing to act promptly. On February 28, 1916, General Braun wrote that "further cooperation with this government and its further functioning lost all importance." He proceeded to say that the local commanders would soon receive orders that "from now on all government members who had remained in Montenegro after King Nikola's departure should be treated as private individuals."[65] What followed was a complete takeover of all state affairs in Montenegro by the Austro-Hungarian military authorities. On March 1, 1916, a provisional military government was established with an Austro-Hungarian officer as the new civilian commissar in Montenegro.[66]

The capitulation of Montenegro in 1916 is still a contested issue among Montenegrin historians, and their views vary according to their ideological preferences. Some are eager to put the blame squarely on King Nikola with his delusions of grandeur and his unrealistic dynastic aspirations that disrupted communication with the Serbian High Command and ultimately resulted in the destruction of the Montenegrin army. Nikola's war aims, which included the preservation of an independent and sovereign Montenegrin state, are thus seen as the main reason for the defeat.[67] Others place blame on the Serbian government and its war aims, which perceived Montenegro as a part of a future Greater Serbian state. They argue that Nikola Pašić, his government, and the Serbian High Command did everything in their power to diminish Montenegro's chances of surviving the war as an independent state.[68] As Jovan Plamenac pointed out in a letter from Paris to King Aleksandar Karadjordjević, French authorities had assisted the Serbian government in preventing Montenegrin soldiers and officers from withdrawing through Albania. According to Plamenac this was a calculated move to destroy the Montenegrin army and to force its surrender. He claimed that "with the help of the French power, official Serbia was determined to destroy the Kingdom of Montenegro in a most disgusting manner."[69] It should be noted that Plamenac's harsh language and negative attitude toward the newly established state were typical of a number of King Nikola's supporters. It should also be pointed out that this long letter to King Aleksandar was accompanied by a short, more personal note expressing Plamenac's desire to return to his native country. This note ended with his pledging allegiance to the new state: "My future political activity will be marked by absolute loyalty because it will be in accordance with the existing laws of the Kingdom of Serbs, Croats, and Slovenes."[70]

It seems that a combination of factors (both domestic and international) would explain the collapse of the Montenegrin army in early 1916. King Nikola tried to preserve his dynasty and his state, whereas the Karadjordjevićes worked to enlarge their own domain, and this clash of dynastic aspirations represents an important segment in every analysis of the capitulation of Montenegro. King Nikola's responsibility should also be taken into account. During the final months of 1915 when it became obvious that the Montenegrin army would collapse under Austrian-Hungarian pressure, Nikola did little to save his soldiers by either disarming their units and sending them home or by ordering them to withdraw from the front lines and retreat toward Albania. Even though he was aware of the upcoming defeat, he maintained his usual heroic attitude and insisted on fighting to the end. With this in mind, one could say that what was lacking in Montenegro at the end of 1915 was a strong and pragmatic leader willing and able to salvage the remnants of a defeated army. Nikola's actions prove that his prime concern was the preservation of his dynasty. On the other

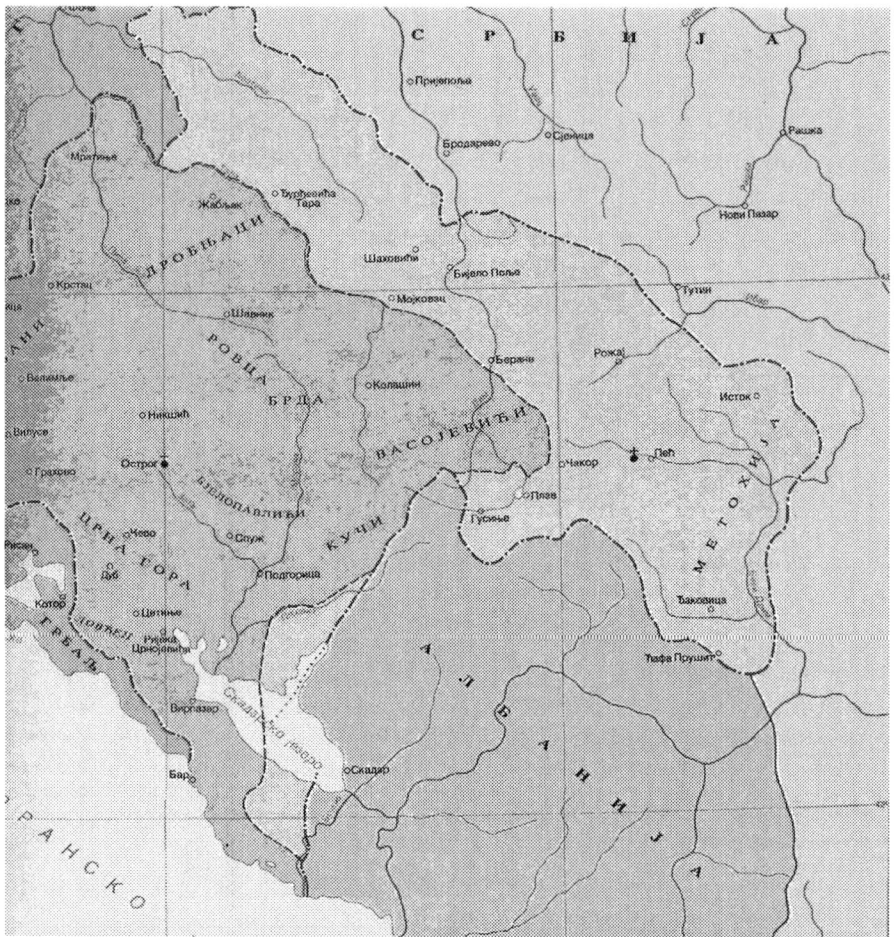

Figure 8. Montenegrin territorial gains after the First Balkan War

hand, the Serbian government did indeed endeavor to marginalize its Montenegrin counterpart and to make sure that no Montenegrin army units reached the island of Corfu and the Allies. From the outset of the war the Montenegrin army fought not only under Serbian command but also according to war aims defined by the Serbian government, and the defense of Montenegrin territory was of secondary importance. Moreover, all of the scarce, irregular supplies that reached Montenegro were under Serbian control, and in wartime food and military equipment could be used as a mighty weapon for pacifying any potential internal opposition. The first two years of World War I in Montenegro suggest that the Serbian government had tried deliberately to exhaust Montenegrin military and economic resources and capabilities. The international aspect of this issue also played a significant role. At the outset of the war, and in spite of the rhetoric, it was obvious that the Great Powers paid much closer attention to the war aims of Serbia than to those of Montenegro. Such an attitude is understandable if one remembers the numerous ill-measured diplomatic and military adventures of King Nikola, especially in light of Serbia's other advantages (a larger population, greater natural resources, a larger army, and more skilful politicians). Last but not least, among the South Slavs of the period it was Serbia and not Montenegro that was looked to as a potential unifying force. These elements could hardly justify the wartime attitudes of the Serbian government and the governments of the Great Powers toward the people of Montenegro, but they should be taken into consideration when assessing the reasons for the military defeat of Montenegro in January 1916.

Notes

1. Vladimir Dedijer, *The Road to Sarajevo* (London, 1966) p. 328.
2. Dedijer, ibid., pp. 418–419, and Luigi Albertini, *The Origins of the War of 1914*, trans. and ed. Isabela M. Massey, vol. 2 (Oxford University Press, 1953), p. 65. Also see Treadway, *The Falcon and the Eagle*, pp. 182–183.
3. On the efforts to accommodate Montenegrin requests and on the dynamics of the initial diplomatic contacts between Austria-Hungary and Montenegro after the Sarajevo murders, see Treadway, *The Falcon and the Eagle*, pp. 186–189.
4. Iu. A. Pisarev, *Velikie derzhavy i Chernigoria v gody pervoi mirovoi voiny* (Moscow: Mezhdunarodnye Otnosheniia na Balkanakh, 1974), p. 136.
5. On July 31, 1914, the Russian envoy to Cetinje, A.A. Girs, reported to his foreign minister (Sazonov) that King Nikola had told him that "unless the Austrians enter Montenegrin territory, Montenegrins will not attack them." Pisarev, *Velikie derzhavy i Chernigoria*, p. 135.
6. D. Šepić, *Italija, Saveznici i Jugoslavensko Pitanje, 1914–1918* (Zagreb, 1970), pp. 40, 106. Dimitrije D. Vujović, *Ujedinjenje Crne Gore i Srbije* (Titograd: Istorijski Institut Crne Gore, 1962), pp. 106–107.
7. Vujović, *Ujedinjenje*, pp. 106–107.
8. Spalajković to Pašić, J.M. Jovanović's Collection, Yugoslav State Archive/Archive FNRJ (hereafter AJ), May 7, 1915.
9. Spalajković to Pašić, AJ, July 3, 1915.
10. Andrijašević, *Kratka Istorija*, p. 201. Also see Rakočević, *Politički Odnosi*, p. 229.
11. *Operacije Crnogorske Vojske u Prvom Svjetskom Ratu* (Beograd, 1954), pp. 63–76. Novica Rakočević, *Crna Gora u Prvom Svjetskom Ratu, 1914–1918* (Cetinje: Obod, 1969), pp. 34–41.
12. Treadway, *The Falcon and the Eagle*, pp. 198–199. According to the prominent unionist, Marko Daković, Montenegro's entering the war as an ally of Serbia was "a sacrifice for its sister Serbia." AIICG, File 63, Marko Daković, *Uloga Crne Gore u Svetskom Ratu* (handwritten), p. 2. Also see "Proklamacija Crnogorskog kralja Nikole," Cetinje, August 7, 1914, in Ferdo Šišić, ed., *Dokumenti o Postanku Kraljevine Srba, Hrvata i Slovenaca, 1914–1919* (Zagreb: Naklada Matice Hrvatske, 1920), pp. 6–7.
13. Vojvoda Radomir Putnik to the Serbian minister of war, Niš, July 3, 1915, Telegraph, AIICG, File 44, Doc. No. 4872. For a more detailed disbursement plan of the Montenegrin forces under General Janković's command, see his report to the Serbian General Headquarters on May 4, 1915. AIICG, File 44, Doc. No. 15689.

14. See *Operacije Crnogorske Vojske u Prvom Svetskom Ratu* (Beograd: Vojnoistorijski Institut, 1954), p. 134. Nikola Škerović, *Crna Gora za Vrijeme Prvog Svjetskog Rata* (Titograd, 1963), pp. 12–20. Dragoslav Janković, *Srbija i Jugoslovensko Pitanje, 1914–1915* (Beograd, 1973), p. 148. Others claim that the plan was drafted on August 6, 1914. See Novica Rakočević, *Crna Gora u Prvom Svjetskom Ratu, 1914–1918* (Cetinje: Obod, 1969), p. 58. *Veliki Rat Srbije za Oslobodjenje i Ujedinjenje Srba, Hrvata i Slovenaca*, vol. 1/1914 (Beograd, 1924), p. 31. Miro Božović, "Crna Gora i Njena Vojna Uloga of 15 Juna 1914 do Kapitulacije," *Slobodna Misao*, no. 47 (November 1936).
15. Miro Božović, "*Crna Gora i Njena Vojna Uloga.*" Also see AIICG, File No. 330. Risto Popović, *Dnevnik*. In 1914 Popović was minister of the interior and deputy war minister in the Montenegrin government. Serbian officers met with the king in Cetinje on August 23 because he was in Nikšić at the time of their arrival in Montenegro.
16. *Veliki Rat Srbije za Oslobodjenje Srba, Hrvata i Slovenaca*, vol. 1/1914 (Beograd, 1924), pp. 31–33.
17. Brigadier General Jovan Bećir studied at the Italian Military Academy and was known in Montenegro as an ardent supporter of King Nikola. He had developed particularly close relations with Nikola's son, Prince Danilo, and was his commanding officer during the First Balkan War (1912–1913). Shortly after the annexation of Montenegro in 1918, Bećir retired not at the rank of general but of colonel. He spent his retirement years in Sarajevo. In 1941, he was taken prisoner and sent to the Jasenovac death camp, where he was killed. Novica Rakočević, *Politički Odnosi Crne Gore i Srbije, 1903–1918* (Titograd: Istorijski Institut SR Crne Gore and Obod, Cetinje, 1981), pp. 236–237. Also see Milorad Ekmečić, *Ratni Ciljevi Srbije, 1914* (Beograd, 1973), pp. 420–421.
18. Dimitrije D. Vujović, *Ujedinjenje*, p. 105.
19. Novica Rakočević, *Politički Odnosi*, p. 251. Also see Vladimir Dedijer, *Sarajevo, 1914* (Beograd, 1966), p. 696.
20. "This should be treated as top secret. The Montenegrin king has dispatched his special advisor, Andrija Radović, so that he could take care of purchasing food for Montenegro. However, it seems that his main goal will be to inform people there about the future borders of Montenegro, which as according to what I was told are to stretch from San Giovanni di Medua all the way to Metković. He will interpret this issue as being of vital interest for Montenegro. I am informing you about this so that you can monitor his activities and report back to me everything you find out." Nikola Pašić to the Serbian representative in Paris, Telegraph, No. 3499, AJ.
21. R. Bojović to the Serbian High Command, Niš, June 19, 1915, AIICG, File 44, Doc. No. 20019.
22. The Chief of the General Staff to the Commander of the Prahovo Port, Kragujevac, June 11, 1915, AIICG, File 44, Doc. No. 15913.
23. Novica Rakočević, *Politički Odnosi Crne Gore i Srbije, 1903–1918*, p. 233.
24. General Vešović to the Commander of the New Territory, Skopje, June 3, 1915, AIICG, File 44, Doc. No. 6526.
25. General D. Popović to General R. Vešović, Skopje, June 4, 1915, AIICG, File 44, Doc. No. 6458.
26. Operations to General B. Janković, May 29, 1915. Urgent and Secret. The Serbian General Headquarters. AIICG, File 44, Doc. No. 15362. San Giovanni di Medua (Šindjon) was the small Adriatic port at the mouth of the Bojana River on the Montenegrin-Albanian border.
27. B. Janković to the Serbian High Command, Cetinje, June 13, 1915, AIICG, File 44, Doc. No. 1091.
28. General Janković to Montenegrin prime minister, Cetinje, June 17, 1915, AIICG, File 353, Doc. No. 1111.

29. In 1968 the Montenegrin historian Risto Dragićević set out to prove that the document was a forgery. Significantly, Danilo Perović, the brother of the author of the forged document, assisted him in doing so. In 1961 Danilo Perović signed a statement refuting the authenticity of this document. The complete text of his statement is stored in the Archives of the State Museums in Cetinje.
30. Radoslav M. Raspopović, *Diplomatija Crne Gore, 1711–1918* (Podgorica and Beograd: Istorijski Institut Crne Gore/NIU Vojska, 1996), p. 597.
31. Vojislav Vučković, "Diplomatska Pozadina Ujedinjenja Crne Gore i Srbije," *Jugoslovenska Revija za Medjunarodno Pravo*, no. 2 (Beograd, 1950). *Glas Crnogorca*, June 21, 1914. Also see *Cetinjski Vjesnik*, Cetinje, June 19, 1914.
32. Dragoljub Živojinović, *Crna Gora u Borbi za Opstanak, 1914–1922* (Beograd: Vojna Knjiga, 1996), p. 14. Also see *I Documenti Diplomatici Italiani*, Serie Quinta, vol. 4 (Roma, 1983), p. 360.
33. Velimir Terzić and others, *Operacije Crnogorske Vojske u Prvom Svjetskom Ratu* (Beograd: Vojno Delo, 1954), p. 21.
34. Petar Pešić to the Serbian minister of war, Cetinje, June 22, 1915, AIICG, File 353, Doc. No. 1130.
35. Pešić, ibid., Cetinje, July 1, 1915, AIICG, File 353, Doc. No. 1169.
36. Petar Pešić to the Serbian minister of war and to the Serbian High Command, Cetinje, August 31, 1915, AIICG, File 353, Doc. No. 1447.
37. One such publication that circulated in Montenegro was R.W. Seton-Watson's *The Yugoslav Question*. Dimitrije D. Vujović, *Ujedinjenje*, p. 114.
38. *Ljubo Bakić's Collection*, handwritten notes, p. 185, AIICG, File No. 145.
39. Dimitrije D. Vujović, *Ujedinjenje*, p. 115.
40. Telegraph from Niš to Cetinje, February 28, 1915, AJMJ.
41. Petar Pešić to the Serbian minister of war, Cetinje, September 18, 1915, AIICG, File 44, Doc. No. 1529.
42. Nikola Pašić to the Serbian minister of foreign affairs, Niš, September 26, 1915, AIICG, File 44, Doc. 10766.
43. "On November 24, 1914 the English steamer *Wigthead* carrying corn from Canada entered the port of Bar. The unloading was done during the night and under the heavy bombardment of enemy planes. We managed to unload some 300 tons of corn, but in the early hours of the morning the steamer was forced to leave the port with some 150 tons of corn still aboard." Niko Hajduković, *Memoari* (Podgorica: CID, 2000), p. 171. Also see Hajduković's report of October 13, 1916, on the food supplies shipped from Thessalonica to Montenegro. Hajduković, ibid., pp. 197–201.
44. Šerbo Rastoder, ed., *Uloga Francuske u Nasilnoj Aneksiji Crne Gore: Dokumenta*, trans. Marina Vukičević (Bar: Conteco, 2000), pp. 118–120. Original title: *Documents officiels publies par le Ministere des Affaires Etrangeresdu Montenegro*, Rome, 1921. Imperiere A. Manuce. Hereafter DOM.
45. P. Plamenac to A. Radović, Cetinje, August 1915, AIICG, File 171.
46. The Montenegrin army had only 155 canons and 107 heavy machine guns at its disposal. Živko M. Andrijašević, *Kratka Istorija*, p. 204. Petar Pešić described the Montenegrin army as "40,000 Montenegrin soldiers that were poorly dressed, without proper shoes, hungry, carrying old rifles and old canons, and using outdated black powder." "Crna Gora u Svjetskome Ratu," *Ratnik* (Beograd, 1925), p. 17.
47. Marko Daković stated that the Serbian troops would have been wiped out if it were not for the efforts of the Montenegrin army. Marko Daković, *Uloga Crne Gore u Svetskom Ratu* (handwritten), p. 9, AIICG, File 63.

48. "On the Mojkovac front the First Sandžak Division began an attack at 6:00 a.m. The fighting lasted until 5:30 p.m., that is, until darkness separated the enemies. According to the reports of local commanders no. 10891 during these operations our losses were as follows: the Kolašin Brigade suffered 400 dead and wounded, and according to report no. 889, other units suffered some 200 dead and wounded. Our army kept its positions and even made some advances against the enemy." Marko Daković, ibid., p. 1, AIICG, File 63.
49. Telegraph from General B. Janković to the Serbian High Command, Top Secret. Cetinje, December 29, 1915, AIICG, File 44, Doc. No. 2339.
50. General B. Janković to the Serbian High Command, Cetinje, December 29, 1915, AIICG, File 44, Doc. No. 2336.
51. Colonel Pešić to the Serbian High Command, Cetinje, December 29, 1915, AIICG, File 44, Doc. No. 163.
52. Janković also reported that the queen and Princess Vera left for Rijeka Crnojevića (on the banks of Lake Scutari) and that some household items from the court had been sent there. General B. Janković to the Serbian High Command, Cetinje, December 29, 1915, AIICG, File 44, Doc. No. 2350.
53. Ilija Hajduković, "Potonji Dani Samostalnosti Crne Gore," typed, pp. 3–4. AIICG, File No. 95.
54. General B. Janković to the Serbian High Command, Cetinje, December 30, 1915, AIICG, File 44, Doc. No. 2452.
55. General B. Janković to the Serbian High Command, Podgorica, December 30, 1915, AIICG, File 44, Doc. No. 2353.
56. Ilija Hajduković, "Potonji Dani," p. 4. AIICG, File No. 95.
57. Ilija Hajduković, ibid., p. 5.
58. Marko Daković, *Uloga Crne Gore u Svetskom Ratu* (handwritten), p. 10. AIICG, File 63.
59. Vujović, *Ujedinjenje*, pp. 118–119. Also see Doc. No. 9006, Colonel Petar Pešić to the Serbian High Command, Podgorica, January 13, 1915; Doc. 26849, General B. Janković to the Serbian High Command, Podgorica, January 13, 1915; Doc. No. 2387, General B. Janković to the Serbian High Command, Scutari, January 16, 1916, AIICG, File 44.
60. Colonel Marković to the Serbian High Command, Scutari, January 20, 1916, AIICG, File 44, Doc. No. 106.
61. Hajduković, "Potonji Dani," p. 29.
62. Memorandum by Lazar Mijušković issued on February 11, 1916, through the Montenegrin representative in Paris. See Hajduković, "Potonji Dani," p. 29.
63. Hajduković, "Potonji Dani," pp. 30–32.
64. Hajduković, ibid., p. 34.
65. Hajduković, ibid., p. 37. AIICG, File No. 95. Doc. No. 700.
66. Hajduković, ibid., pp. 37–42.
67. Good examples of such an interpretation are *Politički Odnosi*, by the Montenegrin historian Novica Rakočević, and works by Svetozar Tomić, *Desetogodišnjica Ujedinjenja*; Jovan Ćetković, *Ujedinitelji Crne Gore i Srbije*; and Radislav M. Raspopović, *Diplomatija Crne Gore*.
68. See Vujović, *Ujedinjenje*; Štedimlija, *Gorštačka Krv*; Drljević, *Balkanski Sukobi*; Šuković, *Podgorička Skupština*; Rastoder, *Janusovo Lice Istorije*.
69. Letter from Paris by Jovan Plamenac to His Royal Highness the King Aleksandar Karadjordjević, Paris, January 31, 1925, p. 49, AIICG, File No. 176/Arhiva Jovana Plamenca.
70. Plamenac, ibid., p. 78.

CHAPTER THREE

The King in Exile

The Montenegrin king and his government left Cetinje on December 29, 1915, never to return. After short stays in Podgorica and Scutari, the king proceeded first to Italy and then to France. Some of Nikola's supporters have tried to present his departure as a decision that was forced on him and have portrayed the old king as a romantic figure and a victim of historical circumstances.[1] What is absent from this romantic portrayal of an ailing monarch is the issue of his own culpability and his unwillingness to recognize a strong pro-Serbian and prounion current in Montenegrin politics. Although King Nikola I Petrovic might have been less than fortunate in his dealings with Belgrade and the Entente, he was far from being an innocent victim in the political game of numbers. When he traveled through Italy without stopping, many interpreted it as a sign of his dissatisfaction with Italy's policy with regard to Montenegro. According to Niko Hajduković, one of King Nikola's close associates, it was clear that the Montenegrin sovereign blamed Italy for the collapse of his country.[2] Italy was indeed anything but supportive to those claiming for Montenegro the right to exist as a sovereign and independent state. After a month-long stay in Lyon, the king proceeded to Bordeaux, where the French government made necessary provisions for his court and his government. Montenegrin politicians, bureaucrats, and officers began gathering in Bordeaux, and Lazar Mijuškovic was able to establish a kind of administrative unit. The Montenegrin government in exile started receiving a monthly subsidy of 400,000 francs from the French government. This subsidy covered administrative expenses and included an allowance for the king and his family members. Nikola immediately started various diplomatic activities in order to publicize his views on the future of the Montenegrin state. During his meeting with a Russian envoy to his court on March 6, 1916, the king maintained his earlier views that the Great Powers should guarantee Montenegrin independence and its territorial enlargement. The Russian envoy surprised Nikola by telling him that this was not the right time to discuss these issues and that the best thing for

Montenegro was to secure as close ties with Serbia as possible.³ Shortly after this meeting, Lazar Mijušković wrote a memorandum outlining Nikola's political desires and territorial aspirations, which entirely corresponded to those he had expressed to the Russian representative. According to the memorandum the Montenegrin borders should be redrawn 10 kilometers south of the mouth of the Drim River (in Albania), and the old border with Serbia should be corrected in Montenegro's favor all the way to Prijepolje (in southeastern Serbia) and farther along the Lim and Drina Rivers all the way to Rogatica (in Bosnia). The western borders should also be corrected so that Montenegro would gain territories in eastern Bosnia, including Sarajevo and the region of the Neretva Valley all the way to the Adriatic coast. Montenegro would acquire towns on the Adriatic coast such as Metković, Dubrovnik, Kotor, and Budva.⁴ Shortly after this memorandum was handed over to the Russian representative, Mijušković proved unable to continue his work because he came into conflict with a number of high-ranking Montenegrin officers. In his attempt to isolate the king, Mijušković tried to get rid of some of the king's closest associates and family members, such as General Anto Gvozdenović, Petar Plamenac, and Princess Ksenija. Mijušković also clashed with Nikola over the issue of who was to blame for the capitulation of Montenegro. Whereas Nikola tried to place the blame on Mijušković, the prime minister accused the king of abandoning his people and his country. In his letter of resignation the Montenegrin prime minister clearly stated his prounionist sentiments and his hope that the people of Montenegro would soon "enter into the great all-Serbian union."⁵

Following Petar Plamenac's suggestion, the king gave Andrija Radović a mandate to form the government. Plamenac was so eager that Radović take over the government that on one occasion he pleaded with the king: "My Lord! You know all too well how loyal I am to you, and I give you my word that Andrija would be immeasurably more loyal and more obedient in everything to you than I could ever be."⁶ Among other new members of the government, Radović selected Pero Vučković as minister of education, Janko Spasojević as minister of justice, and General Milo Matanović as minister of war.⁷ Radović's government

Figure 9. Andrija Radović

was successful in highlighting Nikola's profile on the international political scene and managed to organize a number of activities related to Montenegrin refugees, as well as to establish a relief fund for the people of Montenegro, which was headed by Princess Ksenija. The Montenegrin Red Cross was also established.[8] The new prime minister was very active in dealing with the problematic issue of Montenegrin volunteers from abroad, who were arriving in Thessalonica and Corfu in large numbers. Nikola hoped that these volunteers, together with the remnants of the Montenegrin army that had managed to retreat through Albania, would constitute the core of a future army that might facilitate his return to Cetinje. Over two thousand armed Montenegrins under the command of Danilo Gatalo (the former Montenegrin minister of war) had managed to reach the Albanian port of Durazzo and were later evacuated to Corfu. In early January 1916, a couple of days before the capitulation of Montenegro, the Italian ship *Brindisi* carrying over five hundred Montenegrin volunteers from Canada (Halifax) reached San Giovanni di Medua. The ship hit a mine, and only 164 passengers survived. They were rescued and transported to Biserta in North Africa.[9] But once they reached Corfu, Montenegrin officers were offered various incentives to join the Serbian army and continue fighting at the Thessalonica front. General Gojnić was offered a promotion to the rank of brigadier general while Majors Matanović, Djukanović, Djurišić, Djurović, and Martinović were offered the rank of colonel. Gojnić and Matanović refused the offer, claiming that the new ranks did not correspond to those they had had in the Montenegrin army, and together with fifteen low-ranking Montenegrin officers, they left Corfu and joined the Montenegrin government in exile. Others accepted offers and entered the ranks of the Serbian army. Commander Danilo Gatalo reached a separate agreement with Balugdžić, the Serbian representative in Athens, and was sent to Paris to assist the Serbian ambassador Milenko Vesnić.[10] Because of constant pressure from the Serbian government and its military authorities to join the ranks of the Serbian army, the Montenegrin representative in Thessalonica, Niko Hajduković, urged the new prime minister in Neuilly to intervene with the French government with regard to the establishment of the separate Montenegrin unit in Corfu:

> This unit could serve as the core of the future Montenegrin army for all those that are now in Italy and for those who are willing to come here from America. Soldiers would like that. You could give command of this unit to Danilo Radović. . . . It is necessary to act quickly.[11]

Because it took a long time for Radović to respond, Hajduković entered into negotiations with the French Colonel Jackmont and the commander in chief of the Eastern Army, General Maurice Sarai. He obtained their permission to form a Montenegrin battalion whose soldiers and officers would be allowed to display all of the insignias (coats of arms, flags, etc.) of a traditional army unit from Montenegro.

King Nikola and Andrija Radović agreed with these steps and encouraged him to continue. Hajduković's immediate concern was to find a suitable location for this unit, and he chose the Thessalonica suburb of Zeitinlik. According to his report to Andrija Radović, distancing the Montenegrin battalion from the Serbian troops and their camp was necessary to prevent further spreading of pro-Serbian and prounionist propaganda among the Montenegrin soldiers.[12] In spite of Hajduković's efforts to separate the Montenegrin battalion from the Serbian troops and in spite of his plans to use it later as a force that would enter and liberate Montenegro, the Serbian High Command persuaded French military authorities that this unit should be joined with their forces and positioned toward Bulgaria at the front line overlooking Dojran Lake. A few months later, and again under the pressure of the Serbian High Command, the French General Sarai decided to ship the Montenegrin battalion to Corsica, thus preventing its soldiers from ever reaching Montenegro.[13] Serbian authorities continued to lobby among the soldiers in Corsica to join the Serbian army, and in November 1917, Boža Milanović reported from Bastia to the Serbian military attaché in Paris, Colonel Dušan Stefanović, that recruitment was going according to plan and that he treated Montenegrin soldiers in the same manner as other citizens of Serbia:

> If we treat them in the same way as we do our citizens we will achieve an important political objective. Moreover, a few other useful things for us might come out of it. I hope that they will inform their relatives and friends in America about the proper treatment they are getting here and that it might make it easier for us to recruit volunteers there.[14]

While recruiting Montenegrin soldiers for his cause, Milanović took great care to monitor all those who refused his offer and managed to prevent them from communicating with Nikola's government in Neuilly. In a letter of November 30, 1917, he stated that "we have all the main points in the depot, such as the mailroom and the censor's office, under our control, and we have cut off all connections between them and their agents."[15]

Back in France, the newly appointed prime minister, Andrija Radović, arranged an audience for the Montenegrin king and queen with French President Raymond Poincaré. Soon afterward the French government agreed that the Montenegrin king and his government could move from Bordeaux to the Paris suburb of Neuilly. It also provided Nikola with numerous insignias of power, including an honorary French adjutant and a French secretary, as well as two luxury automobiles and a special police unit for protection. Nikola was allowed to display his dynastic flag on the roof of his residence while the Montenegrin flag was hoisted on the government building. Furthermore, French, Italian, British, Russian, and Serbian representatives and ambassadors were accredited to the Montenegrin court. Keeping in mind the policy of the French government toward the future of the Montenegrin state, one could interpret this sudden granting of signifiers of statehood to Nikola as an exercise in diplomatic politeness. Aside from maintaining the appearance of benevolence toward the Montenegrin king and his government in exile, the French government together with the other Great Powers never modified its stand on independent and sovereign Montenegro. On the contrary, it did everything to marginalize Nikola and his efforts to prevent the annexation of Montenegro.

It was at this time that Radović was encouraged by his close friend Danilo Gatalo to meet and socialize with the Serbian representative in Paris, Milenko Vesnić, who was known as a strong advocate of the unitary South Slav state and a confidant of the Serbian prime minister, Nikola Pašić. It seems that his subsequent friendship with Vesnić marked the turning point in Radović's political career and his attitude toward the future of Montenegro. It has been alleged that the Serbian representative facilitated numerous financial transactions for Radović, including his purchase of a large amount of stock of the Serbian People's Bank below the official price, and that such "favors" were the main reason for Radović's "change of heart."[16] Regardless of the validity of such claims, the fact is that shortly after his initial meeting with Vesnić, the Montenegrin prime minister started showing less interest in his work and began delaying the payment of financial aid to refugees and the payment of scholarships to Montenegrin students. Many low-ranking bureaucrats in the government resigned their posts, and a growing number of students refused scholarships from the Montenegrin government-in-exile. Many of them turned to the Serbian Representative Office in Paris and were given much higher scholarships and salaries.

On August 5, 1916, Andrija Radović wrote a memorandum to King Nikola proposing the unification of Montenegro with Serbia. He stated that an Allied victory was certain and the liberation of all South Slavs inevitable. With this in mind, Radović asserted, a renewed Montenegrin state along the lines of Nikola's plan would not be able to survive. He pointed out the existence of democratically minded movements in Montenegro that might threaten the king's stay in power. As a solution, Radović proposed unification with Serbia. He also proposed the manner in which it should take place: King Nikola should abdicate in favor of the Regent Aleksandar Karadjordjević, but in the future the male members of both dynasties should take turns on the throne. All members of the cabinet with the exception of the minister of war, Matanović, agreed with Radović's memoranda. The king replied that he was also in agreement but that he would prefer to decide on the matter after his return to Montenegro. He also pointed out that if the people of Montenegro were not in favor of unification he would then abdicate in favor of his son, Prince Danilo.[17] Radović realized that the king had refused his proposal as soon as Nikola ordered all Montenegrins living abroad to mobilize in order to establish a new military unit. This sudden development worried the Serbian government; Pašić instructed his associates in the Montenegrin government to act against King Nikola:

> Convey my message to Mr. Janko Spasojević, the Montenegrin minister of justice, that now is the time and the perfect opportunity for him to ask his colleagues in writing to collectively hand in their resignations to the king because the mobilization of Montenegrins in one separate unit is in direct opposition to the text of the memorandum on abdication, which they presented to King Nikola some months ago. If Mr. Radović does not agree to do so and if he does not agree that the entire cabinet should resign, then Mr. Spasojević has to hand in his prepared resignation to Mr. Radović at once with the explanation that he is doing so because he intends to remain true to the nature of the proposal on Nikola's abdication in favor of a union between Serbia and Montenegro. After resigning Mr. Spasojević could continue to lead the movement among Montenegrins working toward unification. In this effort all of us will accept and welcome him: the government of Serbia and the Serbian people from all regions.[18]

Spasojević followed the instructions but found it difficult to persuade the prime minister to resign and resorted to handing in his own resignation and initiating a crisis in the cabinet. In the meantime, Radović continued to pressure King Nikola to accept his earlier memorandum on unification. On January 4, 1917, he submitted another memorandum on the same issue and threatened to resign if the king rejected it.[19] And he did resign, that very day. The resignation of the prime minister was a serious blow to the king. Over time, Andrija Radović became the most prominent and hard working unionist and was instrumental in preparing the Podgorica Assembly.[20] It should be mentioned that at the time of his resignation Radović was in constant contact with the Serbian Representative Office in Paris. He promised Vesnić that he would do everything in his power to make sure that no respectable Montenegrin would accept the king's mandate, and he pointed out that accomplishing this would require considerable funds. Radović also suggested that any financial compensation of those refusing Nikola's offer to form a new government should be disguised to look like Allied financial aid rather than like a payoff from Serbia. Radović managed to persuade Duke Simo Popović not to accept the king's offered mandate. Furthermore, Radović managed to convince the French authorities and other Allied governments to lower their monthly subsidy payments to the king and his government from 400,000 francs to just over 100,000. Radović accomplished this by presenting a false financial report that excluded the amounts needed to cover financial aid to Montenegrin students and refugees.[21] On March 4, 1917, Andrija Radović, together with the former Montenegrin ministers Djurović, Gatalo, Spasojević, and Vučković, established the Montenegrin Committee for Unification in Paris in cooperation with the Serbian government.[22] The committee immediately issued a proclamation announcing its existence and formulating its political credo and sent it to Corfu to be approved by the Serbian government. This first public document was not to Pašić's liking, however, because it referred to "the unification of Montenegro with Serbia and Yugoslavia." Pašić immediately sent a telegram to Paris saying that

> the Montenegrin Committee's proclamation should not include words such as *Yugoslavia* and *Yugoslavs* and should not include any kind of similar references. The committee is working with us on the unification of Montenegro and Serbia and on achieving the unity of the Serbian people regardless of other Yugoslavs ... the phrase "the unification of Montenegro with Serbia and with other Serbian lands" should be used.[23]

The new Montenegrin government was formed on January 4, 1917, under the premiership of Brigadier General Milo Matanović, but it lasted a scant five months until May 29. Matanović and his ministers were under constant pressure from the Serbian government to abandon the king. The issue of the future of the common South Slav state and the unification of Montenegro with Serbia came to the political forefront; no government was able any longer to avoid declaring its position on the issue, and Matanović's was no exception. Its main focus was on proving that the king and the government were not enemies of unification but rather that all aspects of the process needed to be discussed at greater length.[24] Engagement of this kind gained in importance particularly after the establishment of the Montenegrin Committee for Unification because the committee tried to present itself as the only legitimate advocate of the unification of the two countries. But in spite of the rhetoric, Nikola maintained the position that his dynasty was the only legitimate protector of Montenegrin distinctiveness. The government issued a memorandum on May 2, 1917, demanding that the king, in cooperation with the Serbian government, take some practical steps toward unification with Serbia. Nikola refused, and the government resigned on May 29, 1917.[25]

Yet another government in exile was formed on May 29, 1917, under the leadership of Evgenije Popović, who was working at the time as the Montenegrin general consul in Rome and was considered to be an Italophile.[26] He chose Milo Vujović as finance minister, Veljko Milićević as justice minister and minister of education, and Niko Hajduković as interior minister and the representative of the minister of war. The new government issued a proclamation publicizing its program and addressing the question of future unification. It stated that "the royal government remains loyal to Russia, and it will in cooperation with Serbia work toward the betterment of Serbdom. The liberation and the unification of all our brothers who are under foreign rule was always the priority of Montenegro and its rulers and will remain so." According to the government's program, the issue of unification should be addressed with respect to the provisions and legislations outlined in the Montenegrin Constitution. With this in mind, on June 18, 1917, Evgenije Popović dispatched a note to the Serbian representative in Paris, Tihomir Popović, expressing his desire to work together on the issue. The note emphasized that the Montenegrin king and his government were focused on accomplishing the ultimate goal of uniting Serbdom and that they were willing to do so in cooperation with the government of Serbia. He reminded Popović that during World War I Montenegro had fulfilled its duties and sacrificed itself for this common goal and asserted that Montenegro was ready to do so again. Popović's government suggested that the two governments should work together to achieve a common policy on the idea of South Slavic unity and the future state.[27] The government of Serbia did not respond to this note but decided to cooperate with the Montenegrin Committee for Unification because it considered that organization to be the only legitimate representative of the people of Montenegro. Moreover, the Serbian government did not want to alienate the president of the committee, Andrija Radović, and his colleagues because it had already given them a mandate to work freely on the issue of unification. According to Nikola Pašić the committee was established to lead the unionist movement "in the spirit of general Serbian interests and according to our program."[28] Instead, what followed was the Corfu Declaration, which was signed by the leaders of the Yugoslav Committee from London (representing South Slavs from Austria-Hungary), the Serbian government, and representatives of the Montenegrin Committee for Unification. The Corfu Declaration outlined a framework for the new post–World War I South Slav state, emphasizing the principle of national unity among Serbs, Croats, and Slovenes and invoking the principle of self-determination that constituted the basis for the struggle for the liberation of the South Slavs and their unification into one "free, national, and independent state."[29] The Montenegrin government in Neuilly was never consulted or invited to participate in this process and did not appear as a signatory on any documents important for the establishment of the future state. Considering the turn of events during 1917 and 1918, it is safe to say that the government of Evgenije Popović was unable to do much to change their course. The two most important achievements of this government were the securing of U.S. support for the future Montenegrin representative in Washington, General Anto Gvozdenović, and the French government's decision to prevent distribution of *Ujedinjenje* (the official journal of the Montenegrin Committee for Unification) on French territory. All of this, however, proved to be too little, too late. The fate of the Montenegrin state would be determined by the Podgorica Assembly.

Montenegro, the Great Powers, and the Paris Peace Conference

The relations between Montenegro and the European powers and the United States during and immediately after World War I resembled a political and diplomatic seesaw and were conditioned by the immediate interests of the Great Powers in the region. A number of factors led the Great Powers to concentrate their efforts on strengthening Serbia's position in the region and, by doing so, to marginalize Montenegro, thus determining the future of the Montenegrin state to a greater extent than the policies of the Serbian government. Examination of Montenegrin foreign policy showcases the important role of the Great Powers in gradually dismantling the Montenegrin state. King Nikola's relations with the Great Powers are the story of his struggle with the Serbian government over the issue of dynastic rule and the structure of the future South Slav state. It is also important to note that King Nikola and his government contributed to the deterioration of Montenegro's position abroad by constantly shifting their policies in an attempt to achieve their primary goal: the preservation of the Petrović dynasty. The future status of Montenegro seems to have been of secondary importance to King Nikola, and his insistence on due process in the establishment of the new South Slav state appears to have been just a tool to secure his dynasty's survival.

At the outset of World War I, Montenegro did not have very fruitful relations with the Allied governments. An atmosphere of mistrust marked the policy of the Great Powers toward Montenegro throughout the war years until the establishment of the Kingdom of Serbs, Croats, and Slovenes. There were several reasons for the Allies' political distancing from Cetinje. One was the attempt of King Nikola and his government to enlarge their state territory by occupying northern Albania. Another was the effort of the Montenegrin High Command to separate its military actions from those of Serbia. The Great Powers were eager to see Montenegro develop closer ties with Serbia, mainly due to persistent rumors about Nikola's secret and prolonged contacts with Austria-Hungary and Germany during the first two years of the war. Learning about these rumors provoked strong reactions among the Allied governments even though their actions fell short of issuing the king any direct warnings. The Great Powers were concerned that if they openly accused Nikola of collaborating with the enemy he would then pull Montenegro out of the war. In order to avoid a direct confrontation they took a different approach to Montenegro, concentrating their political attention and military assistance on Serbia, a course of action they maintained until the end of the war.

Montenegro and Italy

At the end of the nineteenth century, relations between Montenegro and Italy were particularly good. After the military defeat at Adowa (Adua) in 1896, and after it was forced to abandon plans to annex all or part of Abyssinia, the Italian government began paying close attention to the Balkans and to Montenegro. In 1896 the daughter of then Prince Nikola Petrović, Princess Jelena, married the heir to the Italian throne, Victor Emanuel. Attempting to minimize Austro-Hungarian influence in the region, and also because of its geopolitical interests in the Eastern Adriatic and Albania, Italy tried to establish close relations with Montenegro and encouraged every anti–Austro-Hungarian policy in the region. In October 1909 it signed a treaty with Russia on the issue of the South Slavs, the first clause of which stated that "Russia and Italy must endeavor to maintain the status quo in the Balkan Peninsula"; the second clause confirmed that, regardless of future developments in the Balkans, both countries "must adhere to the nationality principle and support the development of the Balkan states in order to eliminate any kind of foreign domination."[30] Italy was hoping to replace Austria-Hungary in the region and, with that goal in mind, it encouraged the establishment of a strong and unified South Slav state.

> Italy wants Montenegro to remain free but wants it even more to remain independent of Austria. Italy would prefer to see Montenegro united with Serbia than to remain connected to Austria. Lovćen should definitely remain Montenegrin so that Austria cannot turn Kotor into its naval base. It is necessary to economically assist the Montenegrin king and prevent him from reaching out to Austria.[31]

It seems that Italy was in favor of the future unification of the two countries. During 1913 and 1914 Italian officials made repeated references to the unification of Montenegro with Serbia. On October 30, 1913, the French ambassador in Rome reported that Italian officials had informed him that they believed King Nikola would be the last sovereign of his dynasty because the Montenegrins loved the Serbs and were very much in favor of unification with Serbia. Furthermore, he reported that the interests of Italy were not in opposition to this unification even though the government in Rome would be satisfied with the preservation of the status quo in the region.[32] The Italian government conveyed a similar message to the Serbian representative in Paris, Milenko Vesnić.[33]

As soon as war broke out, Italian diplomats began bargaining with both warring sides in an attempt to secure territorial expansions at the expense of the South Slavs. Baron Sidney Sonnino, the Italian foreign minister, even offered a free hand to the Austro-Hungarian government with regard to Serbia and Montenegro in exchange for certain territorial compensations.[34] As the war continued, the attitude of the Italian government toward the future unification of the South Slavs changed to strong disapproval. Italy was eager to include Montenegro in the process of writing and later signing the London Treaty that outlined the territorial expansion of Montenegro at the expense of Austria-Hungary. This activity of the Italian government on behalf of Montenegro was aimed at marginalizing Serbia. Italy had little to fear from Montenegro. In terms of political influence Montenegro was of secondary importance. In fact, Italy already completely controlled the Montenegrin economy and was able to exert significant influence over the Petrović dynasty. What worried Italian policy makers was Serbia. The government in Rome was aware that the eventual unification of Montenegro and Serbia would mean Serbian domination in the region. They were conscious of the fact that Serbia could easily jeopardize Italian plans to expand in the

Balkans. Immediately after the signing of the London Treaty, the Serbian government complained bitterly about not having been invited to the talks and accused Italy of trying to divide the South Slavs and minimize future Serbian political and territorial gains in the region.[35] Soon after, Italy turned into a strong advocate of an independent and sovereign Montenegrin state and maintained such a position throughout the war years. In late 1916 and early 1917 the Italian envoy at the Montenegrin court in Neuilly initiated a campaign aimed at "saving Montenegro from Serbia" and worked to establish a Montenegrin-French committee that advocated the independence of Montenegro.[36] The activities of the Italian government on behalf of King Nikola and the idea of an independent Montenegrin state had nothing to do with actual independence and sovereignty issues. Italy's engagement in "resolving" the so-called Montenegrin Question represented a tool for its diplomacy to successfully deal with its other allies, and it aimed primarily at pressuring Serbia into making various concessions.

"God Is High Above Us and Russia Is Far Away"

Aside from Austria-Hungary, Russia was a Great Power with an intense interest in the Balkans. St. Petersburg saw the Balkans as its area of influence, and almost all of the political and military happenings in the region from the mid-nineteenth century until 1918 were marked by the rivalry between the Ottoman empire, Russia, and Austria-Hungary. Russia's role as supporter of all South Slavs and its strong advocacy of their regional and local aspirations served the purpose of pressuring Austria-Hungary whenever it became necessary. To minimize the impact of Austro-Hungarian policy in the Balkans, Russia supported the establishment of a strong South Slav state and was in favor of the unification of Montenegro and Serbia. Because Russia wanted to remain in control of the political happenings in the Balkans, the issue of Montenegrin-Serbian unification was of particular importance. St. Petersburg would often switch sides, backing first the Montenegrin dynasty and then the Serbian. By doing so it maintained control over the process and created a climate of mistrust and animosity between the two dynasties. While the Serbian ruler, Prince Mihailo Obrenović, was still alive, Russia saw him as an individual who could unify the South Slavs and supported every action he took in that direction. After he was assassinated, Montenegro and the Petrović dynasty became the focal point of Russia's attention. Following the Berlin Congress, the political climate in Serbia became ever more oriented toward Vienna, and this political shift on the part of Milan Obrenović prompted Russia to stress even more the role that the Montenegrin Prince Nikola could and should play in the process of South Slav unification. Official Russia spoke about Montenegro as the Piedmont of Serbdom, and Emperor Alexander III referred to Prince Nikola as his only true friend.[37] The Russian government's Balkan policy again shifted away from Montenegro when a new dynasty (the Karadjordjevićes) came to the throne in Serbia. The Karadjordjevićes proved to be loyal followers and exponents of the Russian policy in the Balkans, and the rivalry between the Montenegrin and the Serbian dynasties once again came to the political forefront. Belgrade and Cetinje argued over numerous issues on many occasions and even broke off diplomatic relations for a short time. In all of these regional dynastic conflicts, St. Petersburg sided with Belgrade and the Karadjordjević dynasty.[38]

Russian diplomats were eager to see the two countries unify and openly advocated the absorption of Montenegro by Serbia. On February 3, 1914, the French ambassador to Vienna reported to his superiors that Russia was pleased that Serbia would absorb Montenegro in a short while.[39] In 1914 Russian foreign minister, Sergei Sazonov, formulated his government's policy regarding the unification of Montenegro and Serbia as follows:

> We are pleased by the prospects for the unification of the two states of the Serbian race. In accomplishing this, a new Slavic wall will prevent Austria's future advancement toward Thessalonica. Austria will not tolerate Serbia's expansion toward the Adriatic coast, and they will risk going to war in order to prevent it. Therefore, it is necessary to be patient.[40]

The Russian position on unification did not change either after the occupation of Montenegro or after King Nikola went into exile. Before leaving for Italy, Nikola asked to travel to Russia and remain there as the emperor's adviser at the rank of Russian field marshal. The government in St. Petersburg refused to accommodate this request, and on March 8, 1916, the emperor wrote a brief note stating that his officials had to "prevent by all means necessary the arrival of King Nikola in Russia during the war."[41] In later years Russia acted benevolently toward Andrija Radović and his work on unification, but after the October Revolution the impact of the "Russian factor" on the South Slavs was greatly diminished.

France and Montenegro

On December 20, 1920, Delaroche-Vernet, the representative of the French government at the court of the Montenegrin king in exile, delivered an official note informing the Royal Government of Montenegro that after the Yugoslav elections of November 28, 1920, France recognized the unification of Montenegro and Serbia as a fait accompli. The letter further stated that

> under the circumstances, the government of the Republic does not recognize any viable reasons for further continuing its diplomatic relations with His Royal Highness King Nicholas and it decided to close down the French diplomatic mission in Montenegro. Therefore, my mission is concluded.[42]

On January 10, 1921, the exiled government of Montenegro issued an official statement refusing to acknowledge the right of any foreign government to decide the fate of the Montenegrin state. This refusal was based on conclusions reached during the Paris Peace Conference, confirming the international character of the Montenegrin Question. The Royal Government of Montenegro viewed the French memorandum as a sign of a benign and temporary diplomatic incommunicado between the two countries:

> The Royal Government of Montenegro is very surprised that the government of the Republic has publicly and without a doubt supported the crime that Serbia committed against Montenegro, since it has never been in the tradition of the noble French people to encourage a destructive war that would jeopardize the freedom of small nations. . . . The surprise of the Royal Government is even greater since it knows that your government has acutely been aware of the fact that, if completed, such an act would represent a clear violation of the principles of justice and morality of all the civilized people.[43]

This exchange of letters between the two governments marked the final months of the Royal Government of Montenegro's futile struggle to reverse the course of events that followed the annexation of Montenegro by Serbia in 1918 and its later incorporation into the Kingdom of Yugoslavia. The initial question that needs to be answered is what significance Montenegro had within the French foreign policy agenda in general. The second question is why France's political attitude toward Montenegro changed at the end of the World War I.

During the middle of the nineteenth century France showed considerable interest in the Balkans in general and in Montenegro in particular. This interest was motivated primarily by the attempts of the French government to maintain balanced foreign relations with Russia and Austria. After the Crimean War (1853–1856) and the Congress of Paris (1856), France became a dominant political force in Europe. At the time France also had a significant influence on Montenegro's foreign policy. This was partly due to the pro-French sentiments of the Montenegrin ruler, Prince Danilo Petrović. From 1852 until the late 1860s French foreign policy rather favored the issue of applying the nationality principle among small nations. This had an enormous initial impact on Montenegro. However, once France began advocating the idea of preserving the Ottoman state, its influence in Montenegro began to decline,[44] and Russia became the main point of reference in Montenegro's foreign-policy actions. Russia's encouragement of the Balkan peoples in their struggle against foreign rule guaranteed it the dominant political position among the South Slavs. This turn toward Russia marked the beginning of a new phase in Franco-Montenegrin relations. From then on, instances of France's political benevolence toward Montenegro can be traced only to the times when Montenegro more directly attempted to side with Russia. With this in mind, it can be said that the dynamics of Franco-Montenegrin relations reflected to a large extent those of France and Russia. On the other hand, it was in Montenegro's interest that good relations between France and Russia were maintained. The signing of an alliance between those two countries in 1893 was celebrated with cheers on the streets of Cetinje because Montenegro's ruling elite saw it as an opportunity to enlarge their own territory at the expense of the Ottomans and the Austro-Hungarians. However, the political attitude of France toward Montenegro can be characterized as generally benevolent but never one that included any political risk on the part of the French government.[45] This approach was particularly apparent with regard to issues such as the Eastern Question and the preservation of Austria-Hungary. The only instance when French foreign policy took any risks with respect to Montenegro was its support for annulling Article 29 of the Berlin Congress.[46] It can be noted that, until the outbreak of the World War I, the intensity and quality of Franco-Montenegrin relations varied considerably within the context of global political happenings and trends. As far as France was concerned, its position toward Montenegro was that of a somewhat interested but still distant observer.[47]

The attitude of French foreign policy toward Montenegro went through two distinct phases during World War I. From the outset of the war in 1914 until the capitulation of Montenegro in January 1916, France treated Montenegro as its war ally. The two armies even discussed plans to undertake a joint military action in and around the Bay of Kotor, and those plans were bitterly opposed by the Serbian government. When Montenegro occupied the town of Scutari in June 1915, French opposition was less vigorous than that of Serbia, Italy, and England.[48] However, France refused to encourage further expansionist actions by Montenegro by declining to provide large loans to its government[49] and, as was related earlier, Montenegro was forced to capitulate in January 1916. Montenegrin authorities assigned to the Great Powers significant responsibility for the capitulation of Montenegro. In a letter to George Clemenceau, King Nikola I Petrović stated:

> During 1915, my Government repeatedly asked our powerful allies to assist us in obtaining enough food and weapons. Our requests remained unanswered. In the final days of 1915 Montenegrins and their army found themselves lacking in everything. There was not even enough bread to go around. From the very start the Allies treated this theater of war as marginal and not worth paying attention to. Because of the dreadful conditions in Montenegro at the end of 1915 I personally intervened on several occasions with His Royal Highness the Emperor of Russia and His Royal Highness the King of Italy and asked for help in obtaining food and the provisions needed for the army. I have pointed out the inevitable negative consequences of the delay of much needed help to Montenegro. Unfortunately, my interventions did not have a positive outcome. The

aforementioned reasons, paired with the unbearable strategic and tactical position of the Montenegrin army (as the protector of the retreating Serbian army), resulted in catastrophe for Montenegro in January 1916.[50]

When King Nikola and his government found refuge in France (Neuilly) and France became an active participant in the decision-making process regarding the future of the Montenegrin state, Franco-Montenegrin relations entered a new phase. This phase was characterized by ardent French support for the idea of a common South Slav state and the facilitation of the Serbian government's political agenda. While formally playing host to the exiled Montenegrin king and his government, and while subsidizing their stay in Neuilly, the French government prevented official Montenegro from having any impact on the decision-making process at the Paris Peace Conference. This was partly due to the increased propaganda campaign against Montenegro and its king by the representatives of the Serbian government in Paris. This propaganda campaign targeted King Nikola in particular and misrepresented his role in the final collapse of the Montenegrin army in late 1915. Serbian representatives in Paris and the advocates of the unitary South Slav state portrayed Montenegro as a less-than-loyal war ally of France and accused its officials of secretly collaborating with the Austro-Hungarians during the first years of World War I:

> King Nikola left the country without taking with him the army or the government. Therefore, he does not have the right to speak on behalf of Montenegro. He does not even recognize the principles of nationality and, most of all, he does not have an army. We request that the Great Powers do not consider him their ally. He does not have the right to do anything on behalf of the Montenegrin people.[51]

A change in political course with regard to Montenegro could be detected in the attempts of the French government to delegitimize Montenegrin representatives in Paris. At the same time, French officials spared no effort in assisting all those who advocated a unitary new South Slavic state. They made all the provisions needed for the advocates of the future Yugoslav state to travel to Montenegro and campaign in favor of the unification of Serbia and Montenegro. Janko Spasojević was one of the principal organizers of the Podgorica Assembly in 1918. French authorities allowed him to leave for Montenegro even though other Montenegrin expatriates in France were denied the right to possess any travel documents. The same restriction applied to the official representatives of the Royal Government of Montenegro in exile. Spasojević left Toulon and reached Thessalonica in October 1918 on board a French navy vessel. Another central figure in the unionist movement, Andrija Radović, reached Montenegro in the same manner in early December 1918.[52] France was also an avid supporter of the so-called empty chair with respect to Montenegro's participation at the Paris Peace

Conference. According to a decision made by the Allied Commission in Versailles on January 13, 1919, Montenegro's case was to be argued at the Peace Conference "by one representative but the mechanism for choosing this delegate will be established only after the political situation in that country is cleared up."[53] The question of who was going to represent Montenegro's interests in Paris was hotly contested, with King Nikola and the officials of his Royal Government in exile on one side and the representatives of Serbia and those favoring the representation of the newly formed Kingdom of the Serbs, Croats, and Slovenes, on the other. Protracted military conflict between the Serbian occupational forces in Montenegro and Montenegrins opposing union with Serbia on the one hand and the unwillingness of the Great Powers to make a firm decision on the issue of Montenegro's representation at the Conference on the other hand resulted in its being represented by an "empty chair."[54]

Without his own army on Montenegrin soil and living in exile, the king and his government were isolated from the entire decision-making process at the Peace Conference. They were entirely dependent on the subsidies provided by their host, and their image was badly damaged by negative propaganda. Of particular importance was the Serbian Bureau for Journalism, established in Geneva in the spring of 1916. It was headed by Božidar Marković, a professor from Belgrade University. Staff members and associates included Milan Grol, Frano Cvjetiša, Mirko Kosić, Veljko Petrović, and others. The Serbian government set up this bureau as its propaganda office. Its publications were distributed to various organizations and individuals in France (approximately 120 copies), and approximately 50 copies each were sent to England and Russia. Furthermore, the news agencies of the Great Powers received copies of the same material. Another important media outlet was the Geneva-based *La Serbie*, the newspaper closely associated with the Serbian prime minister, Nikola Pašić, and his party.[55] According to the Royal Government of Montenegro, the entire propaganda campaign was coordinated and paid for by the government of Serbia.[56] Under such circumstances the Montenegrin government in exile could do no more than write memoranda and official letters expressing its disagreement with the events taking place in Paris and in Montenegro. Toward the end of World War I, King Nikola insisted on forming a military unit composed of Montenegrins exiled in France that would be sent to the port of Valona (in Albania) and placed under Italian command. The prominent unionist and former prime minister of the Montenegrin government in exile, Andrija Radović, opposed this idea and suggested that this unit, if formed at all, should be sent to the Thessalonica front and placed under the direct command of the regent, Aleksandar Karadjordjević. The French government favored inaction in this respect and prevented Nikola from establishing such a military unit at all. When he attempted to do the same thing in the United States through his representative in Washington, General Anto Gvozdenović, French diplomats intervened and prevented the plans from being carried out.[57] Available sources suggest that the French government acted in this matter in cooperation with the government of Nikola Pašić, who sent one of his agents to the United States to prevent recruitment.[58] At the beginning of November 1918 King Nikola made plans to leave for Montenegro. Upon learning of Nikola's plans, the French representative at his court informed him that his return to Montenegro "could have negative repercussions on the military operation in the Balkans."[59] Similar caution resonated in a letter from the French minister of foreign affairs, General Stéphen-Jean-Marie Pichon:

> Your Highness mentioned that the representative of the French republic at your Court informed you about the memorandum on the position of the French government regarding your return. I should add that other Allied governments share these views about your intended return to Montenegro. Under the current circumstances it would be unwise to undertake such a trip. I believe that the memorandum convinced Your Highness that it is indeed better for him to cancel the trip and that there are no better guarantees for achieving peace in your country than the orders given to the Supreme Allied Commander of the Armies of the Orient. . . . You should rest assured, Sir, that the troops under the command of the General Franchet d'Esperey will not spare any efforts to secure stability in your kingdom and that they will respect the elected power structure and the freedom of the Montenegrin people.[60]

French President Raymond Poincaré reiterated the same points in a letter he wrote to King Nikola twenty days later, again assuring him of the loyalty of Allied troops in Montenegro:

> It would seem better for Your Highness to wait before returning to your Kingdom until these objectives are met and life in Montenegro takes its usual course. The presence of Allied troops and the help that they will provide to the population will without a doubt bring closer that moment of return that Your Highness is so eagerly awaiting. Sir, as soon as that time comes, the government of the Republic will be happy to facilitate your return.[61]

It has been suggested by some Montenegrin historians that the French authorities prevented Nikola's return to Montenegro at the specific request of the Serbian government.[62] Nikola Pašić's government convinced the French that Nikola's return would greatly destabilize the fragile military balance in the region. Moreover, his return was presented as the potential cause of long-lasting instability.[63] The only option left to King Nikola was to request certain guaranties for Montenegro from the Great Powers. France provided these guaranties in an official letter to the Royal Government of Montenegro, which stated that

> the government of France does not intend to interfere in the domestic affairs of an allied state. It is therefore clear that upon its arrival in Montenegro the

French military contingent could not act in a manner other than that of recognizing the legal authority of King Nikola. Therefore, Allied forces will act as an administrative power on behalf of this sovereign. After all, it is not the intention of the French government to harm the feelings of the population or to become an instrument preventing the implementation of policies created by the government of King Nikola. Even though we might want to exercise caution in this regard, we are dealing with a recognized power structure. That power structure is the one established by King Nikola, and we intend to respect it.[64]

The Allied Commission in Versailles made the decision that its troops should enter Montenegro. The country was divided into five occupational zones (French, British, Italian, American, and Serbian) with general headquarters located in the coastal city of Kotor. The first commander-in-chief was General Venell, who was later replaced by General Taon. General Venell had been relieved of his duties after the Montenegrin government in exile and King Nikola himself complained about the political actions of the Allied forces in Montenegro and their interference in the conflict on the side of the government in Belgrade.[65] The general headquarters' staff was formally in charge of all the Allied troops stationed in Montenegro and was to report to the Allied commander of the Armies of the Orient, General Louis-Félix-Marie-François Franchet d'Esperey. French troops were stationed in Dubovik near Cetinje (the Montenegrin capital) and in Bar, as well as in Virpazar, Zelenika (in the Bay of Kotor), and the town of Nikšić in northern Montenegro. Serbian troops were stationed in various garrisons throughout Montenegro.[66] The mandate of the international forces was the preservation of peace and stability in Montenegro. Following the guidelines outlined in Woodrow Wilson's Point XI, which stated that "international guarantees of the political and economic independence and territorial integrity of the several Balkan states should be entered into," the Allied forces were supposed to create a safe environment in Montenegro and facilitate the process of political decision making by its citizens.[67] Despite being formally under a unified command structure, however, each military contingent acted in accordance with the interests and the instructions of its respective national government. Italian forces assisted those who opposed the unconditional unification of Montenegro with Serbia and aided some of those who participated in the 1919 Christmas Eve Uprising in Montenegro. French troops, on the other hand, were for the most part at the disposal of the Serbian government and its representatives in Montenegro. The prominent unionist Andrija Radović was in constant contact with the Serbian representative in Paris, as well as with the leader of the Yugoslav delegation at the Paris Peace Conference, Nikola Pašić. This line of communication was established and maintained through the French army communication center in Kotor. As far as the Serbian army was concerned, it followed the instructions of its government in Belgrade. Prior to sending its troops to Montenegro, the Serbian government managed to obtain a rather broad mandate from the Allied forces for completing its mission in Montenegro. The character of that mission was more political than military; it was thought important to acquire the assistance of General Franchet d'Esperey "as often and as much as possible."[68] It is apparent that the French troops stationed in Montenegro greatly influenced its internal political climate by favoring the political agenda of the advocates of a unitary state of all South Slavs.

General Franchet d'Esperey played a particularly interesting role in assessing the situation in Montenegro. He arrived in Montenegro for a three-day visit at the end of January 1919, shortly after the armed insurrection had started.[69] Prior to taking this trip, d'Esperey sent a message to the Regent Aleksandar Karadjordjević and his government, urging them to have confidence in French attempts to advocate the unionist cause in Montenegro.[70] According to Colonel Petar Pešić, who was the Serbian military representative in Paris at the time, General Franchet d'Esperey expressed a wish to be greeted upon arrival in Dubrovnik by the commander of the Second Army. Pešić's report further states that d'Esperey thought that it would be best if "in Dubrovnik, Kotor, and in Cetinje in particular, he was greeted by large groups of people. Such mass gatherings would represent a clear sign of strong support for unification with Serbia."[71] Pešić instructed Andrija Radović to treat d'Esperey with all appropriate honors and requested that these instructions be kept secret, in particular the fact that they were coming from d'Esperey himself.[72] After this three-day visit, d'Esperey left Montenegro via Scutari. On February 3, 1919, five days before d'Esperey's report on the situation in Montenegro was made official, Andrija Radović informed Nikola Pašić of its contents. Radović's message replicated the forthcoming report almost verbatim and included all six crucial points later emphasized by d'Esperey.[73] The report was indeed very supportive of the unionist agenda in Montenegro. Among other things it stated that the army in Montenegro was a Yugoslav army, not a Serbian one, and that the elections for the Podgorica Assembly had been free and transparent. Moreover, the report stated that Montenegrins were in favor of unification with Serbia. With regard to the insurrection, the author of the report was rather categorical in stating that it had been started by several agents of the former Montenegrin king, who were supported by the Italian generals. Shortly after the publication of d'Esperey's report, the prime minister of the Royal Government of the Kingdom of Serbs, Croats, and Slovenes, Stojan Protić, extended his warmest greetings to the author. Two years later, in 1921, General Franchet d'Esperey was awarded the title of Honorary Yugoslav Vojvoda (Duke).[74] The government of France was particularly keen on following through with its earlier promises to the Regent Aleksandar Karadjordjević and his government.

France's benevolence toward Serbia was primarily of a geopolitical nature, but significant financial interests also determined the course of French policy toward Serbia and the future common South Slav state. Before World War I, French investment capital enjoyed a strong presence in Serbia. This became particularly apparent in the period after 1905 and during the outbreak of the trade war between Serbia and Austria-Hungary. French companies and the French government had substantial investments in the Serbian meat industry, railroad, and mining industry. The Franco-Serbian Bank dominated the financial market in Serbia to the extent that some specialists on the subject spoke of a French monopoly in Serbia.[75] It seems that in the early 1890s the French government had shown a tendency to influence Serbian domestic and foreign policy through various government loans and other financial arrangements. Over some thirty years, the French government had approved a number of loans to the Serbian government totaling more than 1 billion francs. As a point of comparison, it might be noted that France invested in the Ottoman empire some 3 billion francs over a period of one hundred years. As Ljiljana Aleksić-Pejković argued, Serbia's financial dependence on France (and to a somewhat lesser degree on Great Britain) and France's need to protect its investments resulted in a rather strong political bond between the two governments.[76]

The Lion and the Eagle

Britain was never interested in the Balkans to the extent that Russia, Italy, and Austria-Hungary were (not to mention France, of course). Its interests in the region were conditioned by its less than friendly relations with Russia during the second half of the nineteenth century and its concern over potential Russian influence over the Balkan peoples. It was opposed to Russian patronage of any movement working toward political and national consolidation in the region because it feared that such events might trigger similar movements in the Middle East. That was one of the reasons why Britain initially insisted on preserving the Ottoman state. Only after its relations with Germany had worsened and after it had become clear that the Ottoman state was coming ever closer to Germany did Britain adjust its approach to the Eastern Question and begin advocating the division of the Ottoman state among the Balkan states.

The British government was aware of the bitter political divisions in Montenegro during and immediately after World War I but chose to avoid addressing the problem directly. It viewed the resolution of the Montenegrin Question as part of the larger issue of South Slav unity. Once it became clear that the Austro-Hungarian empire would dissolve, the attention of the Foreign Office turned toward facilitating the creation of a common South Slav state. Montenegro was affected by British policy on the Balkan Peninsula mainly by default, that is, via Whitehall's attitude toward Serbia. British policy toward Serbia was marked by cautious support of the nationality principle and was conditioned by the imperial and strategic interests of the British Crown. These interests often overlooked the aspirations of the Montenegrin dynasty.

The recurring theme in the relations between Montenegro and the Great Powers that deeply undermined the support to the independent Montenegrin state was the

Allies' belief that King Nikola had maintained secret contacts with Austria-Hungary throughout the war. These fears and suspicions very much colored the British political attitude toward Montenegro. In September 1914 the British representative in Cetinje, Count John de Salis, accused King Nikola and his government of delaying military action against Austro-Hungarian troops. He commented that Nikola was playing a political game in the hope that the eventual military success of Austria-Hungary would facilitate his taking over Albanian territory and the town of Scutari. It would seem that the Foreign Office endorsed de Salis's view but decided not to act upon it immediately.[77] After Commander Jovan Bećir resigned as Montenegrin representative to the Serbian High Command in October 1914, the Foreign Office intervened and pressured Montenegro into settling the dispute.[78] Sources indicate that the British government aided Montenegro during the war for two reasons: first because Montenegro was included as part of the assistance package provided to Serbia, and second because, until January 1916 and the capitulation of Montenegro, the Foreign Office feared that King Nikola might conclude a separate peace agreement with Austria-Hungary if he were abandoned by the Allied powers. In a letter to Count de Salis in October 1915, Sir Edward Grey commented that Britain would not benefit at all from aiding Montenegro. On the other hand, Grey stated that if Serbia were to request assistance it would be promptly provided.[79] With this in mind, it is understandable that the British politicians were the first to endorse the policy of the unification of Montenegro with Serbia in order to solve the Montenegrin Question.[80] Isolating, and later removing, the Petrović dynasty from the political scene was the first step in that direction.

British diplomats did not engage fully in the issues of Serbo-Montenegrin relations during and after World War I but rather tried to maintain cordial relations with King Nikola and his government. Britain even shared with France the cost of subsidizing Nikola's stay in Neuilly.[81] Immediately after the end of World War I, Britain's initial reluctance to intervene in Montenegrin affairs gave way to a more engaged attitude. During 1919 and 1920 numerous British parliamentarians spoke in the House of Commons on the issue of Montenegro, and the government was forced to take a position and dispatch its representative to Cetinje. Regarding disturbing reports coming from Montenegro, Sir Eyre Crowe wrote to Earl George Curzon that he felt "that the conditions in Montenegro are now such as to require the urgent attention of the Peace Conference."[82] The British commissioner dispatched to Montenegro was Count John de Salis; he reached Cetinje in early September 1919. In his rather comprehensive report, Count de Salis comments on the character of his mission and that of American Colonel Sherman Miles:

> Its objective was to ascertain as far as possible the circumstances which attended the Montenegrin elections of November 1918, and the decision taken to unite with Serbia which resulted from them. . . . To my great surprise, Colonel

Sherman Miles informed me, on his arrival on the following day, that he had no instructions whatever to undertake in Montenegro any investigation such as that defined in the telegram sent to me. . . . As I have mentioned above, my instructions were explicit as to an American commissioner being sent to Montenegro to report on the situation. Colonel Miles was equally positive that he had no such instructions, and his stay in Montenegro, limited to one day, was occupied solely with formal visits to the Serbian general and the civil governor.[83]

Contrary to the assessment of the situation made by d'Esperey in February 1919, Count de Salis's findings were critical of the Serbian policy in Montenegro. In his report, de Salis stated that Montenegro was occupied by a strong force of Serbian troops "stated officially to be a division"[84] and that the government in Montenegro was purely one of military force. Furthermore, he pointed out that the elections to the Podgorica Assembly had not in any way been legal and that the elections "were held, and the assembly decided, under the bayonets of the Serbian forces; behind them bands of lawless komitajis."[85] Regarding the armed uprising of those opposed to the annexation of Montenegro, de Salis's report stated that

> the proceedings of the assembly are declared on the Serbian side to have been unanimous and to have been the unanimous will of the people. The most convincing argument on the opposite side appears to be the fact that very shortly afterwards there was a formidable rising which without the help of the Serbian army and the support of the French would have swept away the Provisional Government elected by the assembly.[86]

As for the manner in which the situation in Montenegro could be brought under control, de Salis appeared to be rather skeptical about the prospects for lasting peace in the region and acknowledged the difficult position in which the Allies found themselves:

> In seeking to regularize the situation, it appears to me impossible to get away from the fact that, rightly or wrongly, at their own free choice, the Powers have since 1916 recognized the Government at Neuilly as the legal government of Montenegro and cannot now, with due regard to good faith and consistency, proceed to ignore it. The decisions of the Podgorica Assembly, illegal and irregular, do not furnish them with a sound basis for any such action. Which of the two, if either, really represents the majority of the Montenegrin people can only be shown conclusively by a free election. Much that is going on suggests that it is by no means the friends of annexation to Serbia who would win.[87]

This report on the situation in Montenegro was circulated to the Allied governments in an abridged form and was never thoroughly debated at the Peace Conference. Following the suggestions made by French General Pichon, the British Foreign

Office advised that the report by Count de Salis should not be made public and that the question of Montenegro should not be discussed until such a time as the general Italian-Yugoslav question was ready for final settlement. According to the British Foreign Office, the publication of de Salis's report "would be an intolerable affront to the Serb-Croat-Slovene Govt. and an advantage only to Italian chauvinists."[88]

The United States and the Montenegrin Question

The American policy makers were not very familiar with the intricacies of Montenegrin-Serbian relations and became acquainted with this issue only during World War I. During 1916 and 1918 King Nikola's government in Neuilly tried to establish diplomatic ties with the U.S. government in the hope that American (political, diplomatic, and financial) support might strengthen the position of Montenegro with regard to Serbia and other European powers. The Montenegrin king and his government were hoping that the U.S. president would advocate Montenegro's right to self-determination in light of Wilson's political philosophy. This was of particular importance because in one of his letters to the Allied governments Wilson mentioned Montenegro.[89] Moreover, the Neuilly government looked forward to influencing Montenegrins living in the United States and neutralizing prounionist propaganda, as well as countering the accusations of the Serbian diplomats in Washington. Furthermore, King Nikola was convinced that the Montenegrins living in America would readily volunteer for his army and assist him in returning to Cetinje. After several failures to acquire American support and after a prolonged period of waiting, Nikola managed to convince the American State Department to accommodate his request to appoint Petar Plamenac Montenegrin ambassador to Washington. On October 8, 1917, Lansing informed the U.S. ambassador to France, Sharp, that the U.S. government would in principle be happy to welcome the accredited ambassador from Montenegro.[90] As soon as this information became available to the British Foreign Office and to the Serbian government, they reacted very strongly against it. In October 1917 the Serbian prime minister, Nikola Pašić, demanded that his ambassador to the United States, Ljuba Mihailović, prevent the arrival of Plamenac in Washington at all costs.[91] Mihailović wrote a personal letter to the U.S. Assistant Secretary of State, William Philips, in which he protested the U.S. government's decision and informed Philips about the attempts by King Nikola to conclude a separate peace with Austria-Hungary at the end of 1915. While stressing that Montenegrins and Serbs were but one people, Mihailović pointed out that "they could never forget King Nikola's treason against the common cause of our allies, for which we have sacrificed all we have."[92] The Montenegrin Committee for Unification in Paris was also very active in persuading American representatives that having Nikola's ambassador in Washington was not a good idea and that Petar Plamenac was the worst possible choice. The president of the Montenegrin Committee for Unification, Andrija Radović, met numerous times with French, British, and American diplomats and politicians and wrote numerous memoranda, trying to prevent the appointment of Plamenac and accusing King Nikola of treason during World War I. He also mailed numerous prounionist articles to foreign diplomats in Paris.[93]

U.S. policy toward Montenegro became proactive only during and immediately after the Paris Peace Conference. With respect to reports containing much incontestable evidence that the Montenegrin independentists were fighting for their lives against Serbian forces and that the country was in a desperate situation, Herbert Hoover wrote the following note to President Wilson on January 15, 1919:

> I am obliged for your letter of the 15, with the enclosures from Mr. Devine, which I am returning. We have been in correspondence with this gentleman for sometime ourselves, and beside the fact that his information about Montenegro is far from exact, as proved by our own army and navy people on the ground, we have a very strong feeling that the solicitude he professes for Montenegro and Montenegrins is not entirely platonic. The British Foreign Office has refused to vise his passport for France.[94]

When the U.S. government requested that Allied troops be withdrawn from Montenegro no later than April 30, 1919, the Serbian government intervened at the Paris Peace Conference in an attempt to postpone this withdrawal. Despite the Serbian government's intervention, British troops left Montenegro on April 29, 1919, while the Italian government pulled out most of its contingent in early October and left the area completely in July 1920. Some of the French troops left Kotor on July 31, 1919, while several units were left behind in Bar (until February 1920) and in Virpazar (until early March 1920).[95] In the meantime, the Serbian forces in Montenegro were renamed the Yugoslav forces, thus acquiring the legal right to be deployed in Montenegro.

Considering the ongoing struggle between unionist and independentist forces in Montenegro, it is obvious that the Allied occupational forces failed to fulfill their mandate as outlined by the Allied Commission in Versailles. The opponents of the annexation of Montenegro organized an insurrection that quickly turned into a full-scale conflict. Moreover, during the first months of this conflict Allied forces did little to mediate between the warring parties. On December 22, 1918, the rebels' committee sent the commander of Allied forces in Montenegro, General Venell, a list of demands signed by one of the rebel leaders, Captain Krsto Popović. In this written statement the rebels demanded that the international commission settle the Montenegrin Question because it was an international issue; they further demanded that the unification proclaimed at the Podgorica Assembly be annulled. The statement emphasized the illegal character of the Podgorica Assembly and asserted that this meeting was conveyed contrary to the provisions of the Montenegrin Constitution and in opposition to the will of the majority of Montenegrins. Independentists did not dispute the validity of the idea of Montenegro's becoming a constitutive and equal member of a larger South Slav state. The issue was the manner in which unification took place.[96] Furthermore, they requested that all Serbian troops evacuate Montenegro and that free elections be held under the control of the Great Powers.

> The French General replied by telling them to go home and to rely on him for their protection; he would forward their proposal to his government. The insurgents then asked for the dispatch of Allied troops to maintain order and peace. This was refused.[97]

The insurrection started on December 24, 1919, with some 4,000 armed independentists surrounding Cetinje, as well as the towns of Rijeka Crnojevića and Virpazar. They declared that their forces would enter Cetinje and take over the entire state apparatus. Even though General Venell half-heartedly attempted to mediate between the warring sides, neither side met his requests.[98] In the meantime, the commander of the Adriatic troops in Cetinje, Serbian General Dragutin Milutinović ordered that the volunteers and the army must "prevent the armed mob from entering the city at all costs."[99] Fighting around Cetinje broke out on December 24, but the rebels did not manage to enter the city. During the fighting around Cetinje, sixteen unionists were killed and sixty-three were wounded. On the rebels' side, twenty-six independentists lost their lives.[100] For the next ten years and with varying levels of intensity, the insurgency was the central feature of the Montenegrin political scene.

The new parliament of the Kingdom of Serbs, Croats, and Slovenes was established after elections on November 28, 1920, and officially recognized by the Allied powers. The questions of Montenegro's annexation by Serbia and the internal restructuring of the new state were placed on the agenda of the new Constituent Assembly. Such an outcome of the crisis corresponded closely with the solution the Allies had proposed during the Paris Peace Conference:

> It would thus appear easy for the Conference to divest themselves of all responsibility by merely stating that they will recognize the union of Montenegro with Jugo-Slavia if and when a freely elected Constituent Assembly decides to that effect. I gather that this is the view which the French are inclined to adopt, but it is not a very honest solution since it is obvious that in present conditions no freely elected Constituent could take place in Montenegro, or indeed, in Croatia, Dalmatia and Slovenia.[101]

The Politics of the Fait Accompli

Between 1918 and early 1922 all of its former allies broke off diplomatic ties with the Montenegrin government in exile. There were three main reasons for the gradual political and diplomatic marginalization of Montenegro. The first had to do with Serbia. On December 15, 1918, the government of Serbia instructed its representative in Neuilly, Tihomir Popović, to inform the Montenegrin government that because Serbia and Montenegro had been unified on the basis of a Podgorica Assembly proclamation, "the diplomatic representative of the Serbian government is ceasing its activities."[102] Other countries justified their diplomatic distancing from King Nikola by invoking the fact that on November 28, 1920, elections for the Constitutive Assembly of the new South Slav state had taken place. The third reason was that the signing of the Rapallo Agreement settling border disputes by the Kingdom of the Serbs, Croats, and Slovenes and the Kingdom of Italy on November 12, 1920, clearly indicated international acceptance of the newly formed state.[103] France broke off diplomatic relations with the Royal Government of Montenegro in exile on December 20, 1920; the United States decided to withdraw its representative on January 21, 1921; Great Britain did the same on March 17, 1921. Diplomatic exchange between the Montenegrin government in exile and the government in St. Petersburg had been almost nonexistent since the October Revolution. Italy was the only country that maintained official diplomatic contacts with the Montenegrin government in exile until early 1922, despite signing the Rapallo Agreement. These contacts had little impact on the future of the Montenegrin state, and it would seem that Italy's prolonged diplomatic activity came as the result of the family connections between the two dynasties.

It appears that the Allied governments tried to avoid addressing directly the question of the annexation of Montenegro in 1918 and to create modalities of its inclusion in the already approved project of Yugoslavia. It is safe to conclude that France and the other World War I Allies strongly supported the Serbian policy of expansion and its long-lasting desire to reach the shores of the Adriatic through Montenegro. Following the logic of protecting their economic and political interests, the Great Powers had to sacrifice Montenegro because it had the least market value. The French and British governments enthusiastically embraced the prospects of a new and unified South Slav state's emerging in the Balkans. They accepted the Serbian government's argument and that of the advocates of the unionist policy in Montenegro that this new state would represent the realization of the centuries-old dreams of all South Slavs. Advocates of a unitary South Slav state argued that the disappearance of the Montenegrin state and its absorption by Serbia were the ultimate political goals of all Montenegrins. In such a political equation the continuity of Montenegrin statehood (in various forms and on various levels during the past 400 years or so) was characterized not as the historical continuity of a real state formation but rather as an aberration and as the product of the constant state of war between the Montenegrins (Serbs) and the Ottomans. The unionists argued that once this external threat ceased to exist with the dissolution of the Ottoman state there was no need for Montenegro to guard its independence and sovereignty any longer. Because they considered Montenegrins to be merely one ethnic branch of the Serbian national body, the unification of Montenegro and Serbia was presented as a natural occurrence. Accordingly, Balkan advocates of a unitary South Slav state maintained that "the Serbians are the most representative of the Balkan Slavs" and that other Yugoslavs "looked to Serbia to lead them towards independence as Piedmont had led the other Italian states in 1860."[104] At the Paris Peace Conference this argument won the day.

Faced with such views on the Montenegrin Question among the representatives of the Great Powers, the Montenegrin government in exile and the now former King Nikola dispatched numerous notes and memoranda protesting in vain against their marginalization during the Paris peace negotiations. Regardless of how complex the reasons might have been for the shift in the policy of the Great Powers toward their World War I ally, it is obvious that it represented a departure from the proclaimed and adopted Wilsonian principles of fairness and equal treatment of small nations. It signaled the final victory of the Allied policy of fait accompli.

Notes

1. "At midnight on December 29 the king mounted his horse in front of his palace. A few minutes earlier his adjutants had driven away in his car. They would wait for him at Crna Greda. That was the place where the road to Podgorica left behind the last houses of Cetinje. The city was silent as a graveyard. The half-dead king rode his horse through the dead city of Cetinje. Alone. Only the fading light of the moon lit the road. His horse walked slowly as if carrying a casket. From time to time the king would stop and look back. He would look back at the monastery and the Orlov Krš, and Lovćen. He would look back at the graves of his ancestors." Sekula Drljević, *Balkanski Sukobi, 1905–1941* (Zagreb: Naklada Putovi, 1944), pp. 84–85.
2. Islavin's report to Sazonov, Paris, April 19, 1916, AIICG, File No. 120. Also see Hajduković, *Memoari*, p. 234.
3. Report of the Russian representative to the Montenegrin Court to the Russian minister of foreign affairs, Bordeaux, March 6, 1916, AIICG, File No. 120, Doc. No. 3.
4. Memorandum of the Montenegrin prime minister to the Russian representative to the Montenegrin Court, Bordeaux, March 6, 1916, AIICG, File No. 120.
5. Vujović, *Ujedinjenje*, p. 158. Also see *Slobodna Misao*, no. 197 (Nikšić, June 27, 1926). During one of the heated debates with Nikola's associates, Mijušković was involved in a fistfight with General Ante Gvozdenović. Hajduković, *Memoari*, p. 235.
6. Hajduković, *Memoari*, p. 236.
7. Milo Matanović was educated at a Russian military academy and later, in 1917, went on to become the prime minister of the Montenegrin government in exile. Pero Vučković was also educated in Russia, and in Montenegro he worked as the rector of the Orthodox seminary in Cetinje. Following instructions from Serbian Prime Minister Nikola Pašić, on December 8, 1916, Janko Spasojević resigned from his government post and initiated a cabinet crisis. Hajduković, *Memoari*, p. 236.
8. Hajduković, ibid., p. 237.

9. Hajduković, ibid., pp. 238–239.
10. Hajduković, ibid., p. 239.
11. Hajduković, ibid., p. 243.
12. Hajduković, ibid., pp. 244–245.
13. Hajduković, ibid., pp. 258–259.
14. Milanović to Stefanović, Bastia, Corsica, November 13, 1917, AIICG, File No. 357, Doc. No. 7/4.
15. Milanovic to Stefanović, Cervione, November 30, 1917, AIICG, File No. 357, Doc. No. 4/4.
16. "They figured out his character flaws and realized that Radović was a self-centered person, very ambitious and politically unstable, as well as very much oriented toward amassing material goods. Radović confirmed this last character flaw of his during the difficult days of the Serbian retreat through Albania. On several occasions he sent his associate, Boro Djurašković, the captain of the Port of Bar, to meet with Serbian refugees and purchase from them gold coins and Italian liras." Hajduković, *Memoari*, p. 266.
17. T. Popović to Nikola Pašić, Geneva, June 15, 1917. Diplomatski Arhiv Dubrovnik, Crnogorski Odsjek, Doc. No. 119.
18. Nikola Pašić to the Serbian Representative Office in Paris. November 20, 1916, Diplomatski Arhiv Dubrovnik, Crnogorski Odsjek, Doc. No. 17.
19. Andrija Radović to King Nikola, "Drugi Predlog o Ujedinjenju Srba, Hrvata i Slovenaca" (typed), Paris, January 4, 1917, AIICG, File No. 156.
20. In the discourse on Montenegrin nationalism, the name of Andrija Radović became a symbol of national treason, much like the name of Benedict Arnold in the United States.
21. Diplomatski Arhiv Dubrovnik, Crnogorski Odsjek, File No. 81, Doc. No. 2153 (December 31, 1916) and Doc. No. 4 (January 2, 1917). Hajduković, *Memoari*, pp. 266–271. Also see Vujović, *Ujedinjenje*, pp. 162–164.
22. "After the establishment of the committee the government of Serbia remained in control of the unionist movement." Dragoslav Janković, *Jugoslovensko Pitanje i Krfska Deklaracija, 1917. Godine* (Beograd: Savremena Admnistracija, 1967), p. 100.
23. Dragoslav Janković, *Jugoslovensko Pitanje i Krfska Deklaracija, 1917* (Beograd: Savremena Administracija, 1967), p. 100.
24. The government-controlled *Glas Crnogorca* published numerous editorials expressing similar opinions. "From its beginnings Montenegro was the standard-bearer of Serbian liberation and unification. At present, Serbian unification cannot be fully achieved by eliminating either of the two Serbian national dynasties." *Glas Crnogorca* (Neuilly, June 16, 1917).
25. Milenko Vesnić to Nikola to Pašić, Paris, May 21, 1917, Diplomatski Arhiv Dubrovnik, Crnogorski Odsjek, Doc. No. 374, and Milenko Vesnić to Nikola Pašić, Paris, May 25, 1917, Diplomatski Arhiv Dubrovnik, Crnogorski Odsjek, Doc. No. 380. Also see Vujović, *Ujedinjenje*, pp. 166–167.
26. Evgenije Popović (1842–1931) was born in Boka Kotorska (Boca di Cattaro). He was an Italian citizen and a member of Garibaldi's movement. Popović was well known as a journalist and a war correspondent in the 1876–1878 Montenegrin-Turkish war. He worked as the Montenegrin consul in Rome and was the Montenegrin prime minister from 1917 to 1919. Hajduković, *Memoari*, p. 272. The Italian government was very pleased with this appointment and tried to assist Popović as much as possible. In September 1917 it provided the loan of 2 million francs to the Montenegrin government in Neuilly. Radović to Ivanović, September 8, 1917, AIICG, File No. 62.
27. Hajduković, ibid., pp. 279–280. Vujović, *Ujedinjenje*, pp. 168–169. Rastoder, *Uloga Francuske u Nasilnoj Aneksiji Crne Gore*, p. 212.

28. Dragoslav Janković, "O Političkoj Situaciji medju Jugoslovenima pred Ujedinjenje (u 1918, do oktobra)," *Istorijski Glasnik* 4 (1964), pp. 174–175.
29. Janković, *Jugoslovensko Pitanje*, p. 288.
30. Vujović, *Ujedinjenje*, p. 132.
31. Vujović, ibid., p. 133.
32. Vujović, ibid.
33. Vesnić to Pašić, June 21, 1914. Diplomatski Arhiv Dubrovnik, Političko Odjeljenje 1914. File: Odnosi Srpsko-Crnogorski, Confidential, Doc. No. 2544.
34. Arhiva V. Popovića, "Anketa o Kralju Nikoli u Crnoj Gori," (handwritten), AIICG, File No. 113.
35. Vujović, *Ujedinjenje*, pp. 134–135.
36. T. Popović to Pašić, January 5, 1917. Diplomatski Arhiv Dubrovnik, Crnogorski Odsjek, Doc. No. 114 and Doc. No. 12.
37. Herman Vendel, *Borba Jugoslovena* (Beograd, 1921), p. 366.
38. Russia was not pleased with the attitude of the Montenegrin government during the famous Bombaška Afera (the Bomb Plot). Diplomatski Arhiv Dubrovnik, Poslanstvo Cetinje, *Ministarstvo Inostranih Poslova*, Top Secret, Doc. No. 1058 (June 7, 1908).
39. Vujović, *Ujedinjenje*, p. 142.
40. Vujović, ibid., p. 143.
41. Vujović, ibid., p. 147.
42. Delaroche-Vernet to Jovan S. Plamenac, Paris, December 20, 1920, in *Uloga Francuske u Nasilnoj Aneksiji Crne Gore: Dokumenta* (Bar: Conteco, 2000). (Original title: *Documents officiels publies par le Ministere des Affaires Etrangeres du Montenegro*, Rome: Imperiere A. Manuce, 1921. Hereafter DOM.)
43. "Memorandum by the Montenegrin Ministry of Foreign Affairs to the French Foreign Minister," January 10, 1921 (DOM, Rome, 1921). Signed by J.S. Plamenac.
44. Michael L. Dockrill and J. Douglas Goold, *Peace without Promise: Britain and the Peace Conferences, 1919–1923* (London: Batsford Academic and Educational Ltd., 1981), pp. 205–207. The reasons why the French supported the idea of the preservation of the Ottoman state were primarily economic. France had significant financial resources engaged in the Ottoman state. Dimitrije D. Vujović, *Ratna Saradnja Crne Gore i Francuske, 1914–1916* (Podgorica: CANU, 1994), p. 10.
45. On the French reaction with regard to the Annexation Crisis in 1908 and Montenegro's role in these developments, see Vujović, *Ratna Saradnja*, p. 14.
46. According to this article, Montenegro was deprived of having access to the port of Bar (on the Adriatic Sea). It was interpreted that such denial of access infringed on the rights of Montenegro as a sovereign state.
47. See Dimitrije D. Vujović, *Crna Gora i Francuska, 1860–1914* (Cetinje: Obod, 1971).
48. For a comprehensive account of the Montenegrin occupation of Scutari and the reaction by the Great Powers, see Vujović, *Ratna Saradnja*, pp. 216–235.
49. Vujović, ibid., pp. 235–280.
50. "King Nikola Petrović to Georges Clemenceau," August 26, 1919 (DOM, Rome, 1921).
51. Statement by Andrija Radović, the president of the Montenegrin Committee for Unification, on August 3, 1917. Quoted in Janković, *Jugoslovensko Pitanje*, pp. 391–392.
52. Vujović, *Ujedinjenje*, p. 285.
53. DOM, Rome, 1921.
54. Montenegro suffered ten years of armed conflict between the opponents and the proponents of unification. Starting on Christmas Eve 1919, the insurrection quickly turned into a full-scale civil war, which varied in intensity and form and lasted until 1929. See Šerbo

Rastoder, *Skrivana Strana Istorije: Crnogorska Buna i Odmetnički Pokret, 1918–1929. Dokumenti*, vols. 1–4 (Bar: Nidamentym Montenegro, 1997).
55. See Janković, *Jugoslovensko Pitanje*, p. 109. French newspapers such as *Les Journal des Debats* (allegedly financed by the Serbian governmnet), *Le Temps,* and *L'Exelsior*, as well as *Le Journal*, carried long articles criticizing the Royal Government of Montenegro and King Nikola. "Vodeći Pariski Listovi 1916, 1917, i 1918 Vode Kampanju Kleveta Protiv Crne Gore" (DOM, Rome, 1921).
56. "The campaign was paid for and coordinated by the government of Serbia. For this purpose 36 million francs were spent over a three-year period. It goes without saying that the money was given by the Allies." In "Vodeći Pariski Listovi" (DOM, Rome, 1921).
57. Dimitrije D. Vujović, *Podgorička Skupština* (Zagreb: Školska Knjiga & Stvarnost, 1981), p. 52.
58. Paulova, *Jugoslavenski Odbor* (1925), p. 236; also see George J. Prpić, "The South Slavs," in Joseph P. O'Grady, ed., *The Immigrants' Influence on Wilson's Peace Policies* (Lexington: University of Kentucky Press, 1967), pp. 173–203.
59. Vujović, *Podgorička Skupština*, p. 59.
60. General Pichon to King Nikola Petrović, Paris, November 4, 1918 (DOM, Rome, 1921).
61. Poincaré to King Nikola Petrović, Paris, November 24, 1918 (DOM, Rome, 1921).
62. Janković, *Jugoslovensko Pitanje*, pp. 391–392. Also see Vujović, *Podgorička Skupština*, p. 59, and Rastoder, *Skrivana Strana*, vol. 1, Doc. No. 140, p. 236, and Doc. No. 141, p. 237.
63. Vujović, *Ujedinjenje*, p. 303. It is interesting to note that the same thesis about Montenegro's being a new point of crisis in the region had been one of the central arguments of the Serbian government of Slobodan Milošević. Since Montenegro began distancing itself politically from the Milošević regime in 1997, the advocates of a Yugoslav unitary state argued that the potential secession of Montenegro from the FR Yugoslavia would cause a domino effect and initiate further fragmentation (the secession of Kosovo and Vojvodina, for example). A similar analytical framework with regard to the dissolution of the former SFRY also could be detected in many Western European political circles. One is tempted to compare the political attitude of the international community toward Montenegro in the late 1990s with the political agenda of the Great Powers toward the Balkans that characterized the early decades of the twentieth century.
64. Memorandum of the Government of France to the Government of Montenegro, Paris, October 22, 1918. Signed by Delaroshe-Vernet (DOM, Rome, 1921).
65. Savić Marković Štedimlija, *Gorštačka Krv, Crna Gora, 1918–1928* (Beograd, 1928), p. 132.
66. Vujović, *Ujedinjenje*, pp. 379–380.
67. Woodrow Wilson, "Address on the Condition of Peace Delivered at a Joint Session of the Two Houses of Congress, January 8, 1918," in James Brown Scott, ed., *President Wilson's Foreign Policy: Messages, Addresses, Papers* (New York: Oxford University Press, 1918), p. 361.
68. Vujović, *Ujedinjenje*, p. 303.
69. Andrija Radović to General Venell, Podgorica, February 3, 1919, AIICG, File No. 122, Doc. No. 1. In this handwritten report Radović described Franchet d'Esperey's visit to Cetinje.
70. Vujović, *Ujedinjenje*, pp. 385–387.
71. Petar Pešić to the minister of defense, Letter No. 15, January 1, 1919, Paris. In Rastoder, *Skrivana Strana*, vol. 1, Doc. No. 63, pp. 161–162.
72. Rastoder, *Skrivana Strana*, vol. 1, pp. 161–162.
73. Andrija Radović to the Serbian Representative Office in Paris, Rastoder, *Skrivana Strana*, vol. 1, Doc. No. 118, pp. 215–216. This telegram by A. Radović was dispatched from the French Navy vessel *Lorraine* anchored in Kotor, via the French Navy headquarters to Nikola Pašić in Paris. Pašić attended the Peace Conference as the leader of the Yugoslav

delegation. For the report by General Franchet d'Esperey, see Rastoder, *Skrivana Strana*, vol. 1, Doc. No. 129, p. 224.
74. Vujović, *Ujedinjenje*, p. 387.
75. Ljiljana Aleksić-Pejković, *Odnosi Srbije sa Francuskom i Engleskom, 1903–1914* (Beograd, 1965), p. 819.
76. Aleksić-Pejković, ibid., pp. 819–820.
77. Count de Salis to Sir Edward Grey, Cetinje, September 21, 1914, FO, File No. 371, General Correspondence, Series 46533/51613, Public Record Office, Kew.
78. Arthur Nicolson called it "the stupid conflict" and suggested that Britain should support France in demanding that Montenegro cooperate with Serbia. Sir Edward Grey agreed with Nicolson's suggestion and instructed Count de Salis to warn the Montenegrin foreign minister, Petar Plamenac, about the consequences of Montenegrin refusal to cooperate. Plamenac assured de Salis that the Montenegrin government would do everything in its power to continue coordinating its military operations with Serbia. Nicolson to Grey, October 19, 1914; Grey to de Salis, October 20, 1914; de Salis to Grey, October 26, 1914, FO, File No. 371, General Correspondence, Series 61711/61711, 63823, Public Record Office, Kew. On the resignation of Commander Jovan Bećir, see chapter 3 of this book.
79. Count de Salis to Edward Grey, Cetinje, November 14, 1915, Foreign Office, File No. 371. General Correspondence, Series 152443/177835, Public Record Office, Kew. Grey to de Salis, London, October 14, 1915, Foreign Office, File No. 371, Series 148416. Andrija Radović to the Foreign Office, Brindisi, November 19, 1915, Foreign Office, File No. 371, Series 152433/180595.
80. On the roles of Robert William Seton-Watson, Henry Wickham Steed, Sir Arthur Evans, and other British intellectuals and politicians in shaping Britain's South-Slav policy, see Mark Robert Baker, "A Tale of Two Historians: The Involvement of R.W. Seton-Watson and Lewis Namier in the Creation of New Nation-States in Eastern Europe at the End of the First World War" (master's thesis, University of Alberta, 1993), pp. 6–51.
81. Popović, "*Nekoliko Stranica,*" AIICG, File No. 426.
82. Sir Eyre Crowe to Earl Curzon, September 29, 1919, Doc. No. 6793, FO 608/46, Public Record Office, Kew.
83. Count de Salis to Earl Curzon, Report on Montenegro, September 4, 1919, Doc. No. 124889, Confidential, FO 608/46, Public Record Office, Kew, pp. 1–3.
84. Count de Salis to Earl Curzon, Report on Montenegro, pp. 10–11.
85. Count de Salis to Earl Curzon, Report on Montenegro, p. 10.
86. Count de Salis to Earl Curzon, Report on Montenegro, p. 11.
87. Count de Salis to Earl Curzon, Report on Montenegro, pp. 11–12.
88. Future Status of Montenegro (handwritten note), October 9, 1919, Doc. No. 19476, FO 608/46, p. 130, Public Record Office, Kew. Signature unreadable.
89. In his letter to the governments of the Allies and the Central Powers on January 10, 1917, President Wilson stated that one of the conditions for achieving a peace settlement would be the "reconstruction of Belgium, Serbia, and Montenegro including all reparations that they are entitled to." Wilson made a similar statement a year later in his famous address to the U.S. Congress on January 8, 1918. L. Criscuolo, *Montenegro's Right to Live* (New York, 1928), pp. 21–22.
90. Dragoljub Živojinović, *Crna Gora u Borbi za Opstanak, 1914–1922* (Beograd: Vojna Knjiga, 1996), p. 100.
91. Dimitrije D. Vujović, "Rad Srpske Vlade u Emigraciji na Ujedinjenju Crne Gore i Srbije," *Istorijski Zapisi* 13, no. 17/4 (1960), p. 699.
92. Živojinović, *Crna Gore u Borbi za Opstanak*, p. 101.

93. Živojinović, ibid., pp. 102–103.
94. Herbert Hoover to Woodrow Wilson, Paris, January 15, 1919, quoted in Francis Williams O'Brien, ed., *Two Peacemakers in Paris: The Hoover-Wilson Post Armistice Letters, 1918–1920* (College Station: Texas A&M University Press, 1978), p. 42.
95. Vujović, *Ujedinjenje*, pp. 379–385.
96. Rastoder, *Skrivana Strana*, vol. 1, Document No. 30.
97. Count de Salis to Earl Curzon, *Report on Montenegro*, September 4, 1919, Confidential, Doc. No. 124889, FO 608/46, Public Record Office, Kew, p. 6.
98. Orders of General Venell, Kotor, December 25, 1918, Doc. No. 40, in Rastoder, *Skrivana Strana*, vol. 1, p. 128.
99. General Milutinović to Captain V. Tunguz, Order No. 732, Cetinje, December 22, 1918, in Rastoder, *Skrivana Strana*, vol. 1, Doc. No. 31, p. 123.
100. General Milutinović to the Commander of the Second Army, "Memorandum on the Insurrection in December 1918," Doc. No. 875, Cetinje, January 2, 1919, in Rastoder, *Skrivana Strana*, vol. 1. Also see Doc. No. 56, pp. 144–154.
101. Harold Nicolson to the Foreign Office, "Situation in Montenegro: Transmits Count de Salis' Report," September 16, 1919, Doc. No. 18918, FO 608/46, p. 2, Public Record Office, Kew.
102. Bogdan Krizman, "Pitanje Medjunarodnog Priznanja Jugoslovenske Države, 1919. Godine," in *Istorija XX Veka*, vol. 3 (Beograd, 1962), p. 348. Raspopović, *Diplomatija Crne Gore*, p. 636.
103. Dragoslav Janković argues that the Kingdom of the SHS was first recognized by Norway (January 26, 1919), only to be followed by the United States (February 7, 1919), Greece (February 28, 1919), and Switzerland (March 6, 1919). Dragoslav Janković, "Društveni i Politički Odnosi u Kraljevstvu Srba, Hrvata i Slovenaca uoči Stavarnja Socijalističke Radničke Partije Jugoslavije (Komunista)," in *Istorija XX Veka*, vol. 1 (Beograd, 1959), pp. 10–11. Great Britain formally recognized the new South Slav state on June 2, 1919, and France did the same on June 6, 1919. See Raspopović, *Diplomatija Crne Gore*, p. 637.
104. Woislav Petrovitch, *Serbia, Her People, History, and Aspirations* (London: Harrap, 1915), pp. 241, 158.

CHAPTER FOUR

The Montenegrin Committee for Unification

As related earlier, the prime minister of the Montenegrin government in exile, Andrija Radović, criticized the policies of King Nikola and resigned his post in January 1917. The Serbian prime minister, Nikola Pašić, encouraged Radović to work among the Montenegrin expatriates on organizing a comprehensive prounionist campaign.[1] This chapter will elaborate on the manner in which this work was undertaken and analyze some of the activities of the unionists before and immediately after the end of World War I.

Under the auspices of the Serbian government, in November 1916 a group of Montenegrins stationed in Corfu and Thessalonica established the Montenegrin committee to initiate work on unification among Montenegrins living abroad.[2] The committee proved unable to accomplish this goal, and the Serbian government decided to form a central committee that would coordinate all activities aimed at unification. In early January 1917, Andrija Radović informed the Serbian representative in Paris of his plans to deprive King Nikola of as many of his bureaucrats as possible. He also suggested that it would be necessary to establish a newspaper in Switzerland that would serve the interests of the unionists, and that he, Radović, should remain in Paris in order to regularly brief foreign diplomats about the activities of the unionists. For that purpose, Radović asked for monthly payments of 6,000 francs. These payments were to be presented as donations by various patriotic Serbs so that the direct link between Radović and the Serbian government could not be easily established, even though the Serbian government was in constant contact with Radović through its representative in Paris, Milenko Vesnić.[3]

In January 1917, through his representative in Paris, Nikola Pašić sent lengthy instructions on how to proceed with the Montenegrin Question and what the goals of the future committee should be. Aside from his instructions, which corresponded to Radović's requests and proposals, Pašić stated that it was urgent that the committee should organize a parcel service to Montenegrin prisoners of war interned in various camps in Austria and in Hungary. Furthermore, he suggested that bureaucrats employed by the Montenegrin government in exile resign as soon as possible and that Montenegrin students should refuse scholarships from the government in Neuilly. Pašić concluded by saying that all this had to be accomplished calmly and openly and that there was no need to bother the Allied governments with every little detail of the undertaking because they were aware of the movement and approved of it.[4] In spite of Radović's enthusiasm for unification it would seem that the work of establishing the committee progressed slowly, and Nikola Pašić had to intervene twice in February 1917. Pašić was worried because many Montenegrins were reluctant to publicly declare their allegiance to the unionist cause because they were unaware of the existence of the movement's leadership. For this Pašić blamed Andrija Radović and his colleagues. Such reluctance, according to Pašić, created maneuvering space for King Nikola and allowed him to revive his newspaper, *Glas Crnogorca*, and to form the Montenegrin Red Cross, which had offices in Paris and Geneva. Moreover, Pašić said that there were Montenegrins who demanded decisive action and were ready to work independently of Andrija Radović, if necessary. This was a clear warning to Radović to act quickly and decisively if he intended to remain the leader of the unionist movement among Montenegrins.[5]

Two months after his resignation as the Montenegrin prime minister and just eleven days after Pašić's second intervention, Radović was presiding over the first meeting of the newly established Montenegrin Committee for Unification of Montenegro with Serbia and Other Yugoslav Lands. This meeting took place in Paris on March 4, 1917. Others present at the meeting were the former ministers Pero Vučković, Janko Spasojević, and Danilo Gatalo, and the former judge Miloš Ivanović. The membership later included Luka Pišteljić, S. Djurašković, and Risto Jojić. The committee appointed Radović as its president and decided that the central office should be located in Geneva.[6] It seems reasonable to suggest that the main source of the committee's funding was the Serbian government even though the funds were funneled through individual donors. The documents tell us that during the meeting on March 28, 1917, the president of the committee, Andrija Radović, stated that the committee could count on

> a permanent monthly donation in excess of 40,000 francs to cover various expenses. This money will come from a charitable foundation that was established by those patriotic individuals who are in favor of the unification of the Serbian tribe. Aside from this, for the purpose of aiding prisoners of war from Montenegro and many poor families in Montenegro, our Committee could count on the assistance of various humanitarian organizations and individuals, as well as donations from our expatriates in the United States.[7]

After several unsuccessful attempts to find the right person for the role of the Yugoslav philanthropist who would "donate" large amounts of money to the Montenegrin committee, the Serbian government made an agreement with a wealthy Yugoslav from Chile, Paško Baburica, who agreed to play the role of a donor and facilitated the first transaction of half a million francs. During one of the committee's sessions, Radović announced that Baburica had made a generous donation to the committee. It is interesting to note that only after Radović received the funding did he make the announcement to the committee members because he feared that the truth might somehow be leaked to supporters of King Nikola.[8]

Program and Proclamation

The committee's program outlined the need to bring together all Montenegrins willing to work on unifying Montenegro with Serbia and other Yugoslav lands. In order to initiate this process, the committee decided to issue a proclamation to all Montenegrins explaining the motives behind its actions. The program stressed the need for publicizing committee activities and establishing direct lines of communication with Allied governments. It also emphasized the need for creating regional and local subcommittees that would advocate the idea of unification while the main office in Geneva would publish a newsletter and organize regular press conferences. The aim of the organization was to involve as many Montenegrins as possible in the work on unification. The last article of the committee's program pointed out that "all measures necessary for achieving this goal should be taken."[9] The point of departure for the committee members was the notion that Montenegrins and Serbs are one people and that the Montenegrin state came into existence as the result of historical circumstances but that it never represented anything more than an extension of Serbia. In a sense, Montenegro was a mere military camp where "the best of the Serbs" found a temporary refuge from the Ottoman invasion.[10] The committee argued that the end of World War I created favorable circumstances for Montenegro to achieve its centuries-old desire: unification with Serbia. Radović and his colleagues were convinced that such a state would "provide the best guarantees for building a democratic structure, freedom and equality" of its citizens and that in such a state the nationality principle would be fully implemented.[11] The economic argument featured prominently in the committee's program, which stressed the poorly developed economic structure in Montenegro and contended that the country would not be able to function without significant economic support from abroad. Consequently, it was suggested that Montenegro be fully incorporated into the Serbian economic structure, thus creating a strong economic unit. Furthermore, the program argued that such a strong, politically stable, and economically independent union would play a significant role in European politics and would be a source of stability and security and an obstacle to further German advances toward the East.¹² These notions along with romanticized views of the Montenegrin past were also present in the Proclamation of the Montenegrin Committee for Unification that was issued on the same day as its program.

> United Serbia and Montenegro, united with the still occupied Serbdom and with our Croatian and Slovenian brothers, will be our great motherland of which we dreamt for centuries and for which so many generations have spilled the most precious blood! Montenegrins! Let us rally under the flag of unification! Only through the unification and only in one large people's union will you be happy because only then the ideals of our entire tribe for which you spilled your blood will be achieved. Only in such a union will you be happy and free citizens. Only in such a union will you have the broadest constitutional rights. Only in such a union will your well-being be assured.¹³

Diplomatic Activities

The program was translated into English, French, Russian, and Italian and sent to the Allied governments. The responses Radović received from St. Petersburg, London, and Paris were positive. The foreign minister in Russia's provisional government, Mikhail Tereshchenko, stated that the new Russian government "does not have any reason to be interested in the fate of the Montenegrin ruler."¹⁴ The initial reaction of the British Foreign Office was cautious approval. The first to pledge their support to the program of the Montenegrin committee were British journalists and university professors who rallied around Robert W. Seton-Watson and his journal *The New Europe*.¹⁵ On July 2, 1917, Andrija Radović expressed his gratitude for the support Seton-Watson gave to the Montenegrin committee. In a lengthy letter written from Paris, Radović explained to Seton-Watson the reasons behind his resignation as Montenegrin prime minister. He went on to elaborate on the content of his memorandum to King Nikola and stated that his orders that led to the capitulation of Montenegro clearly proved that Nikola was opposing the war aims of the Allied powers. Radović described the newly formed Montenegrin government under the premiership of Evgenije Popović as a toy in Nikola's hands. He further informed Seton-Watson about the preparations of the English edition of the newsletter *Ujedinjenje* (published in English as the *Montenegrin Bulletin*) and announced his upcoming visit to London.¹⁶ Some months later, in a letter accompanying the first edition of the *Montenegrin Bulletin*, Radović wrote to Seton-Watson that the Montenegrin committee was

> simply the representative of the organization for national union to which belongs the elite of our intellectual world and of our youth. As the one guiding principle in all our actions, we have only the sacred cause of the Montenegrin

people. Indeed, the attempt has even been made to cause the world to believe that the Montenegrin people are some sort of nationality apart, in order to be able, even after the War, to turn the "individuality" of Montenegro to account for the profit of the dynasty. Let the War finish as it may, Montenegro and Serbia *must* henceforth form *one indivisible whole*. And that must be, not only because the two countries are inhabited by the same people and because national traditions require it, but also because economic necessity and every condition of national existence imperatively compel it.[17]

The French government acted benevolently toward the Montenegrin committee while trying to balance support to Radović and diplomatic relations with the Montenegrin government in exile and King Nikola. The Italian government took a stand of disapproval toward the committee and its program. At the same time, Italian Foreign Minister Sidney Sonnino tried to convince King Nikola that Italy would like to see Montenegro enlarge its territory after the war and that the Italian government would support such a postwar arrangement. In spite of the rhetoric, Sonnino was against Montenegrin participation in the future peace conference and even prevented Nikola's visit to Rome in June 1917.[18]

The Newsletter *Ujedinjenje* and the Battle of Spilled Ink

On April 2, 1917, the Montenegrin committee published the first issue of its newsletter *Ujedinjenje* (Unification) and advocated the unification of Montenegro and Serbia. The newsletter devoted its pages to Montenegrin politics, its education, and its economy. *Ujedinjenje* was a four-page biweekly printed in Geneva.[19] The Paris-based Montenegrin committee constituted its editorial board. Since Danilo Gatalo was the only committee member based in Geneva, he was entrusted with the printing and the submissions. According to Dimitrije Dimo Vujović, the proofs of all articles intended for the newsletter were couriered from Paris to Geneva together with the rest of the Serbian diplomatic mail. Vujović argued that the Serbian authorities were directly influencing the editorial policy of *Ujedinjenje*. In a letter to Andrija Radović, one of the appointed editors in Geneva, Ljubo Krunić, reported that the Serbian representative in Paris had contacted him.

> I came back from the printers around 8 p.m. last night and found a telegraph from the Serbian Consul, signed by Mr. Vesnić, who authorized us to prepare the issue ourselves in case the material did not reach us through the Marseille courier. He also suggested that an article on St. Vitus day should appear in print.[20]

There were no professional journalists writing for the newsletter, and the quality of articles published was relatively low. Many sympathizers of the Montenegrin committee noticed this and warned Andrija Radović about it.[21] It is interesting to note that the Serbian diplomatic couriers handled all the mail intended for the committee and all of the written contributions to the newsletter. The Serbian Representative Office in Geneva provided a mailing list for the distribution of the *Montenegrin Bulletin* in Switzerland while suggesting that the comittee itself should do the mailing. The mailing list included the American representative, A. Stovall; the Belgian representative, Baron de Grotte; the Japanese representative, Yaguro Miura; the Dutch representative, Van Panhuys; the Portuguese representative, Antonio Maria Bartholomeu Ferreira; the Swedish Count Ehrensvard; the Russians Mikhail M. Bibikov and Andrei N. Mandelstam; and the secretary of the British legation in Switzerland, Viscount St. Cyres.[22] The Serbian Representative Office in Paris also handled all the committee's financial transactions.

> This time around, instead of through the French mail, I am sending you the material for the newsletter through Mr. Savić, who will be traveling to Geneva. I will send the rest of the material (articles and letters) through Mr. Blagojević.[23]

Together with various propaganda materials the newsletter was mailed to numerous addresses throughout the world. Many Montenegrins sympathetic to the committee's cause subscribed to *Ujedinjenje*. In August 1917, copies of the newsletter were mailed to Paris, Bordeaux, Marseille, Corsica, Rome, Naples, Corfu, Thessalonica, London, St. Petersburg, Washington, and Edmonton. A number of the Montenegrin soldiers attached to Serbian and other Allied units, as well as many Montenegrin prisoners of war in Austro-Hungarian camps, also subscribed to it.[24]

The first issue of *Ujedinjenje* published several articles attacking the policy of the Montenegrin government in exile and King Nikola. The language used against Nikola was so strong that one of the committee members and the coeditor of the newsletter, P. Vučković, resigned from the editorial board, left the committee in protest, and went on to work for the Montenegrin Red Cross.[25] The Swiss authorities also issued a warning to the editorial board about the harsh language, and committee members were forced to tone down the rhetoric in order to avoid having *Ujedinjenje* banned in Switzerland.[26] After a strong protest by the Montenegrin government in exile, the French authorities temporarily banned the distribution of both *Ujedinjenje* and the *Montenegrin Bulletin* in France. The committee decided to continue printing in Paris and tailored both newsletters to fit French laws on censorship, thus persuading the French authorities to lift the ban.[27]

As mentioned earlier, after Vučković's departure, three new members joined the Montenegrin Committee for Unification. They were Luka Pišteljić, a lawyer in St. Petersburg; Jovan Djurašković, a former member of the Montenegrin People's Assembly; and Risto Jojić, philosophy professor.[28] Nikola Pašić approved these new appointments.[29] *Ujedinjenje* continued its campaign of discrediting King Nikola and his dynasty, but its articles and editorials failed to sufficiently address the general issue of unification. The committee decided to devote more attention to this issue and began addressing the relations between Serbia and Montenegro. The editorial published on July 1, 1917, stated that the past mistakes of the Montenegrin ruler were not the only reason why people of Montenegro desired unification with Serbia. The article emphasized that, although such mistakes should not be forgotten, the issue of unification surpassed individual and dynastic interests. The essence of this and many other editorials in *Ujedinjenje* was that one should make a clear distinction between the Montenegrin king and the Montenegrin people and that in spite of the king's activities, unification represented the ultimate expression of the national interest of Montenegro.[30]

Andrija Radović continued to campaign against King Nikola in French and Swiss newspapers. On July 21, 1917, the Paris paper *Le Temps* published an article by Radović titled "L'enigme Montenegrine" in which he again criticized King Nikola and his sons, Danilo and Petar, for their behavior during 1915 and for conducting secret negotiations with Austria-Hungary. This attack provoked strong responses by Princes Danilo and Petar in the same newspapers. The Montenegrin government in exile was not sitting idle. Instead, it coordinated an attack on Radović and the committee in newspapers such as *Glas Crnogorca* (Neuilly), *Tribuna* (Rome), and *La France* (Paris).[31] The response by the two Montenegrin princes and various articles in French and Italian newspapers provided Radović with an opportunity to mount an even harsher attack on the Petrović dynasty, and his new publication indicated the beginning of open hostility between Radović and the Montenegrin committee on one side and the Montenegrin court on the other. As part of this battle of spilled ink, on August 30, 1917, Radović published a long article in the *Gazette de Lausanne* titled "La Question du Montenegro." He began by explaining the program of the Montenegrin committee and elaborating on the idea of the unification of Montenegro and Serbia, together with all Serbs, Croats, and Slovenes, in one common state. Radović stated that, due to his absence from Montenegro during the first two years of the war, he was kept in the dark about all the machinations and political games of the royal family, which inevitably led to the capitulation in January 1916. Only after he was appointed prime minister in the spring of 1916 did he learn about the many political blunders of the Montenegrin king. In the article, he concentrated on what he perceived to be the main political wrongdoing of the Petrovićes: the secret and prolonged negotiations with Austria-Hungary. Radović proceeded to list a number of points, such as the series of allegedly secret meetings between Prince Petar and the Austro-Hungarian officer Major Hubka, at which they discussed the separate peace agreement. According to Radović, a number of foreign diplomats stationed in Cetinje confirmed that these meetings indeed took place. He continued that the evidence of Nikola's treason was overwhelming and that the people of Montenegro recognized the wrongdoing of their ruler. In conclusion, Radović pointed out that the political blunders of the Petrovićes did not prevent many Montenegrins from continuing work on the unification because their dream was the establishment of a common state. He stressed that such a concept was supported by many friends of Montenegro and by Serbia in particular. Furthermore, for the first time Radović had publicly admitted that the Serbian government was providing financial assistance to the Montenegrin Committee for Unification.[32] Aside from publishing this article, Radović mailed a copy of it to Harold Nicolson and George F. Clark in the foreign office and wrote a brief explanation of the reasons for such a harsh attack on the Petrović dynasty. In his letter to Nicolson and Clark, he stated that he was forced to respond to his opponents accordingly. A similar letter and a copy of the article were also mailed to R.W. Seton-Watson.[33]

Faced with united opposition (Serbian, as well as French and British) to his plans for the renewal of Montenegrin independence and sovereignty, King Nikola and his prime minister, Evgenije Popović, decided to ask the U.S. government for permission to send Petar Plamenac as King Nikola's ambassador to Washington.[34] As soon as the State Department indicated that it might approve Nikola's request, the governments of Serbia, France, and Great Britain began pressuring Washington to change its mind. Andrija Radović joined the protest against a Montenegrin embassy in the United States and in late October 1917 sent a long memorandum to the American ambassador to Paris, G. Sharpe in which he made a clear distinction between King Nikola's vision of the Montenegrin state on the one hand and the desires of the Montenegrin people on the other. According to Radović, these two visions stood in opposition to each other. He argued with great passion that the people of Montenegro wanted to unite with Serbia, whereas King Nikola struggled to preserve Montenegrin independence. Radović also referred to Wilsonian principles, arguing that because it was proclaimed that every nation had the right to decide its own fate, such a right should also be extended to Montenegro. Because, according to Radović, King Nikola had acted against such principles, the United States should ignore him. In conclusion, Radović stated that he spoke on behalf of the Montenegrin people and emphasized that, if appointed, the ambassador of King Nikola to Washington "will never be the true representative of the Montenegrin people but will only advocate the agenda of the king, which is contrary to the interests of the Montenegrin people."[35] Radović's memorandum reached Washington long after the State Department had decided not to accept Petar Plamenac as King Nikola's ambassador to the United States. Even though Radović's letter did not influence the decision of the American administration, it did outline the main features of the committee's activities and showcased the political pragmatism of Radović himself. It became obvious that the committee members perceived themselves as true representatives of the Montenegrin people. Moreover, in line with the evolution of political philosophy, they argued in favor of a nationality principle and against dynastic legitimism.

The Montenegrin Committee and the Allied Subsidies to King Nikola

On November 14, 1917, Andrija Radović sent another memorandum to the Allied governments arguing against further subsidies to the Montenegrin government in exile. He accused the king and his government of mismanaging the funds, wasting money on political propaganda, and paying salaries to an unnecessarily high number of officers, bureaucrats, and students. He stated that these salaries and scholarships were excessive and that money should instead be distributed to poor people in Montenegro and to a number of Montenegrin war prisoners in Austria-Hungary. Radović provided the list of expenses of the court and the government in exile and of the Montenegrin Red Cross during 1916 and 1917. He pointed out a sharp increase in spending during a one-year period and proposed that the Allied governments establish a commission that would oversee the financial dealings of Nikola's government and cease further subsidy payments to the Montenegrin government in exile.[36]

Shortly before Radović's memorandum reached Rome, the Italian government agreed to assist Nikola and his government with a monthly amount of 100,000 francs. It is therefore understandable that Radović's memorandum ended up buried under the piles of documents in one of the archives in Rome and that Sonnino never acted on it. He did, however, consult with the British and French governments and decided to remain quiet on the issue. The Foreign Office maintained the position that it was difficult to fully determine the truth of Radović's accusations and decided to officially acknowledge the receipt of the material while seeking an expert opinion from the British Ministry of Finance. In January 1918, the Ministry of Finance wrote back to the Foreign Office describing Radović's memorandum as a product of the political conflict between the Montenegrin government in exile and the Committee for Unification. It also suggested that the representatives of the French and British governments should investigate the financial dealings of Nikola's government. Such a suggestion indicates that the Ministry of Finance ascribed some validity to Radović's statements regarding mismanagement of funds by the government in Neuilly.

Shortly after this exchange of letters, the French and British governments both decided to examine the financial records of the Montenegrin government in exile and formed a commission under the chairmanship of Jean Simone. In December 1917, the French representative at Nikola's court, Delaroche-Vernet, informed the Foreign Office that the commission had ceased its activities because Simone had left for the United States and it would be very difficult to form another commission. He stated that no one knew all of the financial dealings of Nikola's government but that he suspected fraud and financial mismanagement, although he was not able to produce any evidence to back up those suspicions. It is interesting to note that the British envoy to the Montenegrin government in exile, George Grahame, defended Nikola and his government and stated that they lived humble lives and that money was carefully spent. However, Grahame did acknowledge that Nikola used some money on funding political propaganda countering the attacks and accusations by the Montenegrin committee and the Serbian government.[37] It seems that Grahame's letter played a role in settling the issue of the subsidies to Nikola and his government. Further, his letter highlighted a problem that had less to do with either Radović's memorandum or Nikola's creative accounting and more to do with the growing disagreement between Paris and London. Namely, the British and the French governments constantly argued over the amount that each country should contribute toward subsidizing Nikola's stay in France. After a month of negotiations, and thanks to British persistence, the two governments agreed to share the cost equally and continued paying monthly subsidies of 100,000 francs each to the Montenegrin government in exile.[38] That amount was considerably lower than the earlier payments, a fact that was seen by many as a victory for the Montenegrin Committee for Unification.

If one considers the British policy toward Montenegro and the future South Slav state from early 1917 onward, it would appear that the activities of Andrija Radović and his colleagues did not have a crucial impact on the position of the Foreign Office. Even though the British government constantly worked on preventing all political activities of the Montenegrin government in exile, it also tried to avoid being publicly blamed for letting down its war ally. Continuing to financially support Nikola's government was not, however, a true reflection of the British policy toward Montenegro. Even though Lloyd George in a speech to the trade union representatives on January 5, 1918, spoke about the need to restore Montenegro after the war, it is worth remembering that on January 3, 1918, just one day before the agreement on subsidy payments was made, the British War Cabinet decided that Montenegro should be incorporated into Serbia.[39] As Dragoljub Živojinović points out, the War Cabinet's decision "confirmed the long-standing policy toward that country (Montenegro)."[40] From then on the political actions of the British government with respect to Montenegro represented a discontinuity of its earlier policy. A conversation between Lord Hardinge and the Italian Ambassador Guglielmo Imperiale in early summer of 1918 reveals the reason for this policy shift. Responding to Imperiale's comments about the reluctance of the British government to act on behalf of the Montenegrin government in exile, Lord Hardinge explained that because of his 1916 treason King Nikola could not count on the British support. Hardinge also expressed his personal view that "ethnic, geographic, and economic reasons do not provide any justification for the existence of the independent Montenegrin state."[41]

Activities among the Montenegrin Students

The Montenegrin committee devoted much of its attention to promoting unification among the Montenegrin students abroad. One important activity of the committee was winning over as many students as possible by offering them relatively high scholarships if they would renounce earlier financial support from the Montenegrin government in exile.[42] Radović and his colleagues determined that the committee would cover the students' tuition fees and that the monthly scholarship for those attending university would be 200 francs; those attending high school would receive 150 francs.[43] The overall strategy was to distance the students from the Neuilly government and make them financially dependent upon the committee. On September 22, 1917, Andrija Radović instructed his colleague in Geneva, Danilo Gatalo, to complete a list of all Montenegrin students in Switzerland.[44] The committee also asked the Serbian High Command to relieve all Montenegrin students of any military duty so that they could continue their studies. It also pointed out that such an action on the part of the Serbian High Command would provide the committee with the opportunity to undertake significant political work among the students and prepare them for their return to Montenegro.[45] Many students were eager to take advantage of this opportunity and provided the committee with official transcripts from their universities.[46] The committee paid out the scholarships on a regular basis and closely followed the quality of work by individual students. Some students found it useful to declare their allegiance to the committee's cause before asking for further financial assistance.

> At a time when the five-centuries-old desire of our people to unite all Serbian and Yugoslav provinces in one big and powerful state is near completion I would like, from the bottom of my heart, to congratulate the committee on all its activities. . . . I would consider myself happy if, as a member of the association of Montenegrin youth, I could contribute even in a small way to the collective efforts that were always dear to me. . . . I would also like to inform the committee that I have stopped receiving financial assistance from the Montenegrin government, and I am hopeful that the committee will further assist me in that respect.[47]

In order to advance its political influence among students, the committee established an association of Montenegrin youth, Union (*Jedinstvo*), in April 1917, in Paris. The aim of this association was to introduce the committee's policies and views to the students. As indicated in the program, the Union was formed in order to work toward a complete unification of Montenegro with Serbia and to defend the honor of its people by explaining that the capitulation of Montenegro was the result of treason. In August 29, 1917, the Union came out with a resolution that fully supported the Corfu Declaration and the position of the Montenegrin committee with respect to unification.[48] Despite the Union's expressed support for the committee, relations between the two became increasingly strained during early 1918. This parting of ways came as the result of the factors: first, Andrija Radović's desire to control the activities of the Union members and his increasingly authoritarian attitude toward any independent political activity of the Union and, second, the influence of the October

Revolution on many young Montenegrins. Under the spell of the new political ideas being spread by the October Revolution some students embraced Bolshevism. Andrija Radović and the Serbian government were bitterly opposed to such a trend. In a letter to Svetozar Tomić, Radović bitterly complained about the students.

> With regard to our youth, it is regrettable that we intended to give it a role that does not suit youth anywhere in the world. Politicians in Montenegro, as well as around the world, should conduct politics. The duty of the youth is to conduct propaganda activities.[49]

Many Montenegrin students who expressed their approval of the October Revolution had their scholarships revoked. Among them was Jovan Tomašević, who later went on to establish the Communist Party in Montenegro.

After the Montenegrin committee left France for Montenegro on December 1, 1918, the Serbian Representative Office in Paris took over much of its activities and continued to pay scholarships and monitor the work and behavior of Montenegrin students abroad. This trend continued for a limited period after the establishment of the new South Slav state.[50]

The Issue of the Prisoners of War

After the capitulation in January 1916, a number of Montenegrin officers, soldiers, politicians, and bureaucrats ended up as prisoners of war in various camps in Austria-Hungary. Some of them were stationed in Belice (Slovenia) and Zenica and Doboj (Bosnia), and others were sent to Brandau, Karlstein, and Mauthausen (Austria), and Boldogasszony and Szolnok (Hungary).[51] There were also two camps for prisoners of war in Montenegro: Vuksan Lekić and Petrovac na Moru. The two topics of conversation that dominated the daily life of Montenegrin prisoners of war were politics and the wellbeing of their families in Montenegro. Political discussion centered on the conditions that had led to the capitulation of Montenegro, and very soon two opposing groups formed within each camp. One consisted mainly of intellectuals and the old opponents of King Nikola, who believed that the capitulation was the result of King Nikola's treason. This group believed that one should oppose the king in any way possible and that he should not be allowed to return to Montenegro once the war was over.[52] The other group consisted of officers, who tried not to express their opinions about the king and his government in public and maintained that the time would come to seek those responsible for the collapse in 1916. Their reluctance to speak out can also be seen as an expression of concern for their position and not necessarily as a sign of profound opposition to the king.

Both sides of the Montenegrin political divide (the Montenegrin committee and the Montenegrin government in exile) soon realized the importance of working among the prisoners of war and influencing their political views. The most effective way of influencing the opinions of those in the camps was through regular parcel service and mail service. Whoever managed to provide those two essential services for the prisoners of war on a regular basis would be able to secure influence among them. Both the Montenegrin government and the Montenegrin committee tried to provide those services to the best of their abilities, but the Montenegrin committee seemed to be a bit more successful in its effort, and many prisoners relied on the committee's support for their families in Montenegro. On July 6, 1918, the committee established a separate section that dealt with the unionist propaganda among the Montenegrin prisoners of war. Andrija Radović instructed Danilo Gatalo on how to set up the section and suggested that he employ someone who "knows how to do propaganda," even if the person were a Serbian subject.[53] The committee began sending copies of *Ujedinjenje* to all the camps in the fall of 1917.[54]

The epicenter of political activity was the camp in Karlstein, where many former ministers, members of the assembly, and high-ranking officers were detained. By the end of 1917, the daily political discussions and disagreements among the prisoners had turned into heated debates that would sometimes end in fistfights between the opposing sides. Both supporters and opponents of King Nikola began lobbying their fellow prisoners, writing statements and memoranda either for or against their former sovereign. The passing of Nikola's father, Prince Mirko, who died in a sanatorium on the outskirts of Vienna, was the crucial event that finally divided the Montenegrin prisoners of war into two hostile camps. The supporters of King Nikola tried to use this occasion for political purposes and suggested that a delegation of prisoners should attend the funeral. The Austro-Hungarian authorities refused to accommodate this request. The other suggestion was to send a letter of condolence to King Nikola, and the prisoners in Karlstein organized several meetings to draft the letter and collect signatures. Many prisoners opposed certain phrases in the letter, arguing that certain expressions could be seen as pledges of allegiance to the king. Only 62 out of 123 prisoners in Karlstein signed the letter. The opponents, who came from the regions of Morača and Rovca, circulated their own letter and warned the signatories that they could become the subjects of attacks.

> Signatures were being collected for the political statement that is essentially the pledge of solidarity with the well-known act of treason against Montenegro and the Serbian people.... The fact that you found it useful to cover your statement of solidarity with the blanket of condolences for the passing of the Prince Mirko speaks a lot about your sense of taste, while our writing to you represents our sense of duty to the tribes of Rovca and Morača.... If you do not give up on all this you could become accomplices in a crime against our tribes, and when the moment of conflict between us comes (as it inevitably will), together with all others that are guilty, you would also be the target of our attacks.[55]

Aside from the obvious political divisions among the prisoners of war in the Karlstein camp, this letter reveals much about old tribal loyalties and political divisions along the boundaries of tribal land in Montenegro. For centuries, the tribes of Morača and Rovci bordered on either Serbia or the Ottoman state and were incorporated into the Montenegrin state relatively late. Traditionally, members of these tribes considered themselves to be the representatives of Serbian stock in Montenegro and took great pride in that notion.[56]

The advocates of unification paid close attention to the Montenegrin officers detained in various camps and tried to win them over. For that purpose, Sekula Drljević, Nikola Škerović, and Marko Daković wrote a letter to the officers and distributed it in every camp where there were Montenegrin prisoners of war. The letter criticized the propaganda in favor of King Nikola and was particularly harsh on the issue of the alleged treason in 1915–1916. It called on the officers not to fall victims to the propaganda. According to Nikola Škerović, this letter was well received by many officers.[57] Because the war was coming to an end, the supporters of unification organized several meetings of the officers and bureaucrats detained in Karlstein to discuss the future of Montenegro. The first scenario they discussed foresaw Serbia and Montenegro coming out of the war without any territorial expansions. The prisoners concluded that, under such circumstances, everything should be done so that the two states would unite. The other scenario envisaged the return of King Nikola to Montenegro. The prisoners decided that in this case they should fight for unification. They had also formed two committees whose duty was to organize and direct the armed struggle for unification. These decisions were distributed through other camps and from all accounts the reaction of other prisoners of war was positive.[58]

The King Strikes Back

The establishment of the Montenegrin Committee for Unification and its activities, along with the impact of the Corfu Declaration on the South Slavs and the Great Powers, prompted King Nikola to start campaigning more aggressively against Andrija Radović and his colleagues.[59] Nikola's aim was to counter the Montenegrin Committee's public accusations against him and to prevent further diplomatic isolation of his government. On several occasions during August and September 1917, Nikola and George Grahame discussed at length the issues of the unification of Montenegro and Serbia and Allied policy toward Montenegro. Nikola complained to Grahame about persistent attempts by the Serbian government to influence and even bribe his ministers. Nikola stated that such attempts were usually successful because the Serbian government had considerable financial resources that were specifically designated for anti-Montenegrin political propaganda. He was convinced that the Montenegrins were loyal to him and his dynasty and that he was the victim of a conspiracy initiated by Belgrade. Nikola's main argument was that his loyal subjects in Montenegro could not freely express their opinions and their desires for his future return and the country's independence and sovereignty because of the Austro-Hungarian occupation of Montenegro. According to Nikola, the government of Serbia and the Montenegrin Committee for Unification were taking advantage of a difficult situation in Montenegro for their own political gains. The king was also worried about the political actions of the Great Powers and their favorable attitude toward the propaganda in favor of Greater Serbia. During a meeting with Grahame, King Nikola informed the British envoy that he was expecting some kind of support from the British government because it was obvious to him that French authorities were openly supporting Serbia's political agenda. He used harsh language when describing Andrija Radović, who had proposed that Nikola abdicate in favor of Karadjordjevićes.[60] Even though it would appear that Grahame was inclined to support Nikola's complaints about Allied policy toward Montenegro, his views did not reflect the position of the Foreign Office. Since early on in the war, British officials had been suspicious of the circumstances under which Montenegro capitulated and were inclined to believe that Nikola was somewhat responsible for the fall of Lovćen in late December 1915. The position of the Foreign Office toward the future of Montenegro remained unclear, and such an attitude created much-needed maneuvering space for the Montenegrin Committee for Unification.

In the late summer of 1917, the Italian newspaper *Tribuna* (Rome) published an article by the Italian politician and writer Arturo Labriolla in which he confirmed that a movement including Italian diplomats and politicians in Italy supported the Petrović dynasty and the preservation of independent Montenegro.[61] Despite Labriolla's siding with the Montenegrin king in exile, the fact remains that the proindependence campaign in the Italian media had little to do with the preservation of Montenegrin independence. The true aim of the campaign was to strengthen the position of the Italian government with respect to potential post–World War I territorial gains along the Adriatic coast and in Albania.

In the fall of 1918, the government in Neuilly finally managed to secure the appointment of General Anto Gvozdenović as the Montenegrin ambassador in the United States. This appointment was seen as a major diplomatic victory by King Nikola and was enthusiastically supported by the Italian government. Others, however, were opposed. The governments of Serbia, Great Britain, and France, as well as members of the Montenegrin committee, immediately began pressuring Washington to reverse its decision. Andrija Radović wrote a long memorandum to the American representative in Paris, Edward M. House, discrediting King Nikola. He stated that the appointment of the Montenegrin ambassador to Washington was nothing more than the fulfillment of Nikola's "personal agenda" and had nothing to do with desires of the citizens of Montenegro. With this in mind, he referred to the

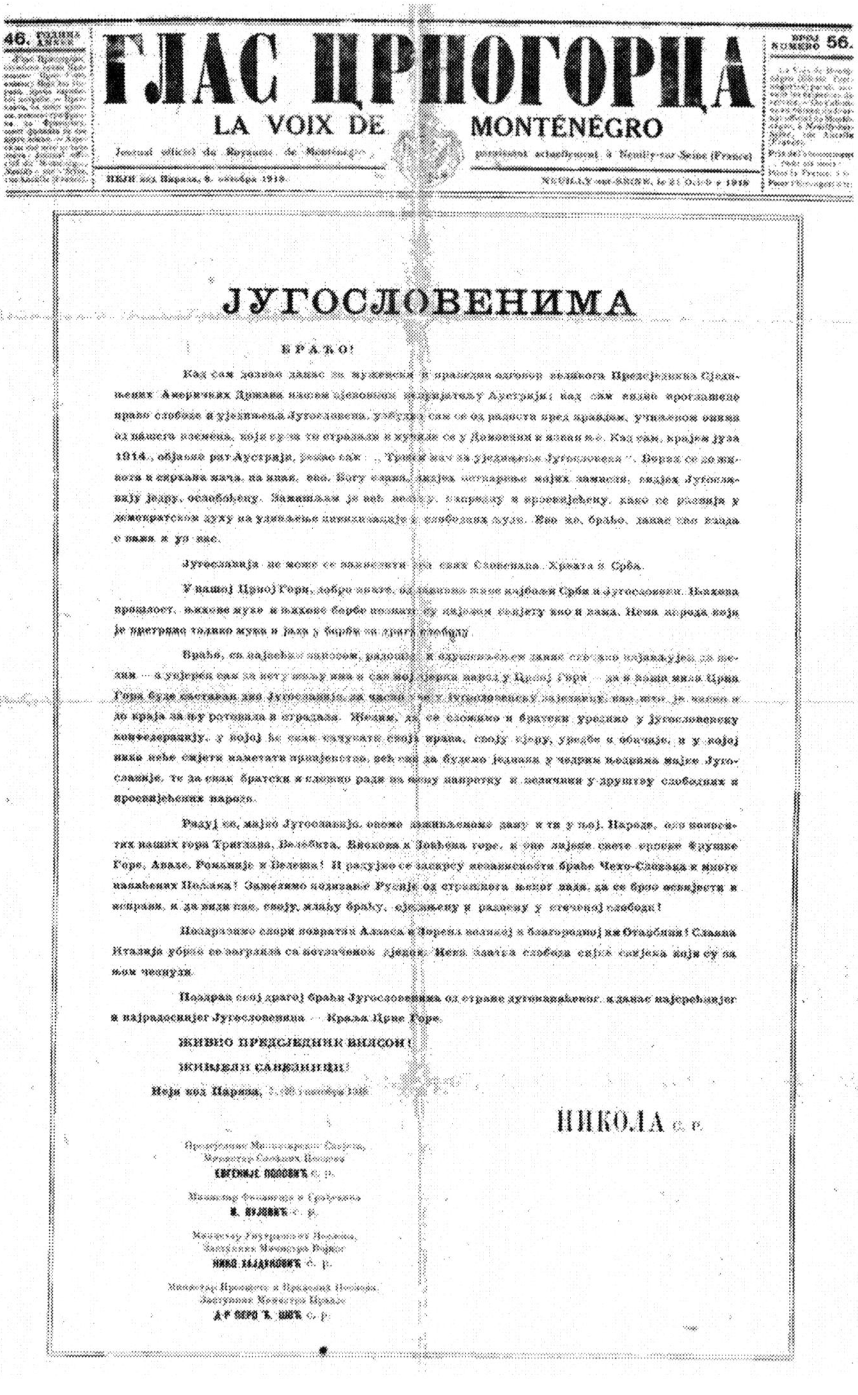

Figure 10. *King Nikola to the Yugoslavs* – Memorandum

new appointment as "unusual" because the majority of Montenegrins were eager to unite with Serbia in one state, whereas King Nikola and his family were opposing the "will of the people." Radović described Nikola as an autocratic ruler, the enemy of democracy, and a collaborator with the Central Powers. He concluded by saying that King Nikola "did not have anything in common with Montenegro" and that the appointment of Gvozdenović would represent an unnecessary luxury and a waste of money on Nikola's political agenda, which was in opposition to that of the United States.[62] Radović sent a similar letter and memorandum to the Serbian representative in Washington and to President Wilson. He instructed Montenegrins living in the United States and their organizations to write letters of protest to the U.S. government.[63] In spite of all this, General Anto Gvozdenović managed to organize and lead a significant campaign in the United States in favor of the Neuilly government and King Nikola, and he successfully organized the celebration of the Montenegrin Day in Washington. Gvozdenović also appointed an American businessman as the Montenegrin consul in New York, and he began establishing new links with various Montenegrin colonies throughout the country. Because of those activities, membership in the U.S. branches of the Montenegrin Committee for Unification began to stagnate, and some members left the organization altogether.[64]

While the campaign against Anto Gvozdenović by the American-based members of the Montenegrin committee was in full swing, the Montenegrin government in exile devised another tactic aimed at discrediting Andrija Radović and his colleagues in the United States. On July 10, 1918, the government in Neuilly sent an official note to foreign diplomats accredited to Nikola's court. The note stated that an assassination plot against King Nikola was being devised in the United States. It further claimed that the Montenegrin Ministry of the Interior had a letter in its possession written by Stevo Djurašković from Arizona that confirmed the existence of the conspiracy. During his conversation with U.S. Ambassador Sharpe after delivering the note, the Montenegrin minister of foreign affairs, Dr. Pero Šoć, cautioned Sharpe about a possible link between the assassination plot and the activities in the United States aimed against King Nikola and designed by Andrija Radović.[65] According to Šoć, it was Djurašković, an avid supporter of unification, who wrote to the offices of the Montenegrin Red Cross in Geneva about the assassination plot. Šoć read Sharpe a segment of the letter.

> You there! You should know that all of us here care about Nikola as much as we care about a stinking piece of shit; he is an old dog and his sons are following in his footsteps, as well as all of you who are licking his heels. You should also know that all of us here do not want to know about any king other than our Yugoslav King Petar; you could send Nikola to Berlin to join the Kaiser. . . . Once again I am telling you, traitors, not to send us those calendars with Nikola's picture on them because we use them as toilet paper and wipe our behinds with Nikola's

face. We are establishing an organization here with the intention of assassinating him so that he would no longer embarrass us."[66]

The Montenegrin government's note continued by suggesting possible accomplices and stating that the entire affair had been designed by Montenegrin expatriates who belonged to the "conspiratorial group gathered around Andrija Radović." The letter pointed out that "back in 1907 Radović was accused and sentenced for conspiring against his sovereign."[67] Miloš Ivanović, Djuro Vukmirović, and Mićun Pavićević were named as Radović's coconspirators in the United States. The note alleged that they had close relations with the officials at the Serbian Representative Office in Washington.[68]

The Montenegrin note did not provoke the expected reaction from the Foreign Office. Even though Grahame pointed out to his superiors the possible existence of a link between Andrija Radović and the assassination plot, British officials did not assign much credibility to the story. The Foreign Office adviser on the Balkan issues, Harold Nicolson, quickly brushed aside the accusations and stated that the entire affair was nothing more than a futile attempt to discredit Radović. He pointed out that there was no proof that any conspiracy to assassinate King Nikola ever existed. Moreover, Nicolson emphasized that solid proof was needed because the accusations were essentially directed against the Serbian government. A number of Foreign Office bureaucrats shared his views.[69] Nicolson's handwritten comment on the margins of the document clearly indicated that the British government had no intention of intervening in the matter on the side of the Montenegrin government in exile. His comment was also an implicit acknowledgment of the direct link between the Serbian government and the Montenegrin committee. The Italian government reacted in a manner similar to the British Foreign Office, refusing to grant any credibility to the story about the conspiracy to assassinate Nikola.[70]

In contrast, the American administration made some attempts to act on the allegations. The U.S. State Department decided to open an investigation and on August 5, 1918, forwarded a copy of the Montenegrin note to the secretary of the Yugoslav committee in Washington, John Grgurević. After reading the material, Grgurević concluded that one letter from the government in Neuilly was not enough to mount an investigation. Moreover, Grgurević made a written statement in defense of the committee members. He pointed out that he knew them very well and that he believed their work and activities to be proper and legal. Grgurević also emphasized that the accused cooperated closely with the Yugoslav committee. On August 8, 1918, the deputy U.S. secretary of state, Frank Polk, requested the original of Djuraškovic's letter. The State Department also contacted the Federal Bureau of Investigation and requested that they look into this matter and try to locate the letter's author, as well as inquire about the activities of Miloš Ivanović, Djuro Vukmirović, and Mićun Pavićević.[71] On August 28, 1918, the FBI agents arrived at the office of the Montenegrin committee in New York at 404 West 23rd Street. They met with Ivanović and informed him that, together with Vukmirović and Pavićević, the Montenegrin government in Neuilly accused him of plotting to assassinate King Nikola. Ivanović maintained his innocence and asked the FBI agents to immediately search the office and the private residences of all three accused. It would seem that the agents were either surprised by his reaction or were aware of the lack of credibility assigned to the Montenegrin note because they decided not to search the office but instead to take a written statement from Ivanović. In his later report to Andrija Radović, the committee representative in New York concluded that the alleged assassination conspiracy was an attempt to facilitate Anto Gvozdenović's work in the United States, and the whole affair was seen as part of a broad attempt to discredit the activities of the Montenegrin committee in the United States.[72] Such a view is supported by the fact that, parallel to the FBI investigation, the Montenegrin government in exile sent a new note to the American government describing numerous activities of Andrija Radović and complaining about his propaganda work. This note paid particular attention to the distribution of various pamphlets and newspapers throughout the United States that contained articles against King Nikola and his government.[73] The FBI investigation lasted until the final days of World War I and ended without any concrete evidence being presented against the committee members. It is very unusual for a conspirator to sign his full name and address on a letter informing the potential victim about assassination plans. Moreover, the Montenegrin committee did not have a branch in Ray, Arizona, and its activities in the area were almost nonexistent. According to Ivanović, the supporters of King Nikola (*gospodarevci*) were in control in that region. There is no information on the identity of the author, and some historians believe that the name might have been invented. The author of the letter was never found, and from Washington's point of view the entire affair seems to have represented nothing more than a tempest in a teapot.[74]

In mid-August 1918, at Nikola's behest, the Montenegrin government made yet another attempt to discredit Andrija Radović and other prominent members of the Montenegrin committee. It decided to initiate a criminal investigation of Radović and his colleagues and charge them with high treason. The accused were former ministers Andrija Radović and Janko Spasojević, as well as the former bureaucrats Danilo Gatalo, Jovan M. Djurašković, and Miloš Ivanović.[75] The indictment stated that the accused had violated Articles 88, 89, and 90 of the Criminal Code and had engaged in an act of high treason. The indictment further stated that the declaration of the Montenegrin committee published in *Ujedinjenje* on July 29, 1917, constituted an attack on Montenegrin sovereignty.

> With this declaration they tried to forcibly incorporate the Montenegrin territory, that is entire Montenegro, into another state, and to impose upon it a

different dynasty. For that purpose, the aforementioned individuals established an association called the Montenegrin Committee for Unification. At the same time, those individuals established contacts with a foreign state. . . . Any action aimed at denying the right of the Montenegrin people and its legal representatives to decide those questions (issues of territorial integrity and statehood) runs contrary to Articles No. 18, 19, 36, 218, 219, and 220 of the Montenegrin Constitution and should be treated as high treason punishable under the Criminal Code. Regarded as high treason and punishable under the Criminal Code are also those activities that through the press either call on the citizens of Montenegro to work on unifying the Montenegrin territory with the territory of another state or call for change of dynasty.[76]

The Montenegrin committee was described as the "sinister five-member-strong gang that was comprised of individuals who took money to betray and inform."[77] The activities and the concept of unification they advocated were characterized as the "Austro-Bulgarian-German concept of solving the Yugoslav question."[78] According to the indictment this concept proposed that Austria-Hungary should maintain its authority over eight million Yugoslavs and that Bulgaria should take over Macedonia and parts of the Old Serbia, while Serbia would be given Montenegro as "compensation."[79] The indictment was signed by the minister of the interior and the interim minister of war, Niko Hajduković, and was published in the government-controlled *Glas Crnogorca* on August 25, 1918. The indictment provoked a negative reaction from the British Foreign Office. Some bureaucrats argued that because Radović was well known as a supporter of independent Yugoslavia the accusations about him advocating the so-called Austro-Bulgarian-German solution were "absolute lies and the most scandalous slander." Lord Cecil and Lord Hardinge shared this opinion.[80] The decision of the Montenegrin government to accuse members of the committee of high treason and the explanation provided for the indictment indicated the level of frustration among the officials in Neuilly and represented a last-ditch effort to save the dream of preserving independent Montenegro and the Petrović dynasty. The indictment was not the main reason for Allies' abandonment of King Nikola and his government, but it did represent the final phase in a long process of marginalization of the Montenegrin government in exile.

Preaching to the Choir: Toward Annexation

By early 1918, it became clear that King Nikola had lost all of his former allies and that the Great Powers, with the notable exception of Italy, were slowly cutting off all channels of communication with the Montenegrin government in exile. Judging by the Great Powers' post-1915 political actions with respect to Montenegro, it is clear that they preferred the establishment of one strong and unitary South Slav state.

In spite of some initial uncertainties among the Allies about the viability of such a state, by late 1917 any opposition to such a concept was bound to fail. King Nikola's limited resources, his unclear political status in France, and his empty rhetoric recounting Montenegro's heroism and past glories were no match for the well-financed and carefully planned diplomatic maneuvering of the Serbian government. As shown in this chapter the Great Powers had evinced sympathy toward the activities of the Montenegrin Committee for Unification because its program corresponded closely to Allied plans for the establishment of the future South Slav state. The formation of the common South Slav state, with Serbia as its focal point and main guarantor of stability in the region, was preferred to the potentially unstable post–World War I fragmentations, which could have resulted in numerous local and regional tensions. The activities of a number of British intellectuals and politicians sympathetic to the idea of the Yugoslav state also had a significant impact on Allied policy makers. Thanks to the political, financial, and diplomatic assistance of the Serbian government, the Montenegrin committee was successful in rallying support among many Montenegrin expatriates. The committee's relatively successful campaign in favor of the unitary South Slav state made a strong impact on the Allies and to a great extent conditioned their views about the manner in which the Montenegrin Question could be solved. The Allied governments were aware that the Montenegrin committee was under the direct supervision of the Serbian government, upon which it depended fully for financial support. After the Yugoslav committee in London, which represented South Slavs from the Austro-Hungarian empire, adopted the Corfu Declaration, the Montenegrin government in exile was isolated even further and was confronted with a united front favoring the common state. By early 1918, the Great Powers had adopted the view that the Montenegrin Question was an internal matter of Serbia. An independent and sovereign Montenegro was perceived as a remnant of the past, while King Nikola was seen as a self-absorbed opportunist who advocated retrograde political concepts. It should, however, be pointed out that the Great Powers and the Serbian government were not the only culprits responsible for the disappearance of independent Montenegro. King Nikola and his administration also bore a burden of responsibility for the final outcome. From the time of his leaving Montenegro in early January 1916 until the end of World War I, Nikola's self-serving political activities were designed and implemented in such a way that they gradually narrowed his maneuvering space and alienated all those who were initially sympathetic to his cause. Persistent accusations about his dishonesty with his war allies, his secret contacts with Austria-Hungary, Italy's carefully calculated and self-serving support for him, as well as his inability to rally significant popular support among the Montenegrin expatriates, also contributed to his demise. As the war was coming to an end, the reasons for the Great Powers to support Nikola's cause were rapidly withering, and the old king remained powerless to prevent the Serbian government and the Montenegrin Committee for Unification from preparing the stage for the Podgorica Assembly. The meeting of the so-called Great People's Assembly in November 1918 in Podgorica represented the final act in the process of the annexation of Montenegro.

Notes

1. Because of Radović's initial reluctance to resign, Pašić suggested that a former minister in Nikola's government, Janko Spasojević, should replace him. Dimitrije D. Vujović argued that the Serbian government was ready to provide financial support to Spasojević. See Vujović, *Ujedinjenje*, pp. 214–215.
2. Diplomatski Arhiv Dubrovnik, Crnogorski Odsjek, Doc. No. 173, February 16, 1917.
3. Vujović, *Ujedinjenje*, p. 216.
4. Vujović, ibid., p. 217. Also see Nikola Pašić to Milenko Vesnić, January 18, 1917, Diplomatski Arhiv Dubrovnik, Crnogorski Odsjek, File No. 122.
5. Pašić to Vesnić, February 16, 1917, Diplomatski Arhiv Dubrovnik, Crnogorski Odsjek, File No. 173, and Pašić to T. Popović, February 21, 1917, File No. 185.
6. Vujović, *Ujedinjenje*, p. 218. Živojinović, *Crna Gora u Borbi za Opstanak*, p. 134.
7. *Zapisnik Odbora*, March 28, 1917, AIICG, File No. 59.
8. Radović to Protić, September 1, 1918, AIICG, Files No. 59 and No. 67. Radović was regularly providing the Serbian government with lists of all budgetary expenses and on special occasions discussed the financial matters directly with Nikola Pašić. Also see Vujović, *Ujedinjenje*, p. 222.
9. *Program Crnogorskog Odbora za Narodno Ujedinjenje, Paris, March 27, 1917*, and *Crnogorski Odbor za Narodno Ujedinjenje—Zapisnici*, AIICG, File. No. 59. Also see Ferdo Šišić, ed., *Dokumenti o Postanku Kraljevine Srba, Hrvata i Slovenaca, 1914–1919* (Zagreb: Naklada Matice Hrvatske, 1920), pp. 88–91.
10. "After the collapse of the Serbian Empire this segment of the Serbian nation kept guarding and cherishing all that was sacred to our nation and never abandoned the idea of the liberation of our entire tribe." Šišić, ibid., p. 88.
11. Šišić, ibid., p. 89.
12. Šišić, ibid.
13. Šišić, ibid., pp. 91–92.
14. The French ambassador to St. Petersburg, Doulcet, reported this in his letter to the French Foreign Ministry dated July 7, 1917. *Guerre 1914–1918, Balkans, Serbia*, vol. 387, Archive of the French Foreign Ministry. The microfilm copy is stored in the Arhiv Srbije (Serbian Archive), Belgrade.
15. The first issue of *The New Europe*, under the ownership and the editorship of Seton-Watson, was published on October 19, 1916. Other contributors included T.G. Masaryk, Henry Wickham Steed, Sir Arthur Evans, and Ronald Burrows. The new journal came out just one day before the official establishment of the Serbian Society of Great Britain, whose first president was the former British governor of Egypt, Lord Cromer. Together with Steed and Evans, Seton-Watson was instrumental in setting up this society. *R.W. Seton-Watson i Jugoslaveni: Korespondencija, 1906–1941*, vol. 1, 1906–1918 (Zagreb and London: Sveučilište u Zagrebu/Britanska Akademija, 1976), p. 27. On the activities of R.W. Seton-Watson and the issue of a common South Slav state, see Documents No. 137, 152, 173, 180, and 182, in the same book.
16. Andrija Radović to R.W. Seton-Watson, Paris, July 2, 1917, in *R.W. Seton-Watson i Jugoslaveni*, ibid., p. 303, Doc. No. 201.

17. Seton-Watson received the first copy of the *Montenegrin Bulletin* in April 1918. A. Radović to R.W. Seton-Watson, Paris, April 1918, in *R.W. Seton-Watson i Jugoslaveni*, p. 313. Doc. No. 209.
18. Živojinović, *Crna Gora u Borbi za Opstanak*, p. 134.
19. The print run of the first issue of *Ujedinjenje* was 4,000 copies. By June 1918 this had increased to 6,500 copies. Danilo Gatalo to Andrija Radović, June 22, 1918, AIICG, File No. 62.
20. Lj. Krunić to A. Radović, Geneva, June 30, 1917, AIICG, File No. 59. Also see Vujović, *Ujedinjenje*, p. 239.
21. Z. Dačić to A. Radović, March 15, 1918, and Dr. Marković to A. Radović, Geneva, May 11, 1918, AIICG, File No. 61.
22. Grujić to Lj. Krunić, Legation Royale de Serbie en Suisse, Confidential No. 974, Bern, July 21, 1917, AIICG, File No. 155, Doc. No. 110.
23. Andrija Radović to Danilo Gatalo, Paris, February 2, 1918, AIICG, File No. 155. Also see A. Radović to Danilo Gatalo, Paris, November 13, 1917, AIICG, File No. 62. Due to the lack of a printing press and paper, the *Ujedinjenje* did not appear in print on a regular basis. With the assistance of the Serbian Representative Office in Paris, the Montenegrin committee purchased letters and other printing material and sent them to Geneva. See Vujović, *Ujedinjenje*, p. 240. Also see A. Radović to the Serbian Representative, Paris, June 15, 1917, and A. Radović to the Serbian Representative, Paris, July 11, 1917, AIICG, File No. 63.
24. Mitar Stankov Tomović to Andrija Radović, Edmonton, July 26, 1918, AIICG, File No. 155, Doc. No. 500, Stevan Srdanović to Andrija Radović, Rossland, BC, November 26, 1917, AIICG, ibid., Doc. No. 502. Radoje Ćulafić to the editors of the *Ujedinjenje*, Sidi-Fath-allah, Tunisia, January 10, 1918, AIICG, ibid. Djordije Marković to A. Radović, Boldogasszony, Hungary, March 10, 1918, AIICG, ibid. Milica Popović to the editors of the *Ujedinjenje*, Srpsko Dobrotvorno Društvo *Zadruga Srpkinja*, Chicago, Ill., January 9, 1918, AIICG, ibid.
25. Crnogorski Odbor za Narodno Ujedinjenje, Zapisnik, May 24, 1917, AIICG, File No. 59.
26. Andrija Radović to Danilo Gatalo, Paris, October 20, 1917, AIICG, File No. 122.
27. A. Radovi to D. Gatalo, Paris, October 20, 1917, AIICG File No. 155. A. Radović to L. Marković, Paris, August 9, 1918, AIICG, File No. 61.
28. *Zapisnik*, July 4, 1917, AIICG, File No. 59.
29. Vesnić to Pašić, Diplomatski Arhiv Dubrovnik, Crnogorski Odsjek, Doc. No. 42.
30. "People's Desires above Everything Else," *Ujedinjenje* 1, no. 4, (July 1, 1917). Also see "The Main Reasons for the Unification," *Ujedinjenje* 1, no. 12 (September 1917), and "Montenegrin Honor," *Ujedinjenje* 1, no. 13 (September 1917).
31. Andrija Radović, "L'enigme Montenegrine," *Le Temps*, July 21, 1917. Also see Grahame to Balfour, Paris, July 21, 1917, Foreign Office, File No. 371, General Correspondence, Series: 34053/144899, 144900, Public Record Office, Kew.
32. *Gazette de Lausanne*, August 30, 1917.
33. Radović to Clark, Foreign Office, File No. 371, General Correspondence, Series: 175127/175127, Public Record Office, Kew. Also see Radović to R.W. Seton-Watson, Paris, September 4, 1917, quoted in Živojinović, *Crna Gora u Borbi za Opstanak*, p. 137, n16.
34. The request to the State Department was submitted on August 22, 1917. It proposed that Petar Plamenac should represent Montenegro in the United States. For a comprehensive analysis of this diplomatic action of the Montenegrin government in exile, see D. Živojinović, "Crna Gora u Borbi za Opstanak: Otvaranje Crnogorskog Poslanstva u Vašingtonu, 1917–1918 god," *Glasnik Cetinjskih Muzeja*, no. 5 (1972), pp. 83–135.
35. Živojinović, *Crna Gora u Borbi za Opstanak*, p. 139.

36. Radović also suggested that the insurance (some 1 million francs) for several grain freighters that sank in late 1915 before reaching Montenegro not be paid to the Montenegrin government in exile but should instead be used to purchase food for the population in Montenegro. A. Radović to Balfour, Paris, November 14, 1917, Foreign Office, File No. 371, Doc. No. 6933/219996, Public Record Office, Kew.
37. Grahame to Balfour, Paris, December 8, 1917, Top Secret, Foreign Office, File No. 371, 6399/236310, Public Record Office, Kew.
38. Grahame to the Ministry of Finance, London, December 31, 1917, Foreign Office, File No. 371, 6399/243726, Public Record Office, Kew.
39. C.J. Lowe and M.L. Dockrill, *The Mirage of Power: British Foreign Policy, 1902–1922*, vol. 3 (London, 1972), p. 605. D. Živojinović, "Velika Britanija i Problem Crne Gore, 1914–1918. Godine," *Balcanica* 8 (1977), p. 513.
40. Živojinović, "Velika Britanija," p. 514.
41. Raspopović, *Diplomatija Crne Gore*, p. 620.
42. Vujović, *Ujedinjenje*, pp. 233–234.
43. Minutes from the Committee Meeting, Paris, March 15, 1917, AIICG, File No. 59.
44. A. Radović to D. Gatalo, Paris, September 22, 1917, AIICG, File No. 155.
45. Montenegrin Committee for Unification, Paris, August 3, 1918, AIICG, File No. 61.
46. M. Milošević to A. Radović, Nice, July 17, 1917. Vojislav Kurtović to the Montenegrin Committee, Bordeaux, September 21, 1917. Radovan Marković: Certificate from the Institute Polytechnique, Universite de Grenoble, Grenoble, August 30, 1917. Danilo Tunguz-Perović to the Montenegrin Committee for Unification, Grenoble, August 28, 1917. M. Stojanović to the Montenegrin Committee for Unification, Paris, April 27, 1917, AIICG, File No. 154.
47. Ilija Brahović to the Montenegrin Committee for Unification, Paris, May 14, 1917, AIICG, File No. 154.
48. *Ujedinjenje*, September 14, 1917, p2. . Also see Vujović, *Ujedinjenje*, p. 242.
49. A. Radović to S. Tomić, Paris, May 25, 1918, AIICG, File No. 61.
50. On February 5, 1919, Milosav Raičević telegraphed from Podgorica to remind the newly appointed minister in Belgrade, S. Pribićević, of his promise to Andrija Radović with regard to the continuous payments of scholarships to the Montenegrin students abroad. Milosav Raičević to Minister Pribićević, Podgorica, February 5, 1919, AIICG, File No. 122. Also see Vujović, *Ujedinjenje*, p. 241, nn53–54.
51. On December 31, 1916, there were 956 Montenegrin officers and 780 civilians imprisoned in the camp at Boldogasszony (Hungary), and 153 officers and soldiers were held in Karlstein. According to the available sources it seems that the treatment of the Montenegrin prisoners of war in those camps was unusually good. The officers detained in Karlstein were allowed to receive mail and food packages sent by the Montenegrin committee. One of those detained in Karlstein was Vukašin Božović. In his diary, Božović describes the prisoners' morning routine: coffee was served at 7:00 a.m. every day, and at 8:00 a.m. their rooms were cleaned by the guards. The prisoners paid for these services. They were then sent off to various job sites. Vukašin Božović, *Druženje i Razgovor Dva Stara Crnogorca 1917 i 1918 godine u Internaciji u Karštajnu*, AIICG, File No. 14 (handwritten), pp. 6–13.
52. Nikola Škerović, "Ideja Ujedinjenja kod Crnogoraca u Zarobljeničkim Logorima 1916–1918," *Zapisi* 13 (1931), p. 284.
53. Andrija Radović to Danilo Gatalo, Paris, July 6, 1918, and A. Radović to Danilo Gatalo, Paris, July 20, 1918, AIICG, File, No. 155.
54. A. Radović to D. Gatalo, Paris, November 13, 1917, AIICG, File No. 155.

55. Božović, *Druženje i Razgovor Dva Stara Crnogorca 1917 i 1918 u Karlštajnu*, p. 235, AIICG, File No. 14.
56. It is interesting to point out that this type of political loyalty is still present in Montenegro. The contemporary political alliances in Montenegro (neotribalism) rest upon the same old tribal divisions and loyalties. People from the regions of Morača, Rovca, and Vasojevići consider themselves true Serbs, whereas those belonging to the Old Montenegro tribes, such as Katunjani and Bjelopavlići among others, are in favor of an independent Montenegrin state.
57. Škerović, "Ideja Ujedinjenja," p. 288.
58. Vujović, *Ujedinjenje*, pp. 291–292.
59. In June 1917, under the auspices of the Serbian prime minister, Nikola Pašić, the representatives of the Serbian government and its opposition parties together with the representatives of the Yugoslav committee (based in London) met in Corfu to discuss the future union. The purpose of the meeting was to try to bridge the differences between the Serbian government and the Serbian opposition parties on the one hand and Dr. Ante Trumbić and other representatives of the Yugoslav committee on the other. After six weeks of negotiations they agreed on basic principles upon which the future South Slav state should rest. On July 20, 1917, the Corfu Declaration was published, and Nikola Pašić and Dr. Ante Trumbić signed it. The Corfu Declaration outlined the main features of the future state. The newly formed Kingdom of Serbs, Croats, and Slovenes would be a constitutional, democratic, and parliamentary monarchy with the Karadjordjevićes as its dynasty. For comprehensive analyses of the Corfu Declaration, see Dragoslav Janković, *Jugoslovensko Pitanje i Krfska Deklaracija, 1917. Godine* (Beograd: Savremena Administracija, 1967); Srdjan Budisavljević, *Stvaranje Države Srba, Hrvata i Slovenaca* (Zagreb: JAZU, 1958), pp. 34–41; Dragoslav Šepić, *Italija, Saveznici i Jugoslavensko Pitanje, 1914–1918* (Zagreb: Školska Knjiga, 1970), pp. 189–239; Ferdo Čulinović, "Pravnopolitičko Značenje Krfske Deklaracije," in Vaso Bogdanov, Ferdo Čulinović, and Marko Kostrenčić, eds., *Jugoslavenski Odbor u Londonu* (Zagreb: JAZU, 1966), pp. 165–229.
60. King Nikola called Radović a traitor. Grahame to Balfour, Paris, September 3, 1917, Foreign Office, File No. 371, 75905/195013.
61. *Tribuna*, August 14, 1917.
62. Živojinović, *Crna Gora u Brobi za Opstanak*, pp. 148–149.
63. A. Radović to Lj. Mihailović, Paris, July 16, 1918, and A. Radović to M. Popović, Paris, July 6, 1918, AIICG, File No. 63. Also see M. Ivanović to A. Radović, August 16, 1918, and Crnogorska Organizacija za Jedinstvo—Seattle to A. Radović, Seattle, August 24, 1918, AIICG, File No. 62.
64. The American coordinator for the Montenegrin committee, Miloš Ivanović, was appointed in June 1917 and after his arrival to New York established contacts with prominent Serbs who were in favor of unification. S. Bogdanović to the Montenegrin committee, New York, June 28, 1917, AIICG, File No. 63. In the fall of 1918, Ivanović and his colleague Djuro Vukmirović complained to Andrija Radović about the negative impact of Gvozdenović's work on their organization. M. Ivanović to A. Radović, New York, October 10, 1918, AIICG, File No. 62. M. Ivanović to A. Radović, New York, November 4, 1918, ibid.
65. P. Šoć to G. Sharpe, Neuilly, July 10, 1918, Foreign Office, File No. 371, 7420/123821, Public Record Office, Kew.
66. "To the Montenegrins in Geneva," letter signed by Stevo Djurašković from Ray, Arizona, and dated March 28, 1918, in P. Šoć to G. Sharpe, Foreign Office, ibid.
67. For a detailed analysis of the alleged assassination plot, see Nikola Škerović, *Crna Gora na Osvitku XX Vijeka* (Beograd, 1965), pp. 417, 427.

68. P. Šoć to G. Sharpe, Foreign Office, File No. 371, 7420/123821, Public Record Office, Kew.
69. Handwritten note on the margins of the Montenegrin note. Signed by H. Nicolson. Foreign Office, File No. 371, 7420/123821, Public Record Office, Kew.
70. Živojinović, *Crna Gora u Borbi za Opstanak*, p. 166.
71. Živojinović, ibid., p. 167.
72. Ivanović to A. Radović, New York (no date), AIICG, File No. 62.
73. This new note paid close attention to the editorial policies of newspapers such as *Montenegrin Bulletin, Oslobodjenje* (Los Angeles), and *Americki Srbobran* (Pittsburgh). The Montenegrin government requested that American authorities ban the distribution of these newspapers. P. Šoć to G. Sharpe, Neuilly, August 8, 1918, quoted in D. Živojinović, *Crna Gora u Borbi za Opstanak*, p. 155.
74. See Živojinović, *Crna Gora u Borbi za Opstanak*, pp. 172–173.
75. Hajduković, *Memoari*, p. 360.
76. "Rješenje o Pokretanju Krivičnog Postupka," Neuilly, August 17, 1918, in Hajduković, *Memoari*, pp. 361–362.
77. Hajduković, ibid., p. 364.
78. Hajduković, ibid.
79. Grahame to Balfour, Paris, August 31, 1918, Foreign Office, File No. 371, 7420/151346 and 151347.
80. Živojinović, *Crna Gora u Borbi za Opstanak*, p. 156.

CHAPTER FIVE

The Preparations for the Great People's Assembly in Podgorica

By the fall of 1918, the Great Powers were in full agreement about the future of the Montenegrin state. The idea of establishing a unitary South Slav state based on the principle of self-determination of "one nation with three names" (Serbs, Croats, and Slovenes) acquired full international support. By late 1918, it was clear that Nikola's fate as ruler of an independent and sovereign Montenegro had been decided by his former allies and that the political agenda advocated by the Serbian government and the Montenegrin unionists had prevailed.

Bearing in mind all of the activities of the Serbian government toward unification, the Great Powers' support of this concept, and the divided Montenegrin political body, it was unlikely that the tiny kingdom could have influenced the process of South Slav unification in a significant way. The Serbian historian Andrej Mitrović pointed out that from the Serbian perspective the establishment of a unified South Slav state meant "the transformation of the country into a new state."[1] For politicians in Belgrade, the transformation of Serbia into a "new state" and the introduction of the new system of relations represented the positive aspects of Serbia's power in the region, proper compensation for its war effort, and a reflection of its contribution to the final act of unification. This perception of the Kingdom of Yugoslavia and the Serbian political, military, and economic power behind it made it possible for the ruling political elite in Belgrade to secure primacy when deciding on the nature and the constitutive principles of the future state. For many Serbian politicians and scholars of the period, the new state represented Serbia's generous gift to other South Slavs living in the region.[2] From the Montenegrin perspective, however, the program for unification of the South Slavs looked very different and meant surrendering the country's statehood and independence, as well as renouncing the Petrović dynasty. The model of the future South Slav state designed by Belgrade and supported by the Great Powers did not allow for any expressions (constitutional or otherwise) of Montenegrin distinctiveness. Indeed, the centralized power structure excluded the possibility for any particular region to have autonomy within the new state, so any political manifestation of Montenegro's former statehood and independence was out of the question. Officials in Belgrade applied the same principle to other nations and ethnic groups living in the territory of the newly formed kingdom. The negative effects of this policy were particularly visible in the region of Kosovo. In order to get around the general obligations of the 1919 Treaty on the Protection of Minorities, the officials of the new state maintained that there was no such thing as an Albanian minority in Kosovo.[3]

Despite all the efforts of King Nikola and his government to internationalize the question of Montenegrin independence and sovereignty, the Great Powers remained convinced that the issue had to be settled within Serbia as part of the process of the South Slavic unification. Faced with a formidable opposition to the idea of renewing his country's independence, King Nikola decided to modify his political stand and adopt the Yugoslav rhetoric. His earlier insistence on the preservation of Montenegrin sovereignty and even on the territorial expansion of Montenegro was replaced by his acceptance of a decentralized model for the future state. In his public addresses, Nikola advocated the establishment of "a federal state in which all its constitutive elements would preserve their autonomy."[4] This proposal by the ailing Montenegrin king was in opposition to the unification concept defined by the Corfu Declaration and was contrary to the principles of centralism, which were the main organizational principles of the future South Slav state. On October 7, 1918, Nikola wrote an open letter addressed to all Yugoslavs in which he claimed that his declaration of war on Austria-Hungary in 1914 was the crucial step toward the unification of all Yugoslavs. It is interesting to observe that this open letter to all Yugoslavs indicated yet another political turn because it referred to the future state not as a federation but as a confederation.

> Brothers! With great enthusiasm, happiness and joy I today solemnly declare my desire—and I am convinced that my loyal Montenegrins share the same desire—that our beloved Montenegro become a constitutive part of Yugoslavia and enter the Yugoslav union with the same pride with which it suffered for it . . . the Yugoslav confederation in which everyone would preserve their right, their religion, laws and customs . . . that all of us remain equal and embraced by mother Yugoslavia.[5]

Nikola's policy shift represented a compromise and his realization of who wielded the power behind the political concept of unification, but it also showed his lack of understanding of the political reality of the time. Even though Montenegro was at times an important factor in defining the Yugoslav question, due to its small size and its economic disadvantages, it was unable to take the leading role in the process of unification. Maintaining the image of Montenegro as the leading pro-Yugoslav force in the region proved to be particularly difficult after the military defeat in late 1915 because there was no Montenegrin army left to fight alongside the Allies and the Montenegrin government and its king lived in exile in France. Montenegro was excluded from the Allied war effort, and its fate was left in the hands of the Great Powers. The successful military operations of the Serbian and Allied armies at the Thessalonica front in late September 1918 and the subsequent entry of Serbian troops into Montenegrin territory marked the beginning of the final phase of the annexation of Montenegro.

The Activities in Montenegro: United We Stand!

The Allied offensive along the Thessalonican front began on September 15, 1918, and the Serbian army was able to liberate the Macedonian city of Skopje on September 28. According to the original Plan of Operations, the French government did not anticipate that the Serbian troops would enter Montenegro. Upon the insistence of French General Franchet d'Esperey, this plan was changed, and Serbian troops were positioned along the left flank of the Allied forces, close to the borders of Montenegro and Albania. This movement of troops was intended to prevent possible military activities by the Italian army and the supporters of King Nikola in the region. The president of the Montenegrin Committee for Unification, Andrija Radović, was also suggesting such a movement of troops in early October 1918. In his letter to the Serbian military attaché in Paris, Colonel Dušan Stevanović, Radović argued that it was important to immediately facilitate the entry into Montenegro of Serbian paramilitary units from the Thessalonican front. He also proposed that a municipal government structure in Montenegro be established as soon as possible and that a vote on unification be organized immediately.[6]

Colonel Dragutin Milutinović was appointed commander of the newly established Serbian army units, known as the Scutari Troops (Skadarske Trupe) and later renamed Adriatic Troops (Jadranske Trupe), which were to enter Montenegro. Before leaving Skopje Milutinović had an audience with Regent Aleksandar Karadjordjević and was told that he must prevent King Nikola's return to Montenegro even if he had to resort to "the ultimate measures."[7] Also advancing with the Serbian army into Montenegro were Janko Spasojević, who represented the Montenegrin Committee for Unification, and the Serbian delegate, Svetozar Tomić, who was in charge of the Montenegrin Section in the Serbian Foreign Ministry. Andrija Radović remained in Paris and coordinated the activities of the committee abroad.[8] In order to facilitate the activities of Spasojević in Montenegro, Andrija Radović wrote to the Serbian prime minister, Nikola Pašić, requesting financial support. He also requested money to cover his own expenses for traveling to Montenegro.⁹ Pašić agreed to the request and ordered that funds be made available.¹⁰ Spasojević and Tomić joined Colonel Milutinović in his efforts to prevent Nikola's return to Montenegro and dispatched a telegram to the Serbian government in Corfu requesting further assistance.

> Tomić reports: Preventing King Nikola and his sons from entering Montenegro until November 20 means that unification will be finalized. This has to be done without turmoil and with the help of the French. Explain to the French that the situation in the country is not at all good and that Nikola's return would mean further deterioration of an already difficult situation. As soon as possible, send to Bar the food and other necessary provisions for the people.¹¹

As soon as he arrived in Montenegro, Tomić reported on the initial activities and progress of the committee members. After arriving in Andrijevica (northern Montenegro), the unionists met with several prominent local leaders, such as Duke Lakić Vojvodić, Brigadier Milo Saičić, and Jevrem Bakić, and enlisted their support. On October 24, 1918, they issued a proclamation to all Montenegrins stating that the people of Vasojevići were in favor of unification with Serbia. The letter went on to call upon other Montenegrins to "to embrace the idea of people's unification and to proclaim the unification of Serbia and Montenegro as we have done already, so that we can fulfill an old desire of all the Serbs."¹² After proceeding to the town of Berane, Tomić informed the Serbian Foreign Ministry about the establishment of the local committee in Berane. The man he left in charge was the former government minister Milosav Raičević, a strong supporter of unification and, in Tomić's words, "our man in all respects."¹³

In order to speed up the process of unification, Spasojević and Tomić established the Central Executive Committee for the Unification of Serbia and Montenegro during the meeting in Berane on October 25, 1918. The members of the Central Executive Committee were Svetozar Tomić, Janko Spasojević, Petar Kosović, and Milosav Raičević.¹⁴ The Executive Committee devised the plan for preparing the Podgorica Assembly and

Figure 11. General Dragutin Milutinović

published the rules for the election of the future delegates (see Appendix 3). By issuing this document, the Executive Committee essentially established the Great People's Assembly and provided new rules for electing the delegates. In order to shed more light on the nature of the activities of the Executive Committee and its links with the Serbian government, it is worth elaborating further on how the committee was formed. It is evident that the Kingdom of Serbia established the Executive Committee and facilitated its activities. During the committee session on October 15, 1918, the government of the Kingdom of Serbia decided to appoint Svetozar Tomić as its representative for policy issues in Montenegro. Prior to this appointment, Tomić was in charge of the Montenegrin Section in the Serbian Ministry of Foreign Affairs. He was later responsible for establishing the Executive Committee in Berane. Even though he was a Serbian citizen, Tomić was elected/appointed as the committee's president. The role of this political body was to fulfill the instructions given by the Serbian government and to report exclusively to Belgrade.[15] For that purpose, Tomić was given a special code for communicating with both the Serbian government and the Serbian High Command.[16] Another committee member was Milosav Raičević. As the mayor of Berane, Raičević organized the prounification rally on October 23, 1918, and tried to convince those present that the municipality of Berane should immediately secede from Montenegro and become a part of Serbia.[17] He reported on the rally to the Serbian High Command and urged the Serbian government to immediately recognize the rally as an act of unification. Raičević was also instrumental in securing votes for the unification of Montenegro and Serbia in the municipalities of Berane and Andrijevica.[18]

The committee established in Berane assumed the role of the executive body with the legal capacity and legitimacy to make decisions related to constitutional issues and questions that were of paramount importance to the Montenegrin state and its people. Such decisions and the committee's taking legislative powers for itself meant denying the right to the Montenegrin parliament to act according to its role as defined in Article 36 of the Montenegrin Constitution. This article states that only the Montenegrin parliament, in agreement with the king, has the right to decide on questions of statehood and borders.[19] Moreover, the unilateral decision of the committee to organize an extraordinary assembly session in Podgorica and proclaim unification with Serbia marginalized earlier initiatives of several groups and individuals from Montenegro who lived in exile. Those initiatives were aimed at advocating and eventually introducing the plebiscite as a way for the people of Montenegro to express their feelings about unification with Serbia. Before the Executive Committee had its constitutive meeting in Berane, the option of a plebiscite enjoyed the same appeal within the population as the option of establishing an extraordinary assembly session that would proclaim the unification.[20] Furthermore, the rules published after the Berane meeting were written by the Serbian representative, Svetozar Tomić, and not by any legislative body in Montenegro. Moreover, they were not based on existing electoral legislation in Montenegro.[21]

Montenegrin electoral law made specific provisions with respect to the electoral process. Articles 16–21 stated that only those people named in the electorate districts' lists had the right to vote. In order for those people to be eligible to vote, the lists of their names had to be delivered to local/municipal courts no later than eight days before the elections. On election day, those lists were handed down to the local election committees. Furthermore, Article 22 determined that the list of candidates had to be given to the appropriate authorities no later than twenty-five days before the elections. With regard to the validity of one's candidacy, the following numbers applied: for every province and electoral district, a minimum of seventy-five voters could propose a candidate, whereas for the town of Kolašin, only thirty nominators were required. Article 25 stated that the list of candidates could be signed only by those whose names were listed in the local electoral lists and that the voting and the entire electoral procedure were to be coordinated and headed by the election committee. As outlined in Article 33, this committee had to be selected and verified at least six days before election day.[22]

The Rules did not specify who was to verify the election results. Instead, elections for the Podgorica Assembly were held without lists of eligible voters and without voters being asked to provide valid identification prior to casting their vote. There were no election committees to oversee the elections and verify the results. The necessary percentage of voter turnout needed for the elections to be valid was not determined. The rules and the proclamation of elections were sent to municipalities from Berane on November 8, 1918, meaning that voters had only nine days until the election was to take place. The mayor of Cetinje "ordered" the election of the representatives and the delegates for the Podgorica Assembly on November 13, 1918; therefore, the time frame designated for the preparations of the elections for the representatives in Cetinje was only three days, whereas there was a five-day period for the election of the delegates.[23] The police curfew was in effect in Cetinje prior to and during the elections.[24] These elements clearly show the arbitrary and illegal character of the hastily arranged election process, and because the organizers of the Podgorica Assembly supervised the election process, it is safe to assume that such arbitrariness worked to their advantage.

The issue of the legality of the process and the legitimacy of the decisions lay at the heart of the debate between the unionists and the independentists in Montenegro. Very few people in Montenegro at the time questioned the need for establishing a common South Slav state. What the independentists argued and fought against was the manner in which such a state was to be established. They favored a conditional unification over an unconditional one. They wanted to see Montenegro as a constitutive part of the future state and not as a province of Serbia; however, committee members and their assistants failed to mention the existence of this other option and even deceived the public. While speaking at a preelection rally in Cetinje, Svetozar Tomić stressed the role Montenegro had played during "five centuries of fighting with the enemy of the Serbian tribe." He also pointed out that unification should proceed because it would mean the "fulfillment of Montenegro's old dream of unification." From the scattered reports on his speeches during the preelection campaign in Kolašin and Podgorica, it is apparent that he did not speak in terms of Montenegro's being absorbed by Serbia and that he emphasized that the new state would be democratic and that Montenegro would only benefit from being a part of it. A similar observation can be made about preelection speeches delivered by Kosović and Spasojević.[25] Neither ever explicitly said anything negative about Montenegro nor did they ever come out openly and state that Montenegro would lose its individuality and subjectivity as a political unit in the new state. They also never mentioned that Montenegro would not be a constituent in the common South Slav state. There are no records indicating that the committee members or any of their associates ever considered the merits of an earlier Montenegrin initiative aimed at the unification of Montenegro and Serbia, nor did they ever explain the failings of the proposal for a conditional unification. Their concept of unconditional unification was presented to the general public as the proper measure of patriotism and a sign of high morality, as well as a signifier of one's attachment and devotion to the "centuries-old desires."

While the unionists were staying in Berane, the Montenegrin paramilitary forces (*Komite*), which were five battalions strong, were slowly pushing the Austro-Hungarian army out of Montenegro.[26] After entering Montenegrin territory, Serbian troops marched through territories already liberated by Montenegrin forces and had their first and only battle with the Austro-Hungarian army on the outskirts of Podgorica on October 30 and 31, 1918. They took the city on October 31, 1918. Two days later, independent of Serbian forces, the Komite units under the command of Jovan Radović succeeded in disarming the Austro-Hungarian troops stationed in Nikšić. The Austro-Hungarian forces abandoned the rest of the Montenegrin territory, leaving Cetinje on November 4, 1918, and Serbian troops marched into the already liberated Montenegrin capital on November 6, 1918. The available sources clearly point out that the Serbian troops under the command of Colonel Milutinović did not engage the enemy in Montenegro in any significant way. It is important to keep this in mind for two reasons. First, the fact that almost the entire Montenegrin territory was free of Austro-Hungarian forces before the Scutari Troops (Adriatic Troops) reached Cetinje disproves the persistent unionist claims that Montenegro was liberated by Serbian troops.[27] Second, the Komite troops were perceived by the Serbian High Command and by the politicians in Belgrade as the military force that might be used to facilitate the return of King Nikola. Because they were seen as a potential threat to plans for the annexation of Montenegro, the Komite were dealt with in a harsh manner. Indeed, the commander of the Serbian troops in Montenegro, Colonel Milutinović, resorted to the "ultimate measures" suggested earlier to him by the Regent Aleksandar Karadjordjević.[28]

Following the advances of the Montenegrin Komite, Spasojević, Tomić, and their colleagues proceeded to Kolašin, Nikšić, Bar, Cetinje, and Podgorica to continue their work on unification. Under the protection of the Adriatic Troops, they were successful in organizing several prounification rallies in Kolašin, Podgorica, and Cetinje. The youth of Cetinje were consumed with the idea of a common South Slav state and decided to establish their own organization in order to facilitate the work on unification.[29] Residents of Kolašin showed similar enthusiasm toward unification.[30] On November 6, 1918, Tomić and Spasojević reported to Nikola Pašić on their successful campaign and stated: "The work on the unification progresses splendidly in the four municipalities of Andrijevica, Berane, Kolašin, and Podgorica, where the elections were concluded. All those elected as people's deputies are in favor of unification."[31] He also warned about potential bloodshed if King Nikola were allowed to return to Montenegro. Spasojević and Tomić requested that the Serbian government send them an additional 1 million dinars by plane so that they could continue their work. It is interesting to note that Spasojević also asked for more Serbian soldiers to be sent to every Montenegrin town. His request for additional military presence in Montenegro came two days after the Austro-Hungarian units left Cetinje. If, as Spasojević claimed in his letter to Nikola Pašić, work on unification was progressing "splendidly," why would he feel the need to ask for more troops to be deployed? It is important to remember that the population of Montenegro was not entirely comfortable with the activities of the Executive Committee and that those advocating Montenegrin independence and sovereignty still represented a serious opponent.[32] King Nikola's supporters tried to disrupt the activities of the unionists but had limited success. Nevertheless, the commander of the Adriatic Troops seemed very concerned about the activities of the independentists, and in a report to the Serbian minister of war, Colonel Milutinović spoke about serious antiunification disturbances in southwestern parts of Montenegro.[33] Opposition to the unconditional unification was publicly displayed in Nikšić on November 7, 1918, when a group of citizens chanted slogans in favor of King Nikola, disarmed an army guard, and then occupied several buildings housing state and military institutions before finally being overwhelmed and disarmed by advocates of unconditional unification. Even one of the most prominent unionists, Svetozar Tomić, admitted in his book that during the elections in Andrijevica on November 5, 1918, those who voted were mainly peasants and educated youth, whereas the community leaders and the majority of bureaucrats were absent. Tomić said that "some apologized for this and said that they were too old, while others complained that they were ill, and others argued that they were obliged to follow the military pledge of allegiance given to the

Montenegrin army and King Nikola."[34] He also noted that those present at the pre-election rally appeared restless and that some left early, clearly upset and angry when one of the speakers spoke about King Nikola in negative terms.[35] Jovan Ćetković also noted a considerable popular opposition to the manner in which the preparations were proceeding. According to Ćetković, the peasants were often puzzled and angered by the persistent references to Serbia and were "terribly poisoned by that stubborn Montenegriness." Ćetković wrote that "in some places the Montenegrins were all in favor of the unification regardless of the potential sacrifices, and at other places they remained silent, while sometimes they were openly opposing the idea." He concluded that in spite of the "murky situation" what had won the day was the determined youth who embraced the idea of unification and adopted the slogan "Unification or Death" from the very beginning.[36] Considering the volatile political situation in Montenegro at the time, it is obvious why the unionists needed the backing of the Serbian army to proceed with their work, and Colonel Milutinović obliged.[37] In a letter to the Serbian High Command, he asked for additional troops to be deployed in Montenegro.

> On November 6 of this year, the Montenegrin committee announced elections for the Great National Assembly. The assembly would take place in Podgorica on November 24. Because of this and because of the need to maintain general political stability, it is absolutely necessary to strengthen the Adriatic Troops with at least two more battalions of infantry and one or two artillery units.[38]

Furthermore, the Serbian army prevented a number of Montenegrin officers from returning to Montenegro in time for the elections because they were worried that they might sway public opinion in favor of King Nikola.[39] Cetinje was the center of political activities preceding the assembly sessions. The political divisions among its citizens became evident during the election of the delegates when the two opposing groups presented two different lists of candidates. One list was printed on white paper, the other on green. The candidates from the white list favored unconditional unification, whereas the candidates from the green list argued for a more cautious and less romanticized approach to the issue of unification. During the meeting the Greens demanded that all foreign citizens, children, underaged persons, nonpermanent residents of Cetinje, and those ineligible to vote leave the room. This request was met with loud objections and an occasional insult. Even though the Greens were also in favor of unification, albeit from the perspective of Montenegro's being a constitutive element of the new state, their representatives were shouted down and kicked out of the assembly hall in Cetinje. On behalf of the 250 citizens of Cetinje, the representative of those from the Green list submitted a written complaint to the Podgorica Assembly about the illegality of the election process in Cetinje. During the first assembly session on November 24, 1918, the Select Committee (*Verifikacioni Odbor*) ruled that the complaint was groundless and stated that the Greens left the meeting because they realized that they were in the minority.[40] These two lists of candidates would later be used to describe the two opposing political forces in Montenegro (independentists/Greens and unionists/Whites).

The election of the delegates went according to plan, and on November 17 Janko Spasojević reported to Nikola Pašić that the Great People's Assembly would meet in Podgorica on November 24 to "proclaim the unification with Serbia."[41] He wrote this optimistic letter even though elections were not held in the provinces of Ulcinj, Krajina, Mrkojevići, and Vladimir (Bojana).[42] The day before the assembly's first session, Colonel Milutinović informed the High Command that the Great People's Assembly would proclaim the unification of Montenegro with Serbia.

> This should be understood as a sure thing. It is necessary, however, that our government immediately accept and formalize the proclamation of the Montenegrin People's Assembly on unification, so that the power structure in Montenegro can be organized in accordance with our laws. Future developments depend on the speed with which this decision is accepted and implemented.[43]

God's Messengers

On Sunday morning, November 24, 1918, in the hall of the Tobacco Monopoly in Podgorica, 165 delegates gathered for the first preliminary session of the Great People's Assembly.[44] The delegates came from nine Montenegrin provinces. Among them were teachers, priests, bureaucrats, bankers, landowners, former municipal officials, and a few farmers.[45] The first to address the assembly session was the oldest among the delegates, the priest Nikola Simović. He invited delegates to partake in a collective prayer in the town church. Upon their return, the assembly resumed work and selected Simović as its interim president. During the two preliminary sessions, the delegates verified mandates, selected the interim secretary, and divided themselves into five groups that would select the verification committee. They also agreed on the text of the solemn oath. During the second preliminary session, 158 delegates voted to elect the president, vice president, and several secretaries of the assembly. Savo Cerović won the presidency with 82 votes, and Lazar Damjanović was elected vice president with 135 votes, while Ljubomir Vuksanović, Milan Bajić, Radovan Bošković, Luka Vukotić, Novica Šćepanović, and Mihailo Jovanović were elected as secretaries.[46] The issue of the solemn oath had resulted in a brief debate among the delegates. Specifically, Janko Spasojević proposed that a priest with the cross and the Bible be brought in to read the oath. Some delegates saw this as putting an unnecessary religious emphasis on the entire process. The Metropolitan Gavrilo Dožić reminded the delegates that "rituals such as this one are performed according to religious practices by every assembly" and that "this People's Assembly is not a legislative body. I believe that this People's Assembly was not gathered here by the people to debate this issue but to follow the forms established earlier."[47]

The first regular session of the Great People's Assembly began at 3:00 p.m. on November 25, 1918. The delegates debated the agenda at length, trying to decide whether to (a) first address the dethroning of King Nikola and then (b) discuss unification of Montenegro with Serbia and the establishment of the Executive Committee that would take over the executive powers in Montenegro, as well as decide on the question of appointing the committee to prepare the final resolution.[48] Some delegates, such as Velimir Jojić and the Metropolitan Gavrilo Dožić, pointed out that the issues related to unification and the fate of the Petrović dynasty were closely connected, whereas Lazar Damjanović, Ljubo Bakić, and many others argued dethroning should be the first topic, followed by unification. The speech by Lazar Damjanović serves as a particularly good example of the unionist perception of the role of Montenegro, its history in the broader South Slavic framework, and the prounification faction's understanding of national identity and state formations among the South Slavs. Within such a paradigm, the Montenegrins, as well as the Croats and Slovenes, were seen as ethnic Serbs. For Damjanović, the region that was populated by one people with three names was once fragmented but had become unified in terms of both national identity and political structure. Moreover, Damjanović argued that, unlike the former Russian, German, and Austro-Hungarian empires, the establishment of the new South Slav state represented a stage in a natural progression. Its creation, Damjanović asserted, was not based on political exclusivism, treachery, deceit, and brute force.[49] After fondly reminiscing over the fate of the "great Prince Lazar" and other figures from the Serbian nationalist pantheon, he proceeded to assert that if it had not been for the medieval Serbian state "we would have been a people without a past,"[50] thus clearly positioning Montenegrins as an integral part of the Serbian political, national, and territorial framework. Damjanović saw Montenegro as a part of Serbdom that through unification was rejoining the nation's nucleus. The rest of his speech was devoted to discrediting King Nikola and accusing him of shameful capitulation and of political gambling with the "fate of the Serbian Montenegro." For Damjanović, the assembly represented the practical application of the Wilsonian principle of self-determination. Because, according to Damjanović, they were elected by the free will of the people, all delegates had the duty to dethrone Nikola and save the nation's honor.[51] The twenty-member committee was elected to prepare the assembly's resolution despite the fact that the text of that document had already been prepared by Svetozar Tomić and distributed among the delegates.[52] According to Damjanović, the role of this committee was to prepare the draft of the resolution (proclaiming the unification of Montenegro with Serbia) and to present it to the delegates for debate.

Figure 12. Metropolitan Gavrilo Dožić

After a prolonged debate the delegates agreed on the central point of the agenda—the unification of Montenegro with Serbia—and the first regular session of the People's Assembly concluded its work.

The second regular session started on November 26, 1918, at 10:30 a.m., with the decision not to address various letters of complaint sent to the assembly but to proceed directly to the issue of the resolution.[53] Even though some of the delegates, such as Jagoš Vešović, complained about the total lack of debate on the text of the resolution, the assembly's president decided that the document should be read aloud.[54] The reading of the text was interrupted by loud cheering and singing of the Serbian national anthem and ended with the following resolution:

The Serbian Great People's Assembly in Montenegro, as the true interpreter of the desires and wishes of the entire Serbian people, and true to historical tradition and the solemn oaths of its ancestors who for centuries heroically fought to preserve them, unanimously and by individual votes proclaims that

1. King Nikola I Petrović-Njegoš and his dynasty have been deposed from the Montenegrin throne.
2. Montenegro, together with its brother Serbia, be united in one single state under the Karadjordjević dynasty, and so united they enter the common fatherland of our three-named people: Serbs, Croats, and Slovenes.
3. The five-member Executive People's Committee be elected to coordinate all works until the unification of Serbia and Montenegro is completed.
4. This proclamation is to be forwarded to the former King of Montenegro, Nikola Petrović, and to the Royal Government of Serbia, as well as to all friendly powers and all neutral states.[55]

As soon as the reading was over, the Metropolitan Gavrilo Dožić stepped onto the podium and declared, "[that the] assembly accepted the resolution with such a delight is proof enough that any further debate is pointless." Spasoje Piletić interpreted the singing of the Serbian hymn as proof that all the delegates accepted the resolution.⁵⁶ In spite of these and other similar emotional outbursts, some of the delegates insisted on individually voting on the resolution, and organizers had to intervene to prevent that. Janko Spasojević attempted to rationalize the manner in which the resolution was accepted by saying,

> It is true that under normal circumstances, when a law has to be passed the assembly would vote on each article, as well as on the whole document, but we do not have to follow these regulations because they were established for a time of peace. This resolution was accepted in its entirety by acclamation. Because this is a coup d'etat by peaceful means, it is only necessary to confirm all this with individual signatures.⁵⁷

After a prolonged debate, 160 delegates signed the proclamation. As soon as the voting was over, the organizers sent telegrams to the Serbian king, Petar I Karadjordjević, and to the president of the Serbian People's Assembly, Djoko Braćinac, as well as to the government of Serbia and to all municipal authorities in Montenegro.⁵⁸

The assembly continued its work the next day and debated the election of the five-member Executive Committee that would act as the interim government. The debate concentrated on narrow partisan interests and threatened to destabilize the uniformity of the assembly. To prevent that from occurring, Savo Fatić reminded

Figure 13. Delegates of the Podgorica Assembly

those present that they should leave aside fighting and disagreements over the intricacies of the political history of Montenegro and concentrate on more important issues. He summed up his views of unification by saying that "as far as its political history is concerned, I see it divided in two parts: one until yesterday, and the other since yesterday. We are no longer Montenegrins. We are Serbs. We need to elect those who will have strength to materialize the great idea defined yesterday."[59] In spite of his intervention, the rest of the third regular session was devoted entirely to partisan arguments, and the president was forced to conclude the session without deciding on any points of the proposed agenda. During the fourth session the delegates elected the Executive Committee as the highest governing body in Montenegro. Its members were the Duke Stevo Vukotić (brother of the Montenegrin Queen Milena), Marko Daković, Spasoje Piletić, Risto Jojić, and Lazar Damjanović.[60] They also elected fifteen representatives who would travel to Belgrade and present the resolution to the Serbian government and Regent Aleksandar Karadjordjević.

During the fifth regular session of the assembly (November 29, 1918), the delegates debated the duties of the newly established Executive Committee and argued over how the assembly should deal with the property of the dethroned king and that of the Montenegrin Orthodox Church. In order to prevent lengthy debate, Janko Spasojević suggested that the important questions related to governing Montenegro should be left to the Serbian government to resolve. Spasojević argued that because the decision on unification was accepted unanimously "other issues important to the Serbs will be addressed by the government of Serbia, because after unification that government is our government."[61] Radovan Tomić echoed the sentiment that, after the passing of the resolution, Montenegro became an integral part of Serbia. He complained about the presence of Italian army units in Montenegrin territory and suggested that the Executive Committee demand that the Italians "leave the territory of the Kingdom of Serbia as soon as possible."[62]

The last regular session of the assembly was particularly interesting because it could not avoid addressing the issue of opposition to unification and had to acknowledge that unification did not have unanimous approval in Montenegro. In his address to the delegates, Blažo Begović urged those present to avoid partisan infighting. He proposed that the Executive Committee be empowered to act decisively against any opposition and that courts martial be introduced because "one could not exclude the possibility of civil war breaking out."[63] Mihailo Božović supported this proposal and defined the conditions under which the court martial should be established. According to Božović, "crimes committed with the intention of disturbing or compromising the newly established order" must be punishable by a court martial.[64] The assembly agreed with him and voted in favor of his proposal. An interesting debate then ensued over the property owned by Nikola I Petrović, which some delegates insisted on confiscating and declaring as state property, whereas others argued that the case should be handled according to the existing laws.⁶⁵ Ljubo Glomazić complained about the apparent leniency toward Nikola and argued that the delegates should remain true to the main principle of the assembly: "This is the principle: we are the revolutionary assembly that implements laws by force. If King Nikola could not be held accountable as a king, he could be held accountable as a citizen."⁶⁶ Janko Spasojević seconded this motion and reiterated the revolutionary character of the assembly, comparing it to the French and the Bolshevik Revolutions. He proposed that Nikola's property be confiscated and that Nikola be forbidden from ever entering Montenegro and Serbia again. After several more interventions by Nikola Cemović, Lazar Damjanović, and Milosav Raičević, the assembly voted unanimously to issue a separate document ordering the confiscation of Nikola's property and forbidding him and his family from ever returning to Montenegro. This was the last vote taken by the Great People's Assembly of the Serbian People in Montenegro, and its president, Savo Cerović, adjourned the meeting at 7:00 p.m. on November 29, 1918.

Two days later, Svetozar Tomić reported to Belgrade on the completion of his work in Montenegro and proposed that the Serbian government adopt the resolution from Podgorica and provide economic assistance to Montenegro. He assured the government in Belgrade that economic aid sent from Serbia would have a significant political impact on the citizens of Montenegro.⁶⁷ The delegation, headed by the Metropolitan Dožić, left for Belgrade to meet the representatives of the Serbian government and Regent Aleksandar. Both the government of Serbia and Aleksandar understood Montenegro to be a part of Serbia, and the details of unification outlined in the resolution of the Podgorica Assembly were treated as the formalization of the natural process of the territorial expansion of Serbia. It is for this reason that the Regent Aleksandar did not mention Montenegro in his address during the ceremony proclaiming the new state. While addressing the representatives from Croatia, Slovenia, Slavonia, and Dalmatia, Aleksandar stated:

> On behalf of his Royal Highness King Petar I, I hereby proclaim the unification of Serbia with the territories of the independent state of Slovenes, Croats, and Serbs in one united Kingdom of Serbs, Croats, and Slovenes.⁶⁸

On that day, the first South Slav state was created. The Kingdom of Serbs, Croats, and Slovenes incorporated a number of territories, some of which had been a part of the Habsburg Empire. The new state had almost twelve million inhabitants, most of whom were Serbs and Croats. Other inhabitants included Slovenians, Montenegrins, Albanians, Jews, and Roma.⁶⁹

Because the government of Serbia did not immediately and officially take over the administration of Montenegro even though it controlled the country through the Executive Committee and the army, the Great People's Assembly remained active a while longer. In April 1919, the government of Serbia requested that the assembly meet in Podgorica once more in order to dismantle the Executive Committee so that the representative of the Serbian government could be appointed as the administrator in Montenegro. The assembly met for the last time on April 29, 1919, and agreed to transfer all executive powers to the Serbian administrator in Montenegro, Ivo Pavićević. Once his appointment was secured, Pavićević proclaimed the unification complete.[70]

The resolution sealed the fate of independent Montenegro, marked the end of its sovereignty, and was the final political act in the process of its annexation by Serbia. The decisions reached by the Great People's Assembly assumed constitutional powers even though the meeting in Podgorica was conveyed as the consequence of the decision made by a body (Montenegrin Committee for Unification) that had no legal power to call for such a meeting. The text of the resolution was written in advance, and by an outsider, and then passed to the Executive Committee on November 25, 1918, only one day before the delegates adopted it. This committee was formed on the same day it received the resolution. It is difficult to envisage any kind of a comprehensive debate about the document going on over night. In fact, there are no indications in the available sources, including the minutes from the assembly sessions, that any debate over the content of the resolution ever took place. Before reading the text of the resolution to the delegates, the speaker read all fifty-eight letters of congratulation that were telegraphed to the delegates of the assembly. Each letter expressed support of the assembly's goal and the resolution. Such a move clearly seems intended to influence the delegates and to give the impression that the entire population of Montenegro supported the ideas expressed in the resolution, whereas this was not the case. It should be noted that city mayors and local officials, as well as regional officials and groups of bureaucrats, signed the majority of these letters and that the Central Executive Committee for Unification had, without exception, appointed all those people to their posts.[71] With all this in mind, it can be concluded that the resolution of the Podgorica Assembly was signed without the delegates having participated in its writing, without the majority of the delegates being familiar with its content, and without any debate on its individual points.

The final document was adopted in contravention to the parliamentary procedures and standards of the period. The disregard for the existing laws and parliamentary procedures is even more striking if we consider that the document adopted by the assembly had a constitutional character and had altered the structure of the Montenegrin state, effectively erasing its borders. These decisions were not based on any kind of plebiscite. In light of the entire questionable election process, it is safe to conclude that the final decisions made by the Podgorica Assembly did not truly reflect the will of the Montenegrin people, most especially because their consequences were immediately negative. Naturally, one could not dismiss the consensus in Montenegro on the issue of the establishment of a common South Slav state—the

ОДЛУКА

Велике Народне Скупштине Српског Народа у Црној Гори, донијета на сједници од 13. новембра 1918. г. у Подгорици.

[illegible]

Секретари:

[illegible]

Предсједник,

Саво Церовић.

Потпредсједници:

[illegible]

Посланици:

[illegible]

Figure 14. Proclamation of the Podgorica Assembly

desire to unite with other South Slavs (including Serbia) in one state presupposed the active participation of Montenegro in the process. Moreover, such a unification of equals did not mean either erasing the distinctiveness of the Montenegrin people or surrendering the signifiers of the country's independence and sovereignty. The desire to unite did not automatically grant legality to the decisions made by the Podgorica Assembly because those decisions effectively denied the right of Montenegrins to determine the fate of their own country. The delegates of the Podgorica Assembly failed to test the popular will with regard to the manner in which the common state was to be created. Their decision was based on the assumption that their own longing for the common South Slav state was good enough reason to disregard the existing Montenegrin legislation.

The supporters of unconditional unification attempted to rationalize the deficient legal process by presenting somewhat moot arguments about the "revolutionary character" of the assembly. In spite of the "revolutionary" rhetoric, the fact remains that events that occurred in Montenegro in 1918 were a far cry from a revolution, unless one refers to the "revolution" imposed or imported from the outside. One must not forget that the entire organizational structure surrounding the Podgorica Assembly was set up, funded, and guided (politically and operationally) by a foreign power (Serbia). The Central Executive Committee was established by Serbia, and its representative succeeded (with the generous assistance of the Adriatic Troops) in taking over power in Montenegro. Knowing this, one is tempted to describe what happened as the occupation of Montenegro rather than as a voluntary unification.

The resolution itself did not contain either the word *Yugoslav* or *Yugoslavia*, and its provisions effectively incorporated (annexed) Montenegro into Serbia. This indicates that the organizers remained true to the earlier demand of the Serbian prime minister, Nikola Pašić, that legal documents relevant to the future unification not contain any reference to Yugoslavia. The absence of this terminology from the resolution of the assembly in Podgorica also casts serious doubts over the claims that the Yugoslav idea was the main goal of the whole action. The Yugoslav idea was based on the principle of mutual respect of differences and cultural/political/national specificities. It was also based on the notion that each constitutive element of the future common state should and would contribute to the betterment of the union. In the case of Montenegro and the decisions reached by the Podgorica Assembly, the guiding principles of the Yugoslav idea were suspended. With this in mind, it would be possible to argue that the resolution of the Great People's Assembly of the Serbian People in Montenegro rejected the Yugoslav idea altogether. Its decisions were not part of the documents on unification drafted in Belgrade on December 1, 1918, and did not affect the establishment of the new state. The consequences of the assembly (territorial enlargement of Serbia) did, however, change the existing balance of power among the South Slavs in favor of Serbia and cemented Serbia's position as the most populous and, militarily, the strongest state in the region. Its resolution was aimed toward further centralization of the newly formed state and not toward its development on democratic principles of self-determination. The negative impact of the Serbian position on the future of the common South Slav state, paired with the persistent desire of the Serbian government to dominate the region's political landscape, became apparent from the mid-1920s onward.

With respect to Montenegro, the text of the resolution clearly pointed out the main goal of the organizers: Montenegro and Serbia were to be united in "a single unified state under the Karadjordjević dynasty."[72] This was confirmed in many writings by prominent unionists such as Nikola Djonović. According to Djonović, the decisions reached by the Podgorica Assembly were the result of pressure exerted on Montenegro by political circles in Belgrade to accept the Karadjordjević dynasty, and the "Podgorica Assembly voted the way Belgrade expected it to."[73] Another unionist and former government minister, Savo Vuletić, echoed similar sentiments about the Podgorica Assembly when he wrote, "The assembly was nothing more than a gathering of carefully selected individuals who adopted the previously prepared resolution without discussing it at all."[74]

Winter of Discontent: The Christmas Uprising

During the preparations for the Podgorica Assembly, a relatively popular but poorly organized group of Montenegrins (former officers, soldiers, politicians, and local leaders) opposed the manner in which Montenegro was being annexed by Serbia. By the time World War I ended, most of them were scattered through various camps as prisoners of war or living in exile in France, Italy, or the United States. When the fighting stopped they attempted to return to Montenegro but were prevented from doing so because the organizers of the Podgorica Assembly feared that their presence in the country and influence on the people of Montenegro would jeopardize the unionist agenda. It would be fair to say that the political allegiance of the independentists to King Nikola and the Petrović dynasty came second to their desire to see Montenegro play an active part ("the role well deserved by Montenegro," from their perspective) in the Kingdom of Serbs, Croats, and Slovenes. Even though the dominant historical discourse in the former Yugoslavia and present-day Montenegro still portrays the independentists as exponents of retrograde political ideas, I find it somewhat inaccurate to categorize them as supporters and advocates of authoritarianism and conservativism. More than anything else, they were former bureaucrats and military personnel who were deeply troubled by the loss of Montenegrin independence and sovereignty and who made a desperate attempt to save Montenegro from "drowning in Serbia."

Figure 15. Captain Krsto Popović

From early January 1919 until late 1924, there was an active movement in Montenegro opposing the resolution of the Podgorica Assembly. Yugoslav historiography does not agree on a single name for the events that began in Montenegro on Christmas Eve 1919. The books and the periodicals of the time referred to it as the Cetinje Uprising, Cetinje Christmas Eve, Christmas Uprising, January Uprising, and so on. Some of the books and articles on the history of Montenegro treated those events as episodes in the process of the unification of Montenegro with Serbia, thus minimizing their importance. Sources sympathetic to the unionist cause often spoke of the events as the contrarevolutionary insurrection and the insurrection of the mercenaries. Calling it the Cetinje Uprising unjustly limited the geographic area affected by the armed struggle. On the other hand, using the name January Uprising imposes, again unjustly, a time frame that does not correspond to the events that occurred over a prolonged period.[75] I have decided to use the term *Christmas Uprising* because most of the heavy fighting between the unionists and the Adriatic Troops on one side and the independentist-minded rebel units on the other occurred over the Christmas holidays, between January 5 and January 18, 1919. It is, however, important to remember that the end of the initial large-scale armed conflict did not mean the cessation of violence. In fact, the fighting continued with varying intensity until late 1924, and the nature of the struggle changed somewhat over time. Considering the circumstances in which the uprising took place and the prolonged armed struggle, and keeping in mind the social and political nature of the motives and goals of the independentist movement exemplified by the action of the rebels, it is necessary to distinguish between the two phases of this process. With respect to the motives and the organizational structure, as well as the relatively minor outside influences, the initial phase of the uprising could be characterized as the Montenegrin People's Movement. After the military failure of the rebels, the movement changed its character and began to be influenced by and dependent on outside factors (King Nikola and Italy), which in turn compromised its original goals and dissolved the populist base of the movement. Historian Dragoljub Živojinović believes that some Italian government officials half-heartedly supported the uprising. In his writing, Živojinović pays particular attention to the activities of the Italian journalist Giovanni Baaldacci, who was in Montenegro just before the uprising. On December 27, 1918, Baaldacci forwarded the plan for the uprising to the Italian Ministry of War and requested that this material be sent to the Montenegrin government in exile. There are no available archival documents to clearly show that King Nikola had any prior knowledge of the plans for the armed uprising, but considering the almost daily contacts between his government and Italian diplomats, it is safe to assume that the king had some information about the uprising.[76]

As previously described, the armed insurrection began as a reaction to the resolution adopted by the Great People's Assembly in Podgorica. The rebels interrupted the lines of communication between Cetinje and other towns in Montenegro.[77] They managed to gather a number of armed followers and concentrated their forces around major cities such as Nikšić, Cetinje, and Podgorica. According to Jovan Vujović, the seven army battalions stationed in Nikšić were ready to join the uprising, while some 500 armed men from the region of Piperi and Rovca were preparing to attack Podgorica.[78] News of the uprising in Montenegro spread fast, and the regional administrator of the Herzegovinian town of Gacko reported on January 6, 1919, that the main topics of conversation among the local population were the events occurring in Montenegro. The administrator found it disturbing that many people from Gacko appeared sympathetic toward the rebels.[79] The rebel units laid siege to the town of Rijeka Crnojevića and issued an ultimatum to the local authorities to surrender the town to avoid any bloodshed. Dimitrije D. Vujović estimated that the rebels' army was some 4,000 men strong. Sources sympathetic to the independentist cause mentioned a 20,000- or even 35,000-strong rebel force. These figures appear grossly inflated. Even though there are no archival sources that clearly specify the number of those who participated in the uprising, my own research leads me to believe that the figures presented by Vujović

Figure 16. Savo Raspopović

are closer to the truth.⁸⁰ The rebels focused the bulk of their forces on Cetinje, hoping that once they took the capital other municipal centers would fall quickly. Before closing in on Cetinje, the rebels formed their own committee and issued a declaration explaining the reasons behind the armed uprising and outlining their program. According to the declaration, the uprising was provoked by the unconstitutional decisions of the Podgorica Assembly. The rebels' goal was to revisit the issue of Montenegro's entry into the Yugoslav state by following the rule of law and the provisions of the Montenegrin Constitution. Article 2 of the declaration demanded that some sort of people's court be established to determine who was to blame for the current disastrous state of affairs. The rebels also demanded that the decisions of the Podgorica Assembly be annulled and that new and free elections be held in Montenegro. In order to start implementing this program, the rebels announced that they would enter Cetinje on Sunday, January 5, 1919, and take over the state institutions.⁸¹ In his response to Krsto Popović, General Milutinović stated that he would forward the demands to his superiors and to the French general, Venell. He also announced that units under his command would defend the motherland in accordance with both "your laws and our laws" and would prevent any armed groups from entering Cetinje.⁸² The situation was so tense that one of the most prominent Montenegrins of the time, Janko Vukotić, pleaded with General Milutinović to avoid the loss of life and to compromise by letting the rebel units occupy some sections of the city.⁸³ Milutinović refused to consider such an option and placed the army units in Cetinje on high alert. As soon as the information about the uprising reached the Montenegrin capital, the commander of the Adriatic Troops ordered his units to act decisively against any "band of traitors and robbers" they might encounter. On January 6, 1919, the rebels' army, numbering between 1,500 and 2,000 men, managed to reach the outskirts of Cetinje but after a day-long battle failed to take the city. During the following days, the units of the Adriatic Troops and the volunteer units of the Executive Committee pushed the rebels back from the capital. The fighting around Nikšić and Rijeka Crnojevića also ended after a day-long conflict, with the rebels on the losing side.⁸⁴ On January 12, French units entered Cetinje; they were joined by a platoon of American soldiers on January 15, 1919. The rebel leaders and prominent commanders made repeated attempts to reinvigorate and broaden their activities but, in the face of dwindling popular support, were unable to achieve any measurable success. As Milo Plamenac reported on September 20, 1919, the people of Montenegro faced a difficult choice: "to go up in arms once again and face a certain death, or to save themselves and their families by unwillingly cooperating with the enemy."⁸⁵

    The initial defeats had a demoralizing effect on the insurgents. The majority of them decided to lay down their arms and return home; some went into exile; and some remained active as a guerrilla force. Some left for the Bay of Kotor, whereas others went to Bar and were later transported by the Italian navy to San Giovanni di Medua before being sent to camps in Gaeta and Formi. Some 300 rebels under the command of Djuro Kapa surrendered to American troops in Kotor and were escorted back to Cetinje, only to be arrested afterward.[86] They were no match for the well-equipped units of the Adriatic Troops, however. Still, the small guerrilla units continued to disrupt communications and fight against the volunteer unionist force until late 1924. Even though the military aspect of the uprising was a failure, deep dissatisfaction with the state of affairs remained. In his report on the post-uprising conditions in Montenegro, General Milutinović admitted that the people were deeply disappointed with Serbia, both in terms of politics and in terms of the promised economic aid. He also pointed out the Executive Committee's lack of diplomatic skills in governing Montenegro.[87]

From the outset of the crisis the rebel movement was poorly equipped and loosely organized, and faced two insurmountable obstacles.[88] The first was the mighty military machine determined to defend the decisions of the Podgorica Assembly by all means. The Serbian government publicly referred to the conflict in Montenegro as a minor domestic disturbance instigated by King Nikola, but it put a lot of effort into pacifying Montenegro by military means. After the initial clash ended, the army units and volunteers proceeded to hunt down the insurgents and often killed their families, looted and burned down their homes, and imprisoned a number of those sympathetic to the independentists' cause. Random murders as well as planned assassinations of prominent independentists and their family members were common in Montenegro throughout the early 1920s.[89]

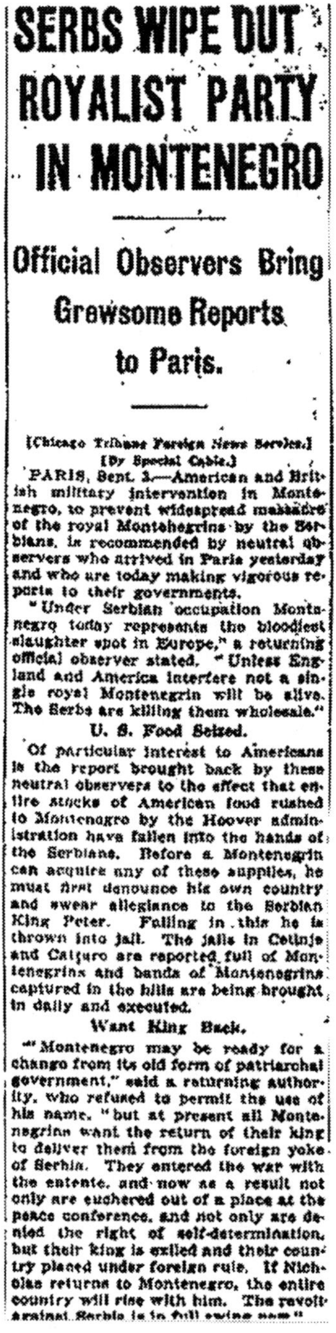

SERBS WIPE OUT ROYALIST PARTY IN MONTENEGRO

Official Observers Bring Grewsome Reports to Paris.

[Chicago Tribune Foreign News Service.]
[By Special Cable.]

PARIS, Sept. 3.—American and British military intervention in Montenegro, to prevent widespread massacre of the royal Montenegrins by the Serbians, is recommended by neutral observers who arrived in Paris yesterday and who are today making vigorous reports to their governments.

"Under Serbian occupation Montenegro today represents the bloodiest slaughter spot in Europe," a returning official observer stated. "Unless England and America interfere not a single royal Montenegrin will be alive. The Serbs are killing them wholesale."

U. S. Food Seized.

Of particular interest to Americans is the report brought back by these neutral observers to the effect that entire stocks of American food rushed to Montenegro by the Hoover administration have fallen into the hands of the Serbians. Before a Montenegrin can acquire any of these supplies, he must first denounce his own country and swear allegiance to the Serbian King Peter. Failing in this he is thrown into jail. The jails in Cetinje and Cattaro are reported full of Montenegrins and bands of Montenegrins captured in the hills are being brought in daily and executed.

Want King Back.

"'Montenegro may be ready for a change from its old form of patriarchal government," said a returning authority, who refused to permit the use of his name, "but at present all Montenegrins want the return of their king to deliver them from the foreign yoke of Serbia. They entered the war with the entente, and now as a result not only are euchered out of a place at the peace conference, and not only are denied the right of self-determination, but their king is exiled and their country placed under foreign rule. If Nicholas returns to Montenegro, the entire country will rise with him. The revolt against Serbia is in full swing now."

Figure 17. *Chicago Tribune*, Sept. 3, 1919

The issue of reprisal against the families and relatives of rebels was the subject of parliamentary debate during the forty-fourth session of the People's Assembly of the new state. Savo Vuletić spoke about many cases of maltreatment of civilians, arbitrary arrests, and executions in Montenegro.[90] The Serbian government was careful not to inform the general public in other parts of the Kingdom of Serbs, Croats, and Slovenes about the events in Montenegro. Newspapers and journals in other parts of the country did not report on the scale of the uprising, the retaliatory actions of the army, or the relentless pursuit of the guerrilla fighters. The first accounts of the situation in Montenegro during 1918 appeared in the book *Crnogorski Političari* by the Belgrade-based journalist Pantelija Jovović, who reported on some 5,000 homes being burned in Montenegro from 1919 on and about families that supported the Greens being forced off of their property. Jovović expressed serious doubts about the nature of the unification process in Montenegro.[91]

The second obstacle was that in spite of being well informed about the situation in Montenegro the international community chose not to act decisively and stop the armed conflict. The Great Powers were aware of the armed struggle, but they regarded it as an internal matter of Serbia and the manifestation of Balkan lawlessness and tried to distance themselves from it as much as possible. It was only the gradual accumulation of bad news coming from Montenegro that made the Great Powers briefly turn their attention to the former kingdom, but even when the Montenegrin problems could not be ignored any longer, the actions of the Great Powers were aimed more toward containment than toward prevention and the remedy of the conflict's causes.[92]

Notes

1. Andrej Mitrović, *Srbija u Prvom Svjetskom Ratu* (Beograd, 1984), p. 236.
2. In time, such a perception of the Yugoslav state ("wherever a grave of the Serbian soldier is, that is Serbian land") became the grounds for claiming territory outside Serbia proper. The most radical and bloodiest manifestation of such a claim was the process of the dissolution of the former SFRY (1990–1995).
3. In a letter to the League of Nations in 1929, the Yugoslav delegation stated: "Our position has always been that in our southern regions, which have been integral parts of our state or were annexed to our kingdom before January 1, 1919, there are no national minorities. That position is still our last word on the question of the recognition of minorities in Southern Serbia." Noel Malcolm, *Kosovo: A Short History* (London: Macmillan, 1998), p. 268.
4. Dragoljub Živojinović, "Kralj Nikola i Teritorijalno Širenje Crne Gore, 1914–1920," *Istorijski Zapisi* 61, nos. 3–4 (1988), p. 173.
5. *Cjelokupna Djela Nikola I Petrovića Njegoša*, vol. 4 (Cetinje, 1969), p. 202.
6. Andrija Radović to D. Stevanović, Paris, October 13, 1918, AIICG, File No. 61.
7. The Scutari Troops consisted of the Second Yugoslav Division (soldiers from regions that were under Austro-Hungarian rule) and Serbian paramilitary units from the Kosovo region under the command of Kosta Pećanac. Rakočević, *Politički Odnosi*, p. 281.

8. Janko Spasojević left France on board a French navy vessel. G. Grbović to A. Radović, October 18, 1918, AIICG, File No. 61. Svetozar Tomić was one of the leading unionists working in Montenegro at the time. It is interesting to note the development of his career in light of his political orientation. After serving at various government positions in the Kingdom of Yugoslavia, in 1941 Tomić, a Montenegrin by birth, allied himself with nationalist paramilitary troops (Chetniks) operating in Serbia and Montenegro. At the end of World War II, Tomić was the only Montenegrin indicted for war crimes. He consequently spent the better part of his life in exile.
9. On behalf of Spasojević, Radović asked the Serbian government for 1 million dinars to pay the salaries of Montenegrin bureaucrats; for himself he requested "one hundred to two hundred thousand francs for establishing the administration in Montenegro." A. Radović to N. Pašić, November 10, 1918, and A. Radović to N. Pašić, November 14, 1918, AIICG, File No. 61.
10. Pašić to Protić, Paris, October 16, 1918, Državni Arhiv Dubrovnik, Crnogorski Odsjek, File No. 603.
11. Svetozar Tomić to the Serbian Ministry of Foreign Affairs, Political Section, November 1, 1918, Arhiv Srbije, Ministrarstvo Inostranih Dela, PO. 1918, File No. 10, Document No. 34, Confidential.
12. The Proclamation by the Prominent Vasojevićes for the Unification of Montenegro and Serbia. Three pages long, handwritten, and signed by 32 prominent Vasojevićes. Arhiv Vojnoistorijskog Instituta, Beograd, Popisnik No. 3, *Operacijski Dnevnik Vrhovne Komande, od 21. Oktobra do 15. Novembra 1918*, Box. No. 25, Ref. No. 2/1, pp. 554–556.
13. "I arrived in Peć on the 12th of this month. The provisional government was set up by Kosta Pećanac. The municipal administrator is our police bureaucrat, Rista Protić. The municipal and regional powers were established in agreement with the population and according to the instructions provided. Protić has to be fired as soon as possible because everyone is against him. Could you please send someone appropriate for the position of the municipal administrator, someone from the region? The governing bodies were also organized in Berane according to the will of the local population and are headed by Milosav Raičević, the former government minister and our man in all respects." Svetozar Tomić to the Serbian Ministry of Foreign Affairs, Political Section, Arhiv Srbije, Ministarstvao Inostranih Dela, PO. 1918, File No. 10, Dossier No. V.
14. Vujović, *Ujedinjenje*, p. 311.
15. "The Montenegrin Committee for Unification and its branches, if there are any in your regions, must not make any important decision without obtaining prior agreement from the royal government and/or from you. We must not allow their work to dissent from our politics even in the slightest detail." Nikola Pašić to the Serbian Representative Offices Abroad, November 16, 1917, Top Secret, Arhiv Srbije, Ministarstvo Inostranih Dela, Crnogorski Odsek, 1917, File No. 2, Dossier No. IV. It is important to note that there is no mention in any of the sources (archival, secondary, or the Montenegrin newspapers of the period) of either Spasojević or Tomić establishing any communication with any Montenegrin state institution from the time of their arrival in Montenegro until the conclusion of the Podgorica Assembly.
16. Mijat Šuković, *Podgorička Skupština* (Podgorica: DOB, 1999), p. 26.
17. Šuković, ibid., p. 29.
18. Raičević later changed his mind and abandoned the tactics of partial unification of individual Montenegrin municipalities with Serbia. On December 21, 1918, he was appointed minister in the first government of the newly formed state. Mijat Šuković, ibid., p. 29.
19. *Ustav Knjaževine Crne Gore*, Cetinje, 1905.

20. Šuković, *Podgorička Skupština*, pp. 52–53.
21. "During my voyage to Peć, I worked on the concept and by the time I reached the town the plan was ready." Svetozar Tomić, *Desetogodišnjica Ujedinjenja Crne Gore i Srbije* (Beograd, 1929), pp. 22–23.
22. Šuković, *Podgorička Skupština*, p. 48.
23. Šuković, ibid., p. 49.
24. The curfew was imposed on November 1, 1918. Šuković, ibid.
25. Šuković, ibid., pp. 51–52.
26. The Komite liberated Andrijevica (October 13, 1918) and Berane (October 14, 1918), and during the next couple of days they took Plav, Gusinje, Rožaje, Bijelo Polje, and Kolašin. In Andrijevica and Berane, these self-organized Komite units disarmed around 2,500 Austro-Hungarian soldiers.
27. Within the Greater Serbian nationalist paradigm of the period, a particular territory became an integral part of the Serbian land by virtue of being "liberated by the Serbian army."
28. Acting upon orders from the Serbian High Command, the commander of the Adriatic Troops in Montenegro disarmed five battalions of the Komite, many members of which were later either imprisoned by the Serbian authorities or executed as outlaws and supporters of King Nikola. Vujović, *Podgorička Skupština*, pp. 25–35. Valuable documents on the fate of Komite are available in Šerbo Rastoder, *Skrivana Strana Istorije: Crnogorska Buna i Odmetnički Pokret, 1918–1929*, vols. 1–4 (Bar: Nidamentym Montenegro, 1997).
29. In November 1918 the owner of the restaurant *Evropa* in Cetinje changed the name of his establishment to *Jugoslavia*. *Novo Doba*, no. 2, November 5, 1918.
30. Colonel Milutinović to the High Command, AIICG, File No. 22, Doc. No. 32282, Cetinje, November 6, 1918. Milutinović informed the Serbian High Command that a number of people from the region of Morača, together with their leaders Momir Lakušić and Miloš Medenica, proclaimed unification with Serbia. According to Milutinović's report, they cheered, "Long Live Greater Serbia! Long Live Yugoslavia! Long Live Aleksandar!"
31. Tomić and Spasojević to N. Pašić, Podgorica, November 6, 1918, Arhiv Srbije, Ministarstvo Inostranih Dela, Popisnik, 1918, File No. 10. Also see V. *Božović's File*, AIICG, File No. 22, Doc. No. 32149.
32. Vujović, *Ujedinjenje*, pp. 315–316. Also see "Proglas 250 Punopravnih Glasača Cetinja," Cetinje, November 8, 1918, in Rastoder, *Skrivana Strana*, vol. 1, pp. 98–100.
33. Commander of the Adriatic Troops to the minister of war, Cetinje, November 29, 1918, IICG, File No. 22, Doc. No. 33204. Also see Milutinović to the Serbian High Command, Cetinje, November 28, 1918, AIICG, File No. 22, Docs. No. 33346 and 33581.
34. Tomić, *Desetogodišnjica*, p. 24. Also see Šuković, *Podgorička Skupština*, pp. 56–57.
35. Šuković, ibid., p. 24.
36. Ćetković, *Ujedinitelji*, p. 285.
37. The Serbian High Command was worried about leaked reports of the "Serbian killings committed in Podgorica" and instructed the commander of the Second Army stationed in Montenegro to "avoid repeating" such actions. Serbian High Command to the commander of the II Army, Belgrade, November 15, 1918, AIICG, File No. 22, Doc. No. 32602.
38. The Commander of the Adriatic Troops to the High Command, AIICG, File No. 22, Doc. No. 3257, October 29, 1918.
39. Montenegrin army Generals Radomir Vešovic, Jovan Bećir, and Jakov Jovanović, and Majors S. Radović, Radovan Radović, Živko Nikčević, and Vlado Vrbica, as well as standard-bearers Marko Popović and Marko Martinović, were kept in Bosanski Brod (Bosnia) and prevented from entering Montenegro.
40. "We are also in favor of unification, but a conditional one: Montenegro should participate in the process of unification of Yugoslavia as an independent kingdom and in the

same manner as Serbia and other regions would." V. Božović, *Dnevnik, 1918*, AIICG, File No. 39. "Izvještaj Verifikacionog Odbora o Poslaničkim Mandatima," *Zapisnici Podgoričke Skupštine*, Podgorica, November 24, 1918, AIICG, File No. 319. Also see Vujović, *Ujedinjenje*, pp. 321–322. The main candidate on the White list was the Montenegrin Metropolitan Gavrilo Dožić, who went on to become the patriarch of the Serbian Orthodox Church. Bojović, *Podgorička Skupština*, p. xvi.

41. Spasojević to Pašić, Cetinje, November 17, 1918, Command of the Adriatic Troops, Confidential Doc. No. 222, AIICG, File No. 359.
42. "Izvještaj Verifikacionog Odbora," Podgorica, November 24, 1918, *Zapisnici Podgoričke Skupštine*, AIICG, File No. 319.
43. Commander of the Adriatic Troops to the High Command, Cetinje, November 23, 1918, Doc. No. 293. AIICG, File No. 359.
44. There were two preliminary and five regular sessions of the Great People's Assembly. Vujović, *Ujedinjenje*, p. 324. Bojović, *Podgorička Skupština*, p. xvi.
45. The delegates came from the following provinces: Metohija, Andrijevica, Berane, Pljevlja, Kolašin, Nikšić, Podgorica, Bar, and Cetinje. Out of 165 delegates, only 14 were farmers. See "Izvještaj Verifikacionog Odbora o Poslaničkim Mandatima," Podgorica, November 25, 1918, *Podgorička Skupština, Zapisnici*, AIICG, File No. 319.
46. "Rezultati Glasanja," *Podgorička Skupština. Zapisnici*, AIICG, Files No. 318 and 319, Podgorica, November 25, 1918. "I swear by almighty God that during this assembly session I will work solely for the good and happiness of my people. So help me God!" "Zakletva Poslanika Podgoričke Skupštine," *Podgorička Skupština, Zapisnici*, Podgorica, November 25, 1918, AIICG, File No. 319. The pages of the entire document are unnumbered.
47. "Stenografski Zapisnik sa Druge Prethodne Sjednice," *Podgorička Skupština, Zapisnici*, Podgorica, November 25, 1918, AIICG, File No. 319.
48. Zapisnik I Redovne Sjednice, November 25, 1918, *Podgorička Skupština: Zapisnici*, AIICG, File No. 319.
49. In order to discourage any potential opposition, the Assembly's president made sure that a couple Serbian army platoons were at hand in the backyard of the building where the Assembly took place. See Dragoslav Janković, *Jugoslovensko Pitanje i Krfska Deklaracija, 1917 Godine* (Beograd: Savremena Administracija, 1967), p. 329.
50. "Lazar Damjanović to the Delegates of the Assembly," Janković, ibid., p. 329.
51. Janković, ibid.
52. The organizers did not want to leave anything to chance, and some of the most prominent unionists—the Metropolitan Gavrilo Dožić, Milosav Raičević, Janko Spasojević, Mihailo Božović, Mirko Vujisić, Jevto Popović, Dr. Jakov Zarubica, Bogdan Bojović, and Risto Jojic—were selected as committee members. *Zapisnik I Redovne Sjenice*, ibid. Also see Tomić, *Desetogodišnjica Ujedinjenja*, p. 161.
53. The delegates decided that only letters of congratulation sent to the Assembly should be read. *Zapisnik II Redovne Sjednice*, Podgorica, November 26, 1918, Podgorička Skupština: Zapisnici, AIICG, File No. 319.
54. "I wonder on what bases the resolution was adopted? I think that it was necessary for the delegates to first exchange their opinions and then decide on the resolution." Jagoš Vešović, during the second regular session of the Assembly. *Zapisnik II Redovne Sjednice*, ibid.
55. On behalf of the Executive Committee, Jevto Popović read the Resolution. Jovan R. Bojović, *Podgorička Skupstina: Dokumenti*, pp. 188–189. Also see *Novo Doba* 1, no. 12 (November 27, 1918), p. 1.
56. Bojović, *Podgorička Skupstina*, pp. 188–189.
57. Bojović, ibid.

58. Tomić, *Desetogodišnjica Ujedinjenja*, pp. 169–170. On page 50 of his book, Tomić cited part of the telegram that was sent to the government of Serbia in which the organizers of the Assembly pleaded with the Serbian government to adopt the resolution and to "introduce necessary and urgent measures in order to implement this decision. The enemy who is working on preventing this great work of the people is not sitting idle, and our efforts must be great, our actions swift and united if we want to save it." Also see Vujović, *Ujedinjenje*, p. 325, and Ćetković, *Ujedinitelji*, p. 302.
59. "The address of Savo Fatić to the Delegates of the Assembly," *Zapisnik III Redovne Sjednice*, Podgorica, November 27, 1918, AIICG, File No. 319.
60. *Zapisnik IV Redovne Sjednice*, Podgorica, November 28, 1918, AIICG, File No. 319. After learning about the resolution of the Podgorica Assembly, King Nikola expressed some doubts about the authenticity of some of the signatures on the document. According to some reports, the signature of the priest Petar Hajduković was forged. After Pero Šoć read the name of the queen's brother, Stevo Vukotić, from the list of signatories, the king remarked, "Dear God! Stevo Vukotić, who might that be?" Hajduković, *Memoari*, p. 443.
61. *Zapisnik V Redovne Sjednice*, AIICG, File No. 319.
62. *Zapisnik V Redovne Sjednice*, ibid.
63. *Zapisnik V Redovne Sjednice*, ibid.
64. *Zapisnik V Redovne Sjednice*, ibid.
65. Stevo Jovićević proposed that property owned by Nikola I Petrović be confiscated by the Executive Committee and put at the disposal of the state and its people. With regard to Nikola's fate, Jovićević acted as the judge, jury, and executioner and suggested that "every citizen of Montenegro could catch and kill Nikola Petrović and members of his immediate family as traitors because this Great People's Assembly cannot presently bring him to justice, put him on trial, and execute him for high treason." Risto Vujačić insisted on the legality of the process and argued that by dethroning Nikola the Assembly did not put him on trial for high treason and thus was not able to confiscate his property. *Zapisnik V Redovne Sjednice*, ibid.
66. *Zapisnik V Redovne Sjednice*, ibid.
67. Vujović, *Ujedinjenje*, p. 329.
68. Srdjan Budisavljević, *Stvaranje Države Srba, Hrvata i Slovenaca* (Zagreb: JAZU, 1958), p. 171. On October 29, 1918, the Croatian parliament passed the resolution announcing the establishment of the new independent state of Slovenes, Croats, and Serbs. This new state included the territories formerly ruled by Austria-Hungary: Dalmatia, Croatia, and Slavonia, as well as the municipality of Rijeka (Fiume). Slovenian representatives also joined the newly formed state. The representatives of this state traveled to Belgrade for the final unification ceremony of the Kingdom of Serbs, Croats, and Slovenes, which took place at 8:00 p.m. on December 1, 1918. For a detailed account of the relations between Serbia and Croatia (Nikola Pašić and Ante Trumbić) and the disagreements over the nature of the future union, see Milada Paulova, *Jugoslavenski Odbor: Povijest Jugoslavenske Emigracije za Svjetskog Rata od 1914–1918* (Zagreb: Prosvjetna Nakladna Zadruga, 1924), pp. 541–582.
69. Šerbo Rastoder, "Tri Jugoslavije," *Vijesti*, no. 204 (1998).
70. Vujović, *Ujedinjenje*, p. 330.
71. Bojović, *Podgorička Skupština*, pp. 149–179.
72. See note 60 of this chapter.
73. Nikola Djonović, *Marko Daković sa Svojim Drugovima*, Legat Nikole Djonovića, State Archives, Cetinje (handwritten), p. 150.
74. Savo Vuletić (1871–1945) was educated in Belgrade, worked as teacher in Cetinje, and was later elected mayor of Cetinje. He was also the president of the Regional Court and a

The Preparations for the Great People's Assembly in Podgorica ◆ 173

member of the Central State Control. From April 1914 until December 1915, Vuletić was the Montenegrin minister of the interior. He was a prolific writer and published numerous articles, essays, and short stories. In 1918, just before the armed uprising began, Vuletić was arrested and sent to prison. While in prison he was visited by Franchet d'Esperey, to whom he said that "barbers instead of surgeons" performed the unification of Montenegro with Serbia. Savo Vuletić, *Članci i Rasprave* (Bijelo Polje, 1998), p. 171.

75. See Vujović, *Ujedinjenje*, p. 331.
76. Živojinović, *Crna Gora*, pp. 295–296.
77. "The supporters of King Nikola, gathered near Njeguši, cut off the telegraph and telephone lines between Cetinje and Kotor, and occupied Njeguši.... With regard to the issue at hand I have issued the following order: 'Follow the orders of your commanding officer and make sure to disperse the Montenegrins as soon as possible, and reestablish order and communications.'" Report by the Commander of the Serbian and Adriatic Troops, January 3, 1919, AIICG, File No. 22, Doc. No. 34071.
78. Jovan Vujović to Djuro Šoć, Dob-Župa, December 31, 1918, in Rastoder, *Skrivana Strana*, vol. 1, pp. 107–108.
79. The Municipal Administrator from Gacko to the II Army, January 6, 1918, AIICG, File No. 22, Doc. No. 34231.
80. Djuro Šoć to Stevo Jovićević, Čista Strana, January 3, 1919, and Djuro Šoć to the Town's Mayor, Čista Strana, January 3, 1919, in Rastoder, *Skrivana Strana*, vol. 1, pp. 118–119. Also see Dimitrije D. Vujović, *Podgorička Skupština* (Zagreb: Školska Knjiga & Stvarnost, 1989), pp. 174–175.
81. Rebels' Declaration to the Executive Committee in Cetinje, Bajice, January 4, 1919 (signed by Krsto Popović on behalf of the Rebel's Committee), in Rastoder, *Skrivana Strana*, vol. 1, pp. 121–123.
82. General Milutinović to Krsto Popović, Cetinje, January 5, 1919, Order No. 734, in Rastoder, ibid., pp. 124–125.
83. Janko Vukotić to General Milutinović, Bajice, January 5, 1919, AIICG, File No. 360.
84. Report by General Milutinović to the Commander of the II Army, Cetinje, January 15, 1919, AIICG, File No. 360.
85. Milo Plamenac to Jovan Plamenac, Gaeta, September 20, 1919, AIICG, File No. 80.
86. Vujović, *Ujedinjenje*, p. 366.
87. Report by General Milutinović to the Commander of the II Army, Cetinje, January 15, 1919, AIICG, File No. 360.
88. According to Dimitrije D. Vujović, some of the rebels did not have rifles but used various farming equipment as weapons. Vujović, *Ujedinjenje*, p. 368.
89. International observers reported the following to the Paris Peace Conference: "Under Serbian occupation Montenegro today represents the bloodiest slaughter spot in Europe." In "Serbs Wipe Out Royalist Party in Montenegro," *Chicago Tribune*, September 3, 1919. On the killing of Savo Raspopović, the pillaging of Montenegrin villages in the region of Rovca, and the repressive measures of the Serbian army units under the command of Colonel Besarabić and Commander Borivoje Rosandić, see *Balkan*, no. 259, August 23, 1922, and no. 270, September 4, 1922.
90. Vuletić provided graphic details about the slaying of the five members of the Zvicer family in 1922 (including a grandmother who was one hundred years old) and about the murders of the prominent Montenegrin officer Major Šćepan Mijušković and his brother Stevan in 1924. In February of that year, a patrol of five gendarmes under the command of Captain Milan Kalabić arrested the Mijušković brothers and a couple of their relatives and friends for no reason whatsoever. After being tortured for some time, both Mijušković

brothers were killed, and Captain Kalabić informed their relatives that they had frozen to death on the way to prison. Seventy-five days later a passerby discovered the body of Šćepan Mijušković, and Kalabić was forced to flee Montenegro and go to Kosovo. In 1930 Kalabić was tried and sentenced to eighteen years in prison but was pardoned and appeared in Belgrade in 1940. Captain Milan Kalabić was the father of Nikola Kalabić, the notorious leader of the Serbian Chetniks during World War II and a close associate of Draža Mihailović. "Savo Vuletić to the Delegates of the Peoples' Assembly," Belgrade, July 27, 1925, Minutes from the Forty-Fourth Session of the People's Assembly, No. 603–605, in Rastoder, *Skrivana Strana*, vol. 4, pp. 2220–2225. Also see Commander of the Zeta Division to the Royal Administrator: Report on the Measures Taken against the Families of Rebels in the Region of Cuce, Cetinje, December 4, 1919, AIICG, File No. 366, Doc. No. 5499, and the Commander of the II Army Group to the Commander of the Zeta Division, Sarajevo, December 4, 1919, AIICG, File No. 366, as well as Ivo Pavićević to the Municipal Authorities in Cetinje, Cetinje, December 5, 1919, Confidential, No. 2483, Montenegrin State Archives (DACG), ONC, File No. 1. Doc. No. 229/1919.

91. "Witnessing such bloodshed, one must ask if Montenegrins were truly for the Unification." Pantelija Jovović, *Crnogorski Političari* (Beograd, 1924), p. 74.
92. For example, the report on the situation in Montenegro by Count John de Salis was never tabled or discussed in the British Parliament.

CONCLUSION

Abiit ad Plures

◆ The New State Is Born ◆

The Christmas Uprising was the most radical attempt by the supporters of independence to reverse the already completed process of the annexation of Montenegro, which was formalized by the resolution of the Great People's Assembly of the Serbian People in Montenegro. Initially, the uprising enjoyed considerable public support, and its goals were the preservation of Montenegrin political and cultural distinctiveness within the newly established Kingdom of Serbs, Croats, and Slovenes. After a swift military defeat, the movement was used and manipulated by both the Montenegrin government in exile and the government of Italy to achieve short-term political goals, and it ended up as a minor domestic disturbance in one of the provinces of the newly formed South Slav state. Even though the Great Powers had shown no interest in preserving Montenegrin independence and sovereignty, King Nikola and his government, as well as many participants in the uprising, hoped that their activities would somehow affect the final outcome of the Paris Peace Conference. Their hopes and dreams remained just that. From 1917 onward, the Allied governments adopted the idea of the new common state of the South Slavs and supported the efforts of the Serbian government in achieving this goal. Once military operations on the Thessalonica front were successfully concluded, Serbia came out of the war as the strongest state in the region and was seen as a force of stability. Its politicians and diplomats skillfully presented to the Great Powers their case for a unitary state and rationalized their requests as the only logical and just outcome of World War I. The forceful advocates of the unification of South Slavs (both domestic and foreign) portrayed the independent Montenegrin state as a remnant of past times and its king as a self-centered and power-hungry autocrat. The fact that King Nikola left the country in early 1916 under suspicious circumstances and remained isolated in exile in France had diminished his influence on events in Montenegro. He was further marginalized by the actions of his former prime minister, Andrija Radović, and persistent rumors about Nikola's wartime collaboration with Austria-Hungary did not endear him to his World War I allies. The unionist propaganda machine further fueled those rumors. Under the supervision and guidance of the Serbian government and with the support of the Great Powers, the Montenegrin Committee for Unification succeeded in preparing the ground for the formal act of annexation. With generous financial assistance from Belgrade and the backing of the Serbian army stationed in Montenegro, Andrija Radović and his colleagues worked tirelessly on organizing the assembly in Podgorica. Unlike their opponents, the unionists were well organized and focused on achieving their main objective: the annexation of Montenegro. The dubious legality of the entire process and the hastily organized elections for the assembly, as well as the unconstitutional character of the resolution of the Podgorica Assembly, were of no consequence for the unionists because they saw their work as revolutionary activity that should not respect old rules. Montenegro lost its independence and sovereignty and, in reality, became a part of Serbia instead of becoming a constitutive segment of the Kingdom of the Serbs, Croats, and Slovenes.

Between 1920 and 1924, the Montenegrin government in exile made several more attempts to revisit some aspects of the Paris Peace Conference and internationalize the Montenegrin Question with the League of Nations. All efforts proved to be in vain. As far as the League of Nations was concerned, the question of Montenegro was answered, and the last memorandum submitted by the Montenegrin government in exile in 1924 ended up in the Library of the League of Nations Secretariat. The Montenegrin Question was put *ad acta*.

Montenegro: Polity in Turmoil

Montenegro is not only one of the smallest but also one of the oldest Balkan polities. The chronicle *Regnum Sclavorum* (1183) mentions Montenegro as part of the former Roman province of Prevalitanis, also known as Doclea (later called Zeta). Since the fifteenth century the name Černagora has been used to describe this principality and its territory. Centuries before it was formally recognized as an independent state by the Great Powers at the Berlin Congress in 1878, the Montenegrin principality existed on the political map with various levels of independence.

Throughout its turbulent history, Montenegrin sovereignty and statehood depended on the ability of its rulers to strike the right balance between the contesting territorial and political claims of its neighbors and the desire to preserve Montenegrin political independence and the cultural specificities of its people. From the fifteenth century onward, Montenegrin history was characterized by numerous and self-serving political and military alliances. Depending on the potential political gain for the Montenegrin ruling elite at any given time, those alliances shifted among

Venice, Austria, Russia, and Serbia. Frequent and devastating military incursions by the Ottomans, as well as the predatory nature of the foreign policies of its neighbors, determined to a great extent the course of the Montenegrin history and defined the central question of its historical and political identity: could Montenegro exist as an independent state, or was its independence only a functional element of a different and larger political process? On one hand, the historical memory of the long-lasting armed struggle with neighboring Ottoman forces was a potent motif for preserving the independence of this tiny principality. On the other hand, the harsh reality of a small, economically disadvantaged, and politically isolated country spoke in favor of embracing the idea of a broader ideological and state framework, either pan-Slavic or pan-Serbian. These conflicting and contesting visions of the Montenegrin future represent the constant features of its history. Different Montenegrin rulers offered different solutions to this problem, thus aiding the construction of conflicting political loyalties and multiple identities of their subjects.

By the mid-nineteenth century, the ruling elites adopted the view that the Montenegrin Question could be successfully resolved only through the liberation and unification of the South Slavs. Influenced by nineteenth-century French ideas of national integration, the last ruler of independent Montenegro, King Nikola I Petrović, advocated the one-nation, one-state principle in the Balkans. For him, that meant the struggle to unite the Serbian nation and revive the long-lost medieval Serbian state. Nikola viewed Montenegro as a part of the medieval Serbian empire that had never been conquered. Therefore, it seemed only natural to him that Montenegro be an important part of this revived empire. Such a vision fit comfortably into the mythologized all-inclusive grand narrative of the Montenegrin state as the continuation of a medieval Serbian empire and corresponded to Nikola's portrayal of the Petrović dynasty as the rightful heir to the medieval throne. By proclaiming the Kingdom of Montenegro in 1910, Nikola hoped to see his dream materialize. The territorial enlargements of Montenegro after the Balkan Wars further fueled his ambition to become the self-styled supreme ruler of the South Slavs.

The events of World War I in the Balkans and the marginal role assigned to Montenegro during the military operations meant that the reality of the economically undeveloped and militarily weak Montenegrin state quickly dispersed all notions of grandeur that were so dear to its ruling elite. Even though the poorly equipped Montenegrin army fought valiantly during the first two years of the war, its government was forced to capitulate in late December 1915. This military defeat, however, was in no small measure caused by the political intrigues and calculations of the government of Serbia. The activities of the Serbian military representatives in Montenegro were tailored to discredit King Nikola and his government and ultimately to destroy the Montenegrin army. The country that was once hailed as *Srpska Sparta* (Serbian Sparta) ended up occupied, while its ruler, who was often referred to as *Car Junaka*

(Emperor of Heroes), went into exile. The catastrophic outcome of World War I for the Montenegrin state, its peoples, and its king was the most radical negative manifestation of the long-cherished notion of self-sacrifice for the greater good.

Post–World War I relations between Montenegro and its former war allies were a political and diplomatic seesaw that led to the relatively swift dismantling of the Montenegrin state. The Great Powers supported the Serbian policy of expansion and its long-lasting desire to reach the shores of the Adriatic through Montenegro and enthusiastically embraced the prospect of a new and unified South Slav state's emerging in the Balkans. Advocates of a unitary South Slav state argued that this new state would represent the realization of the centuries-old dream of all South Slavs, and this argument won the day at the Paris Peace Conference. Nikola's empty rhetoric of Montenegro's heroism and past glories was no match for the well-financed and carefully planned foreign policy actions of the Serbian government. The activities of the Montenegrin Committee for Unification were carefully designed, financed, and supervised by the Serbian government. The Great Powers supported the unitarist agenda of the Montenegrin Committee because they preferred the formation of the common South Slav state, with Serbia as its focal point, to potentially unstable post–World War I fragmentation in the Balkans.

For the politicians in Belgrade and for many Montenegrins, as well as the representatives of the Great Powers, Montenegro was an integral part of Serbia's geopolitical and cultural sphere of influence. The unification of the two states was, thus, seen as the logical step in the process of establishing the first common South Slav state. Many people in Montenegro, however, viewed those plans from a different perspective and opposed the unconditional unification of Montenegro with Serbia. While the Montenegrin Committee for Unification was busy laying the groundwork for the 1918 Podgorica Assembly meeting that would formalize the annexation of Montenegro by Serbia, new dividing lines appeared among the population. The initial disagreement and later open hostility (resulting in the armed rebellion and the long-lasting struggle) between the Greens and the Whites over the manner in which the so-called unification was achieved divided the population of Montenegro for decades to come. It should be emphasized that the conflict between the two sides arose neither from the lack of desire to establish the common South Slav state nor from the lack of enthusiasm of many Montenegrins to contribute to its creation. No Montenegrin (including the king) ever argued against establishing the unified South Slav state. What was disputed, however, was the way in which the unification between Montenegro and Serbia should take place. The ideological bases and the political motivation of the unitarists, and the backing they got from the Serbian government, as well as the speed with which they completed their activities in Montenegro, clearly point to the annexation of Montenegro rather than unification with Serbia. The preparations for the Podgorica Assembly were designed in such a way as to deprive the Montenegrins of their right to self-determination. The inability of Montenegrin institutions, politicians, and intellectuals to unite against the annexation, the poorly organized state apparatus, and the fact that the ruling elite were in exile were some of the factors that contributed to the relative ease with which annexation was accomplished. Naturally, one should not discount the defeat of Montenegro in 1915 and the strong Serbian military presence in Montenegro after World War I.

The result of the proclamation adopted by the Great People's Assembly of the Serbian People in Montenegro in 1918 was the complete disappearance of Montenegro's distinctiveness as a political and historical entity. The decisions adopted by the Podgorica Assembly did not reflect the complexity of the Montenegrin political and social landscape. On the contrary, it highlighted the contested nature of the ideas of a common South Slav state, which polarized the population for decades to come. The Montenegrins, Albanians, and Muslims living in Montenegro were neither presented with the choice nor given a chance to participate fully in the decision-making process. The country lost its independence and sovereignty and became part of Serbia. The immediate consequences of the assembly did not seem to contribute to the prosperity of Montenegro. On the contrary, the impact of the assembly was harmful on many levels. It created the bloody demarcation lines within Montenegro and ignited the armed conflict that lasted until late 1924. On a more general level, the legacy of the Podgorica Assembly and the conflicting nature of its proclamation left many scars in Montenegro, some of which are clearly visible to this day. Due to the nature of the decisions adopted by the Podgorica Assembly, Montenegro entered the newly formed state in a position of socioeconomic and political disadvantage. Montenegro was neither represented in the new South Slav state in any plausible way nor able to contribute to its progress.

The negative impact of the Podgorica Assembly was not limited to Montenegro but spread throughout the new South Slav state. The annexation of Montenegro indeed meant territorial enlargement for Serbia, but it also meant the strengthening of the unitary discourse that envisaged Serbia as the core of the future state and the initiator of the very idea of a unitary South Slav state. The negative effects of such unitarism and centralism projected from Belgrade and embraced by the Serbian ruling elite became clearly visible during the first decade of the common South Slav state and impeded the development of the Kingdom of Yugoslavia. This, in turn, created serious doubts among other South Slavs about the viability of the unified state. The bitter harvest of the 1918 Podgorica Assembly also had a negative impact on Serbia. In the minds of the assembly's contemporaries in Montenegro, Croatia, Slovenia, Bosnia, and Macedonia, the manner in which the new state was created imprinted the image of the Kingdom of Yugoslavia as nothing more than an enlarged Serbia. Such a perception of the common South Slav state resulted in a gradual distancing between its constitutive elements and, in time, the coining of the motto

"Strong Serbia—Weak Yugoslavia. Weak Serbia—Strong Yugoslavia." The negative connotations of such a view of the Kingdom of Yugoslavia only perpetuated further Greater Serbian nationalist and expansionist tendencies.

Traditional scholarship in both Serbo-Croat and English approached the issue of the Podgorica Assembly and post–World War I troubled relations between Montenegro and Serbia hierarchically. More often than not, Montenegro was treated as an extension of Serbia, and its state was inevitably positioned lower in the hierarchical order. Within a discourse that prioritizes Serbia and rationalizes such prioritization by invoking the strength of numbers, military might, significant economic potential, and cultural domination, it is only natural that any and every political action of Montenegro that does not correspond to the Serbian political program is seen as separatist, retrograde, or autarchic. Such discourse also limits the analyses of any given activity of the Montenegrin elite of the time because it positions the Montenegrin Question solely against the backdrop of Serbian political aims. I have tried to present a different approach to analyzing postwar relations between the two countries. My assessment of the Podgorica Assembly and its impact differs from the traditional discourse in one important way: my point of departure has been to acknowledge the equality between the two sides in this conflict. This acknowledgment creates the need to revisit the unjustly marginalized and legitimate concerns of many Montenegrins of the period. I have attached equal importance to both the Montenegrin and Serbian states of the time and insisted on equal respect for their sovereignty, their rights, and their legitimate interests. Recognizing this equality in such a way means recomposing the old image of a uniform process of state formation among the South Slavs. The dissent in Montenegro after the Podgorica Assembly is thus recognized as a legitimate endeavor to protect one's right to express a different opinion on the establishment of the common South Slav state and the right to freely choose one's own future. The importance of such an approach also lies in the fact that this heterogeneity of political, cultural, and ideological concepts between the elites in Montenegro and Serbia is far from being a thing of the past. The nature of the present political instability in the region indicates that old and unresolved ideological differences and political rivalries between Montenegrin and Serbian elites lie at the core of current political confrontation.

Appendix 1[1]

Count de Salis to Sir Edward Grey
Cetinje, July 23, 1914

Received: August 5, 1914
Foreign Office
General Correspondence, Montenegro, File No. 371. Series: 36033. Doc. No. 651. Public Record Office, Kew

Sir,
Early in June last the "Pravda" newspaper of Belgrade, commenting on the reply given by M. Plamenatz, the minister for foreign affairs, to an interpellation on the subject of the abandonment of Scutari and the international loan, published a bitter attack on the authorities of this country. "We are not" said the writer "desirous of going deep into recent events but we wish merely to lift the veil and to show to all what sort of 'types' govern in Montenegro and whether they can be believed when they speak in Montenegro in its name. Let Minister Peter Plamenatz therefore answer: who is that wretched Serb who behind the back of the much troubled but thoroughly patriotic cabinet of General Mitar Martinovitch, went to Baron Giesl, the ex-Austro-Hungarian minister at Cettinje on the 25th of October, 1912, and prayed, as a beggar does from a protector (and one knows in whose name!), that the Austro-Hungarian army should enter the Sanjak? On the part of Montenegro there would be no opposition; the two battalions on the Tara were only there to deceive public opinion. Otherwise Servia would become a danger to Montenegrin independence. Who was this man, Peter? Was he of the Left or of the Right ('Klubash' or 'Pravash')? Anyhow Baron Giesl must have noted the name of this hero in his papers. To think that to-day such a man is deciding, making declarations and speaking in the name of Montenegro and the Serb cause!"

A few days afterwards the same statements were repeated in the "Balkan" newspaper of Belgrade. Moreover, General Luka Gojnitch, a former prefect of Cettinje, was accused of treachery to the Servians at Brditza during the siege of Scutari, while the paper continued: "Like Pilate, Peter Plamenatz washed his hands and declared that he was innocent about Scutari. Yet, as governor of the town he sent a telegram to Martinovitch on the 17/30 April that he would not surrender the place but would defend it to the last drop of his blood. When the government fell and he was offered a post, he handed over the town to Vice-Admiral Burney!" The article concludes with the sentence: "Russia knows this well enough." A detailed contradiction of these assertions was published in the two Montenegrin newspapers on behalf of M. Plamenatz who was able to declare that he was not in Cettinje on the 25th of October 1912. His denial may be placed side by side with the information supplied to you in the following January by the Russian Government to the effect that they were aware that negotiations with Austria on the subject of the Sanjak had been initiated by the King. No statement was made to you as to who had conducted them.

More than once it has occurred in the last three years that accusations of unpatriotic conduct and betrayal of the Serb cause, addressed from Belgrade to Cettinje, have been met not only by counter-charges and insults but also by demonstrations of Chauvinism on the part of King Nicolas in the form of a press campaign of abuse against Austria. An outburst of this kind took place in the spring two years ago when, apparently with the approval of M. Milovanovictch, the Belgrade newspapers published the text of an alleged secret agreement between King Nicolas and Austria. On the present occasion the palace may have considered it imprudent to risk an attack on Belgrade but intemperate articles against Austria at once began to appear. Interrupted for a moment by the news of the assassination at Serajevo which evoked a guarded expression of disapproval, the series was continued with greater violence on receipt of news respecting the anti Serb riots in Bosnia. Austria, it was declared, was aiming at the extermination of the Serb race in her dominions while the two independent Serb States were to be attacked and crushed on the pretext that they had abetted the murder of the Archduke. The insincerity of the indignation thus expressed and the evident desire not to be left out of the controversy may be judged by the fact that though the "Reichspost," the "Neue Freie Presse," and doubtless, other Austrian newspapers have freely attacked Belgrade for harbouring conspirators against the life of the Archduke, not a word seems to have been said in this connection against Montenegro. On the contrary, up to a short time before the formation of the Balkan League, King Nicolas was himself leveling the same accusations against the Servian Government and was even declaring that I. Pashitch had taken a direct part in a plot to murder him. On that occasion the bombs seem to have come from the Servian arsenal at Kragujevatz. Whether they were brought here by the enemies or the agents of the Palace is another matter.

Briefly, danger of disturbance in this country may be caused by the desire of the ruling authorities to outdo Servia in any demonstration of Serb patriotism, by the same spirit, in short, with which the King hastened to begin the Balkan war before his allies were ready.

While the Belgrade papers received here have published long eulogies on the service rendered by the late M. Hartwing and by Russian diplomacy to the Southern Slavs, not a word has been said here on the subject. It is nearly two months since the complimentary mission came from St. Petersburg but still there has been no sign of the money for the military subsidy. The Russian Government are, it is understood, favorably disposed in principle but no final decision seems to have been taken. Their hesitation may be solely due to a desire to postpone payment during the uncertainties of the present moment. Or is distrust of the King, based on past experience, leading them to withhold help from Montenegro pending a modification of the present system of government in accordance with their wishes?

I have, & c.
J. DE.SALIS

Note

1. The photocopy of the original document is stored in the Library of the Montenegrin Institute for Historical Research.

Appendix 2[1]

Count de Salis to Sir Edward Grey
Cetinje, July 26, 1914

Received: August 5, 1914
Foreign Office
General Correspondence, Montenegro, File No. 371. Series: 36034. Doc. No. 652. Public Record Office, Kew

Sir,

In my dispatch No. 2 of the 11th of May reference was made to the rumours current with regard to the alleged aims or intentions of the Austrian Government in connection with the strategical positions belonging to Montenegro which dominate the Bocche di Cattaro. The matter has continued to arouse attention both in this country and elsewhere and the King's semi-official organ, the "Vjesnik," reproduces with evident satisfaction a recent article from the Italian "Messagero." "Austria" it is stated (if the translation from the original is correct) "forgets that the question of the Lovtchen is not only a question for Austria and Montenegro but also for Italy. No Italian Government could allow the Lovtchen to fall into Austrian hands; that would mean a capitulation to Austria in the Adriatic and would put arms into the hands of Austria against Italy. It would give here the key of the Adriatic guns which would command our position in the same way as the Austrians imagine that Montenegrin guns can at present fire down on the bay of Cattaro from the heights of Lovtchen. In Vienna they are so much in love with this Lovtchen that they have even suspended work on the new military harbour at Sebenico. . . . We repeat that Lovtchen is an Italian question, or better still, that it is an international one. Italy cannot allow the strategical situation in the Adriatic to be altered to her disadvantage. Lovtchen must remain as it is . . . Montenegrin."

Some military movements in the neighbourhood of Cattaro have given rise to further comment. Reinforcements of troops were moved to posts in the Bocche with the avowed object of preventing collisions between the Croats and the Serbs. In view of recent riots in Bosnia, the explanation might seem to be well founded, but the report was spread here that the movements carried out were such as would be preliminary to an advance across the frontier. The Austrian minister has hastened to give very positive and friendly assurances that no hostile movement is intended while an official communiqué, to the same effect was published in the "Fremdenblatt" on the 21st July. In spite of the recent press campaign against them the Austrian Government are making considerable efforts to be conciliatory.

I have & c.
J. DE SALIS

Note

1. The photocopy of the original document is stored in the Library of the Montenegrin Institute for Historical Research.

Appendix 3

Rules for Electing People's Delegates for the Great People's Assembly

❖ (Montenegro, November 7, 1918. Berane) ❖ No. 32

The military achievements of our allies and our army created the possibility for the Serbian, Croatian, and Slovenian peoples to freely decide their future state. Even before the Serbian and Allied armies entered some of the Serbian and Yugoslav provinces, those provinces managed to free themselves from the oppression of the enemy and seek unification of all Serbs, Croats, and Slovenes in one free and independent state, for which the constitution will be written by the Great People's Assembly, and whose delegates will be elected in a general election and by direct vote in the whole country. The Interim Central Executive Committee for the Unification of Serbia and Montenegro is working toward accomplishing an old desire of our people: the unification of Montenegro with Serbia in order to enable an immediate unification of all other Serbs, Croats, and Slovenes in one indivisible state.

In order to start working among the people on this magnificent project and after the meeting Number 32, on November 7th this year, the Committee decided to call for the election of people's delegates for the Great People's Assembly in the whole of Montenegro on November 17 this year. The elected delegates will meet on November 24 this year in Podgorica in order to decide the future constitutional and legal position of Montenegro and to elect the permanent People's Executive Committee that will further coordinate the work and implement the decision reached by the assembly.

Each province [Kapetanija] in Montenegro will elect two people's delegates, while every municipality [Srez], in the newly acquired regions, will elect three delegates. Towns with less than five thousand inhabitants, such as Bar, Ulcinj, Kolašin,

Berane, and Bijelo Polje, will each elect one delegate, and towns with more than five thousand inhabitants, such as Cetinje, Podgorica, Pljevlja, Peć, and Djakovica, will each elect two delegates.

The elections of people's delegates will be undertaken by an open and direct vote, as indicated below. Provinces will hold rallies and select 10 representatives each, while municipalities will elect 15 representatives each; smaller towns, 5, and larger towns, 10 representatives each. These elections have to start and be completed on November 4th this year. The representatives from the provinces and municipalities, as well as towns, will meet separately on November 6th this year and elect their delegates. These elections have to be undertaken by open and public voting. The Kapetans [the highest ranking provincial officials], municipal leaders [sreski načelnici], and town mayors will then issue signed affidavits to elected delegates. The three-member regional committees will issue these affidavits: head of the municipality/head of the province, president of the regional court, and the mayor of a particular municipality. The minutes concerning the election process of representatives and the people's delegates will be officially stamped and sent to the Great People's Assembly. Each letter should indicate the character of the election: representative or delegate.

The people's delegate can be any citizen over 25 years of age who has not been convicted of an unlawful conduct. Any citizen over the age of 25 and without a criminal record has also the right and the obligation to vote for representatives and people's delegates. All regional and municipal offices and provincial offices should make sure that elections of the people's delegates for the Great People's Assembly are held according to the aforementioned rules.[1]

Note

1. Svetozar Tomić, *Desetogodišnjica Ujedinjenja Crne Gore i Srbije* (Beograd, 1919), pp. 27–28. The original version of this document does not exist, even though the Rules had been published on many occasions. The first publication occurred in Paris immediately after the Podgorica Assembly. Andrija Radović, Radovan Bošković, and Luka Vukotić, eds., *La Questione Montenegrine* (Paris, 1919). The same document appeared in the Paris-based newspaper *La Volonte du Peuple* on April 14, 1919. The publisher of this newspaper was Janko Spasojević. The Rules were published by the Montenegrin government in exile in *Le Role de la France dans l'annexion forcee du Montenegro* (Rome, 1921), and later in Jovan Ćetković, *Ujedinitelji Crne Gore i Srbije* (Dubrovnik, 1940). The only difference between all the published versions of the document is in the listing of the Montenegrin towns of populations over and under 5,000. Some authors listed Cetinje as a town with less than 5,000 inhabitants, whereas others categorized it as having more than 5,000 inhabitants. Svetozar Tomić listed the city of Cetinje as having more than 5,000 inhabitants. I have used the version published by Tomić.

Bibliography

Archival Sources
This list is confined to those archival sources/manuscripts that have been quoted or referred to in this book. The archives are listed by the abbreviations that have been used in the endnotes, in alphabetical order.

AIICG Arhiv Istorijskog Instituta Crne Gore
Andrija Radović: Korespondencija, 1915–1916 (Typed and Handwritten), File No. 171.
Arhiva Andrije Radovića 1917–1920, File No. 121, and File No. 154.
Arhiva Jovana Plamenca: Pisma; Ugovori; Novinski tekstovi; Memorandumi, 1920–1934, File No. 176.
Arhivska Gradja Andrije Radovića: Sekcije: A–B, File No. 155.
Arhivska Gradja Jovana S. Plamenca, Section 5, File No. 80.
Arhiva Srpske Vojne Misije u Parizu: Dokumenta, 1916–1918, Sections 1–3, File No. 357.
Crnogorski Odbor za Narodno Ujedinjenje: Pisma, Predstavke, Memorandumi (Typed and Handwritten), File No. 156.
Dnevnik Komandira Okružne Žandarmerije na Cetinju, 1918, File No. 39.
Dokumenti Jovana Plamenca, File No. 80.
Ilija Hajduković, "Potonji Dani Samostalne Crne Gore" (Typed), File No. 95.
Izvod Izvjesnih Stvari iz Borbe oko Cetinja 1918 i 1919, File No. 39.
Komanda Budvanskog Otseka-Sektor Tivat, Korespondencija, 1919–1920, File No. 358.
Kraljevsko Srpsko Ministrastvo Vojno: Korespondencija, 1915–1916, File No. 44.
Krsto Popović, Pisma (Handwritten), File No. 81.
Lazar Damjanović: Govor u Cetinju, December 25, 1918, File No. 39.
Marko Daković, "Uloga Crne Gore u Svjetskom Ratu" (Handwritten), File No. 63, Doc. No. 9.
Miro Božović, Crna Gora i Njena Vojna Uloga, and Risto Popović, Dnevnik, File No. 330.
M.M. Martinović, Dnevnik, File No. 304.

Nasilna Aneksija Crne Gore (Handwritten), Sections No. 4, 5, 8, 16, 19, 34, 35, and 42. File No. 113.
Nikola Pašić to Živojin Mišić: Prepiska, 1913, File No. 36.
Pariska Konferencija: Prepiska, File No. 120.
Pavle Popović, Nekoliko Stranica, File No. 426.
Pisma Andriji Radoviću—Narudžbenice, 1917–1918 (Handwritten), File No. 155.
Pisma Odboru za Narodno Ujedinjenje, 1917 (Handwritten), File No.154.
Prepiska Andrije Radovića, 1918–1919 (Handwritten), File No. 122.
Risto Popović, Dnevnik, File No. 330.
Savo Raspopović, Pisma (Handwritten), File No. 81.
S. Popović, Memoari: Crna Gora i Srbija, File No. 137/2.
Spisak Zatvorenika u Podgorici 1919, File No. 390.
Srpska Vrhovna Komanda: Naredjenja i Pisma, 1915, File No. 353.
Srpska Vrhovna Komanda-Komandi Jadranskih Trupa: Božićna Pobuna, 1918–1919, File No. 360.
Uprava Centralnog Kaznenog Zavoda, Podgorica—Andriji Radoviću, 1919, File No. 390.
Zapisnici sa Sjednica Velike Narodne Skupstine u Podgorici, File No. 319.
Zbirka Ljuba Bakića, File No. 318.
Zbirka Ljuba Bakića (Handwritten), File No. 14.
Zbirka Vukašina Božovića: Vojne Depeše 1914–1918, Docs. No. 30597, 31205, 31206, 31227, 31470, 31474, 31551, 31621, 32194, 32257, 32281, 32353, and 32851–38830. File No. 22.

AMC Arhiv Muzeja Cetinje
Fond Nikola I.
Knjaz Danilo.
Ministarstvo Inostranih Djela.
Prinovljeni Rukopisi.

AJ Arhiv Jugoslavije
Kolekcija Jovana Jovanovica Pižona.
Zbirka J.M. Jovanovića.

AS Arhiv Srbije
Crnogorski Odsjek.
Delegacija Mira u Parizu 1918.
Guerre 1914–1918, Balkans, Serbia. Vol. 387. Microfilm.
Ministarstvo Inostranih Dela, File No. 10.

AVB Arhiv Valtazara Bogišića, Cavtat
Rukopisi Bogišićevog Arhiva.
Section 2: Naučni Arhiv.

AVIB Arhiv Vojnoistorijskog Instituta, Beograd
Popisnik No. 3.
Popisnik No. 17.
Popisnik No. 17/2, Zbirka Dokumenata iz Stranačkog Političkog Života Stare Jugoslavije 1919–1929.

DAC Državni Arhiv Cetinje
Legat Nikole Djonovića.

DAD Diplomatski Arhiv Dubrovnik
Crnogorski Odsjek. Files No. 603, 185, 122, and 81. Docs. No. 4, 12, 17, 42, 114, 119, 122, 173, 185, 380, 374, and 2153.
Ministarstvo Inostranih Poslova. Tajno. Doc. No. 1058.
Odnosi Srpsko-Crnogorski, Povjerljivo. Doc. No. 2544.

DADSIP Diplomatski Arhiv Državnog Sekretarijata za Inostrane Poslove SFRJ
Političko Odjeljenje 1903–1914.

FO Foreign Office—Public Record Office
General Correspondence, Montenegro, File No. 371. Series: 46533/51613, 61711/61711, 63823, 152443/177835, 148416, 152433/180595, 608/46, 34053/144899, 144900, 175127/175127, 6933/219996.

NAW National Archives, Washington, D.C.
Correspondence between the Department of State and the Serbian/Yugoslav Legation in Washington. Decimal classifications: 763.71, 701.0072, 860H.01.
Department of State: Correspondence between the Department of State and the U.S. Legation at Corfu/Belgrade, 1915–1919.
Papers of the American Commission to Negotiate the Peace: a/ Committee on Rumanian and Yugoslav Affairs, b/ Central Territorial Committee.

Published Archival Sources
Avramović, Živko. *Britanci o Kraljevini Jugoslaviji 1921–1938*. Vols. 1–2. Beograd-Zagreb: n.p., 1986.
Boban, Ljubo, Mirjana Gross, Bogdan Krizma, Dragovan Šepić, Christopher Seton-Watson, and Hugh Seton-Watson, eds. *R.W. Seton-Watson i Jugoslaveni:*

Korespondencija. Vols. 1–2. Zagreb/London: Sveučilište u Zagrebu i Britanska Akademija, 1976.

Bojović, Jovan. *Podgorička Skupština 1918, Dokumenti.* Gornji Milanovac: Dečije Novine, 1989.

Cetinjski Ljetopis. Cetinje: Fototipsko Izdanje Centralne Biblioteke NR Crne Gore, 1962.

Crna Gora: Izvještaji Mletačkih Providura. Podgorica: CID, 1998.

Crnogorski Senat: Zbornik Dokumenata. Cetinje: Obod, 1997.

Čulinovic, Ferdo. *Dokumenti o Jugoslaviji.* Zagreb: n.p., 1968.

Documents Officiels Publies par le Ministere des Affaires Etrangeres du Montenegro. Rome: Imperiere A. Manuce, 1921.

Dragović, Marko. *Dokumenti o Šćepanu Malom, Spomenik Srpske Kraljevske Akademije.* Vol. 22. Beograd: n.p., 1893.

Državni Kalendar za Kraljevinu Crnu Goru. Cetinje: n.p., 1913.

Hajduković, Niko. *Memoari.* Podgorica: CID, 2000.

Hrabak, B., ed. "Zapisnici Sednica dve Davidovićeve vlade od avgusta 1919 do februara 1920," *Arhivski Vjesnik* XIII. Zagreb: n.p., 1980.

I Documenti Diplomatici Italiani, Serie Quinta. Vol. 4. Rome: n.p., 1983.

Janković, D., and B. Krizman, eds. *Gradja o Stvaranju Jugoslovenske Države: 1.I 1918–1920. XII 1918.* Vols. 1–2. Beograd: Kultura, 1964.

Krizman, B., and B. Hrabak, eds. *Zapisnici sa Sednica Delegacije Kraljevine SHS na Mirovnoj Konferenciji u Parizu 1919–1920.* Beograd: Kultura, 1960.

Listed u Personnel du Gouvernement Royal et de Messieurs les Membres du Corps Diplomatique et Conslulaire au Montenegro. Neuilly-sur-Seine, October 1917.

Luburić, Andrija. *Kapitulacija Crne Gore: Dokumenti.* Vol. 1. Beograd: n.p., 1938.

Luburić, Andrija. *Kapitulacija Crne Gore: Dokumenti.* Vol. 2. Beograd: n.p., 1940.

Montenegro: Political and Ethnic Boundaries, 1840–1920. Vols. 1–2. Slough: Archive Editions, 2001.

Peričić, Eduard. *Sclavorum Regnum Grgura Barskog—Ljetopis Popa Dukljanina.* Zagreb: JAZU, 1994.

Petrović, Nikola I. *Politički Spisi.* Cetinje-Titograd: n.p., 1989.

Petrović, Petar II. *Izabrana Pisma.* Beograd: Prosveta, 1967.

Policijski Pravilnik u Knjaževini Crnoj Gori. Cetinje: n.p., 1907.

Rastoder, Šerbo. *Skrivana Strana Istorije: Crnogorska Buna i Odmetnički Pokret 1918–1929. Dokumenti.* Vols. 1–4. Bar: Nidamentym Montenegro, 1997.

Stenografske Bilješke Crnogorske Narodne Skupštine za 1914. Cetinje: n.p., 1915.

Šišić, Ferdo. *Dokumenti o Postanku Kraljevine Srba, Hrvata i Sovenaca 1914–1919.* Zagreb: Naklada Matice Hrvatske, 1920.

Ustavi i Vlade Kneževine Srbije, Kraljevine Srbije, Kraljevine SHS i Kraljevine Jugoslavije 1835–1941. Beograd: n.p., 1988.

Ustav za Knjaževinu Crnu Goru. Reprint, Podgorica: Službeni List Republike Crne Gore, 1999.
Woodward, E.L., and R. Butler, eds. *Documents on British Foreign Policy, 1919–1939.* Vol. 4. 1st series. London: H.M. Stationery Office, 1952.
Zakon o Ustrojstvu Ministarstva Vojnog. Cetinje: n.p., 1903.
Zakon o Ustrojstvu Ministarstva Unutrašnjih Djela i Administrativnoj Podjeli Države. Cetinje: n.p., 1903.
Zakon o Izdavanju Pasoša. Cetinje: n.p., 1905.
Zakon o Izborima Narodnijeh Poslanika. Cetinje: n.p., 1906.
Zakon o Narodnijem Školama u Knj. Crnoj Gori. Cetinje: n.p., February 2, 1907.
Zakon o Parohijalnom Sveštenstvu od 31.VIII.1909. Cetinje: n.p., 1910.
Zakon o Ustrojstvu Vojske za Knjaževinu Crnu Goru. Cetinje: n.p., 1910.
Zakon o Naseljavanju Novooslobodjenih Predjela Crne Gore od 27.II 1914. Cetinje: n.p., 1914.
Zakon o Kraljevskoj Vladi i o Uredjenju Državnijeh Nadleštava. Cetinje: n.p., May 14, 1914.

Memoirs

Jovanović, Ilija. *Na Dvoru Kralja Nikole: Uspomene iz Mog Života.* Cetinje: Obod, 1998.
Orlando, Vittorio Emanuele. *Memorie, 1915–1919.* Milan: n.p., 1960.
Plamenac, Rade T. *Memoari.* Podgorica: CID, 1997.
Tošković, Janko. *Memoari: Bilješke iz Ustavne Vladavine Kralja Nikole i Njenog Tragičnog Svršetka od 1905. Do 1918. Godine.* Cetinje: Obod, 1974.
Vuković, Gavro. *Memoari.* Vols. 1–3. Titograd: Grafički Zavod, 1985.

Secondary Sources

Albertini, Luigi. *The Origins of the War of 1914.* Translated and edited by Isabela M. Massey. Oxford: Oxford University Press, 1953.
Aleksić, Ljiljana. "O Srpsko-Crnogorskim Pregovorima o Savezu, 1904–1905." *Istorija XX Veka: Zbornik Radova.* Vol. 1. Beograd: n.p., 1950.
Anderson, Benedict. *Imagined Communities: Reflections on the Origins and Spread of Nationalism.* London: Verso, 1983.
Anderson, M.A. *The Eastern Question, 1774–1923.* New York: Macmillan, 1966.
Andrijašević, Živko, ed. *Kratka Istorija Crne Gore, 1496–1918.* Bar: Conteco, 2000.
Andrijašević, Živko M. "Crnogorska Državna Ideja u Vrijeme Nikole I Petrovića Njegoša." *Matica Časopis za Društvena Pitanja Nauku i Kulturu* 1, no. 3 (2000), pp. 43–71.
Andrijašević, Živko M. "O Crnogorskoj Državnoj Ideji." *Matica Časopis za Društvena Pitanja Nauku i Kulturu* 1, no. 2 (2000), pp. 27–45.

Anžulović, Branimir. *Heavenly Serbia: From Myth to Genocide.* New York: New York University Press, 1999.

Avramovski, Živko. *Albanska Država od 1912. Do 1939. Iz Istorije Albanaca.* Beograd: n.p., 1969.

Babović, Senka. "Kulturna Politika u Zetskoj Banovini." PhD diss., University of Montenegro, 1997.

Baiza, Giuseppe de. *La Questione Montenegrina.* Budapest: Casa Editrice Franklin, 1928.

Baker, Mark Robert. "A Tale of Two Historians: The Involvement of R.W. Seton-Watson and Lewis Namier in the Creation of New Nation-States in Eastern Europe at the End of the First World War." MA thesis, University of Alberta, 1993.

Banac, Ivo. *The National Question in Yugoslavia: Origins, History, Politics.* Ithaca and London: Cornell University Press, 1992.

Banašević, Nikola, and others, eds. *Istorija Crne Gore.* Vols. 1–4. Titograd: Redakcija za Istoriju Crne Gore, 1967.

Bandić, Dušan. *Carstvo Zemaljsko i Carstvo Nebesko: Ogledi o Narodnoj Religiji.* Beograd: Biblioteka XX Vek, 1990.

Barac, Antun. *A History of Yugoslav Literature.* Ann Arbor: Michigan Slavic Studies, 1976.

Batovski, Henrik. "Crna Gora i Balkanski Savez 1912." *Istorijski Zapisi* 13, no. 1 (1957), pp. 18–32.

Boehm, Christopher. *Montenegrin Social Organization and Values: Political Ethnography of a Refugee Area Tribal Adaptation.* New York: AMS Press, 1983.

Bogdanov, Vaso, Ferdo Čulinović, and Marko Kostrenčić, eds. *Jugoslavenski Odbor u Londonu.* Zagreb: JAZU, 1966.

Bogdanović, Milan. "Vratimo Njegoša Literaturi." *Srpski Književni Glasnik* 2, no. 16.7 (1925), pp. 21–45.

Bogišić, Valtazar. *Izabrana Dela i Opšti Imovinski Zakonik za Crnu Goru.* Beograd: n.p., 1986.

Bokovoy, Melisa. *Peasants and Communists: Politics and Ideology in the Yugoslav Countryside, 1941–1953.* Pittsburgh: University of Pittsburgh Press, 1998.

Bonsal, S. *Suitors and Suppliants: The Little Nations at Versailles.* New York: Prentice Hall, 1946.

Bošković, Ilija D. *Tragedija Crne Gore i Njeni Životni Problemi.* Beograd: n.p., 1927.

Boym, Svetlana. *The Future of Nostalgia.* New York: Basic Books, 2001.

Božović, Miro. "Crna Gora i Njena Vojna Uloga of 15 Juna 1914 do Kapitulacije." *Slobodna Misao,* no. 47 (1936), pp. 7–14.

Budisavljević, Srdjan. *Stvaranje Države Srba, Hrvata i Slovenaca.* Zagreb: JAZU, 1958.

Bulajić, Žarko. *Agrarni Odnosi u Crnoj Gori, 1778–1912*. Titograd: Grafički Zavod, 1959.
Carter, F.W., and H.T. Norris, eds. *The Changing Shape of the Balkans*. Boulder, Colo.: Westview Press, 1996.
Ćetković, Jovan. *Ujedinjenje Crne Gore i Srbije*. Dubrovnik: n.p., 1940.
Ćetković, Jovan. *Omladinski Pokret u Crnoj Gori*. Podgorica: n.p., 1922.
Clissold, Stephen, ed. *A History of Yugoslavia from Early Times to 1966*. Cambridge: Cambridge University Press, 1966.
Criscuolo, L. *Montenegro's Right to Live*. New York: n.p., 1928.
Crnobrnja, Mihailo. *The Yugoslav Drama*. Montreal: McGill-Queen's University Press, 1994.
Čubrilović, Vasa. *Istorija Političke Misli u Srbiji XIX Veka*. Beograd: n.p., 1958.
Čubrilović, Vasa. "Istorijski Osnovi Postanku Jugoslavije, 1918." *NAUČNI SKUP: U Povodu 50-Godišnjice Raspada Austro-Ugarske Monarhije i Stvaranja Jugoslavenske Države*. Zagreb: JAZU, 1969.
Čulinović, Ferdo. *Jugoslavija Izmedju Dva Rata*. Zagreb: Izdavački Zavod Jugoslavenske Akademije Znanosti i Umjetnosti, 1961.
Čulinović, Ferdo. "Raspad Austro-Ugarske i Postanak Jugoslavenske Zajednicke Države." *NAUČNI SKUP: U Povodu 50-Godinjice Raspada Austro-Ugarske Monarhije i Stvaranja Jugoslavenske Države*. Zagreb: JAZU, 1969.
Cvijić, Jovan. *Balkansko Poluostrvo i Južnoslovenske Zemlje*. Beograd: n.p., 1922.
Cvijić, Jovan. "Izlazak Srbije na Jadransko More." *Glasnik Srpskog Etnografskog Društva* 2, no. 2 (1913), pp. 3–25.
Darby, H.C., and others, eds. *A Short History of Yugoslavia: From Early Times to 1966*. Cambridge: Cambridge University Press, 1966.
Dašić, Miomir. "Pregled Teritorijalnog Širenja Crnogorske Države." *Istorijski Zapisi*, no. 1 (1987), pp. 54–72.
de Somier, Žan-Lui-Klod Viala. *Istorijsko i Političko Putovanje u Crnu Goru*. Podgorica: CID, 1995.
Dedijer, Vladimir. *The Road to Sarajevo*. London, 1966.
Dedijer, Vladimir. *Sarajevo 1914*. Beograd: n.p., 1966.
Dedijer, Vladimir, and others, eds. *History of Yugoslavia*. Translated by Kordija Kveder. New York: McGraw-Hill, 1974.
Dimić, Ljubodrag. *Kulturna Politika Kraljevine Yugoslavije*. Vols. 1–3. Beograd: n.p., 1997.
Dimić, Ljubodrag. "Školsko Pitanje i Odnosi Jugoslavije i Albanije 1918–1939." In *Stanovništvo Slovenskog Porijekla u Albaniji*, conference proceedings. Titograd, 1991.
Djilas, Aleksa. *The Contested Country: Yugoslav Unity and Communist Revolution, 1919–1953*. Cambridge, Mass.: Harvard University Press, 1992.

Djilas, Milovan. *Njegoš: Poet, Prince, Bishop.* New York: Harcourt Brace and World, 1966.
Djonović, Jovan. *Ustavne i Političke Borbe u Crnoj Gori, 1905–1910.* Beograd: n.p., 1930.
Djonović, Nikola. *Crna Gora Pre i Posle Ujedinjenja.* Beograd: n.p., 1936.
Djordjević, Dimitrije. *Izlazak Srbije na Jadransko More i Konferencije Ambasadora u Londonu, 1913. Godine.* Beograd: n.p., 1956.
Djordjević, Dimitrije, and Stephen Fischer-Galati, eds. *The Creation of Yugoslavia, 1914–1918.* Santa Barbara, Calif.: Clio Books, 1980.
Djordjević, Dimitrije, and Radovan Samardžić, eds. *Migrations in Balkan History.* Belgrade: n.p., 1989.
Djukić, Trifun. *Pregled Književnog Rada Crne Gore od Vasilija Petrovića Njegoša do 1918. Godine.* Cetinje: Narodna Knjiga, 1951.
Djurišić, Mitar. "Operacije Crnogorske Vijske, 1915–1916. Godine," *Vojniistorijski Glasnik*, nos. 2–3 (1995), pp. 32–54.
Djurišić, Mitar. "Uloga Kralja Nikole u Prvom Balkanskom Ratu." *Istorijski Zapisi* 18, no. 1 (1960), pp. 64–80.
Dragićević, Risto. "Ugovor Svete Stolice s Knjaževinom Crnom Gorom, 1886. Godine." *Zapisi.* Cetinje: n.p., 1940.
Dragnich, Alex. *Serbs and Croats: The Struggle for Yugoslavia.* New York: Harcourt Brace, 1992.
Dragović, Ž. *Istorija Crne Gore.* Cetinje: KC Ministrastva Vojnog, 1910.
Drljević, Sekula. *Balkanski Sukobi, 1905–1941.* Zagreb: Naklada Putovi, 1944.
Durham, Mary Edith. *Some Tribal Origins, Laws, and Customs of the Balkans.* London: George Allen & Unwin Ltd., 1928.
Durković-Jakšić, Ljubomir. *Njegos i Lovcen.* Beograd: n.p., 1971.
Ekmečić, Milorad. *Ratni Ciljevi Srbije, 1914.* Beograd: n.p., 1973.
Ekmečić, Milorad. "Stavovi Nikole Pašića Prema Američkim Planovima Pretvaranja Austro-Ugarske u Federativnu Državu." *NAUČNI SKUP: U Povodu 50-Godišnjice Raspada Austro-Ugarske Monarhije i Stvaranja Jugoslavenske Države.* Zagreb: JAZU, 1969.
Erdeljanović, Jovan. *Stara Crna Gora: Etnička Prošlost i Formiranje Crnogorskih Plemena.* Naselja i Poreklo Stanovništva 24. Beograd: n.p., 1926.
Evans, R.J.W. "Essay and Reflection: Frontiers and National Identities in Central Europe." *The International History Review* 14, no. 3 (1992), pp. 42–54.
Fleming, K.E. "Orientalism, the Balkans, and Balkan Historiography." *American Historical Review* 105, no. 4 (2000), pp. 31–45.
Frile, Gabriel, and Jovan Vlahović. *Savremena Crna Gora.* Translated from French by Rosanda Vlahović. Podgorica: CID, 2001.
Gellner, Ernest. *Nations and Nationalism.* Ithaca: Cornell University Press, 1983.

Grayson, Benson Lee. "American Diplomacy and the Loss of Montenegrin Independence." *East European Quarterly* 9 (Spring 1985), pp. 13–23.
Greenwalt, Alexander K.A. "The Nationalization of Memory: Identity and Ideology in Nineteenth Century Serbia." Senior thesis, Princeton University, 1994.
Grmek, Mirko, Marc Gjidana, and Neven Šimac. *Le Nettoyage ethnique: Documents historiques sur une ideologie serbe.* Paris: Fayard, 1993.
Hastings, Adrian. *The Construction of Nationhood: Ethnicity, Religion, and Nationalism.* Cambridge: Cambridge University Press, 1997.
Herzfeld, Michael. *Cultural Intimacy: Social Poetics in the Nation-State.* New York: Routledge, 1997.
Hobsbawm, Eric. *Nations and Nationalism since 1780: Programme, Myth, and Reality.* Cambridge: Cambridge University Press, 1990.
Ilinčić, Vukić. "Kapitulacija Crne Gore u Objektivu Karela Podlipnog." *Istorijski Zapisi* 74, nos. 1–2 (2001), pp. 12–34.
Ivelić, Mitar. *Geografija Crne Gore za Treći Razred Osnovne Škole.* Cetinje: Školska Komisija za Rukopis, 1894.
Janković, Dragoslav. "O Niškoj Deklaraciji, 1914. Godine." *NAUČNI SKUP: U Povodu 50-GodišnjiceRaspada Austro-Ugarske Monarhije i Stvaranja Jugoslavenske Države.* Zagreb: JAZU, 1969.
Janković, Dragoslav. *Jugoslovensko Pitanje i Krfska Deklaracija, 1917. Godine.* Beograd: Savremena Administracija, 1967.
Janković, Dragoslav. "O Političkoj Situaciji medju Jugoslovenima pred Ujedinjenje (u 1918, do oktobra)." *Istorijski Glasnik* 4 (1964), pp. 7–36.
Janković, Dragoslav. *Srbija i Jugoslovensko Pitanje, 1914–1915.* Beograd, 1973.
Jelavich, Barbara. *History of the Balkans.* Vols. 1–2. New York: Cambridge University Press, 1983.
Jelavich, Charles. "Nikola P. Pašić: Greater Serbia or Yugoslavia?" *Journal of Central European Affairs* 11, no. 2 (1951), pp. 14–28.
Jelavich, Charles, and Barbara Jelavich. *The Establishment of the Balkan National States, 1804–1920.* Seattle: University of Washington Press, 1977.
Jelušić, Božena. "Otvoreni za Njegoša." *Matica* 2, no. 6 (2001), pp. 47–64.
Jovanović, Jagoš. *Istorija Crne Gore.* 2nd ed. Cetinje/Podgorica: n.p., 1995.
Jovanović, Jagoš. *Stvaranje Crnogorske Države i Razvoj Crnogorske Nacionalnosti: Istorija Crne Gore od Pocetka VIII vijeka do 1918. Godine.* Cetinje: Obod, 1948.
Jovanović, Jagoš. "Veze Crne Gore sa Rusijom od Druge Polovine 16 Vijeka do Danas." *Istorijski Zapisi* 2, nos. 3–4 (1948), pp. 20–56.
Jovanovic, Jovan. *Stvaranje Zajedničke Države Srba, Hrvata i Slovenaca.* Beograd: Zapisi, 1929.
Jovanović, Radoman. *Crna Gora i Velike Sile, 1856–1860.* Titograd: Istorijski Institut Crne Gore, 1983.

Jovanović, Radoman. "Stav Crne Gore Prema Aneksiji Bosne i Hercegovine." *Istorijski Zapisi* 20, no. 1 (1963), pp. 15–38.
Jovanović, Slobodan. "Je li Federalizam kod nas Mogućan." *Srpski Književni Glasnik*. Beograd: n.p., 1920.
Jovanović, Slobodan. "Je li Naša Država Stara ili Nova." *Arhiv za Pravne i Društvene Nauke*. No. 5. Beograd: n.p., 1927.
Jovanović, Slobodan. *Sabrana Dela: Vlada Milana Obrenovića*. Vol. 4. Beograd: n.p., 1990.
Jovović, Pantelija. *Crnogorski Političari*. Beograd: n.p., 1924.
Judah, Tim. *The Serbs: History, Myth, and the Destruction of Yugoslavia*. New Haven, Conn.: Yale University Press, 1997.
Karadžić, Vuk Stef. *Prepiska: Beograd, 1907–1909*. Vol. 1. Beograd: Nolit, 1970.
Karadžić, Vuk Stef. *Život i Običaji Naroda Srpskoga*. Vienna: n.p., 1867.
Kitromilides, Paschalis. "Imagined Communities and the Origins of the National Question in the Balkans." *European History Quarterly* 19, no. 2 (1989), pp. 23–37.
Kostić, M. *Škole u Crnoj Gori*. Pančevo: n.p., 1876.
Kovačević, B. "Djuradj Crnojević i Njegov Značaj." *Bibliografski Vjesnik*. Vols. 1–2. Special edition. 1990.
Kovačević, Mile, and Perović, Lazar. *Istorija Srpskog Naroda za Treći i Četvrti Razred Osnovnih Škola*. Cetinje: Školska Komisija za Rukopis, 1898.
Kovijanić, Risto. *Pomeni Crnogorskih Plemena u Kotorskim Spomenicima XIV–XVI Vijeka*. Vol. 2. Titograd: Istorijski Institut Crne Gore, 1974.
Kulišić, Špiro. "O Etnogenezi Crnogoraca." Titograd: NIO Pobjeda, 1980.
Lainović, Andrija. "Pitanje Skadra u Prvom Balkanskom Ratu." *Istorijski Zapisi* 4, nos. 1–3 (1949), pp. 12–37.
Latković, Vido. *Simo Matavulj u Crnoj Gori*. Skopje: Južna Srbija, 1940.
Latković, Vido, and Jovan Čadjenovic, eds. *Epska Narodna Poezija Crne Gore*. Titograd: Grafički Zavod, 1966.
Lederer, Ivo. *Yugoslavia at the Paris Peace Conference: A Study in Frontiermaking*. New Haven, Conn.: Yale University Press, 1963.
Lowe, C.J., and M.L. Dockrill. *The Mirage of Power: British Foreign Policy, 1902–1922*. Vols. 1–3. London: Routledge,1972.
Macmillan, Margaret. *Paris 1919: Six Months That Changed the World*. London: Random House, 2002.
Malcolm, Noel. *Kosovo: A Short History*. London: Macmillan, 1998.
Mamatey, V. *The United States and East Central Europe: A Study in Wilsonian Diplomacy and Propaganda, 1914–1918*. Princeton, N.J.: Princeton University Press, 1957.
Mandić, Ante. *Fragmenti za Historiju Ujedinjenja*. Zagreb: JAZU, 1956.
Marjanović, M. *Londonski Ugovor iz 1915. Godine*. Zagreb: Jugoslavenska Akademija Nauka, 1960.

Marković, Savić. *Crna Gora u Jugoslaviji.* Zagreb: n.p., 1936.
Marković, Savić. *Gorštačka Krv, Crna Gora, 1918–1928.* Beograd: n.p., 1928.
Marković, Savić-Štedimlija. "Sto Godina Narodne Poezije." *Nova Evropa* 28, nos. 4–5 (1935), pp. 14, 33.
Marković, Vlado, and Radoje Pajović. *Saradnja Četnika sa Okupatorom u Crnoj Gori: Dokumenti, 1941–1945.* Podgorica/Cetinje: Republički Odbor SUBNOR-a Crne Gore, 1996.
Martinović, Dušan, and Šuković Radivoje. *Jovan Pavlović: Život i Djelo.* Novi Sad: n.p., 1988.
Martinović, Niko S., ed. *Rovinski o Njegošu.* Translated from Russian by Radisav Paunović. Cetinje: CNB, 1967.
Mazower, Mark. *Dark Continent: Europe's Twentieth Century.* New York: Vintage Books, 1998.
Medaković, Milorad G. *Život i Običaji Crnogoraca.* Beograd: n.p., 1999.
Mihaljčić, Rade. "Gospodar: Vladarska Titula Ivana Crnojevića." *Istorijski Zapisi* 72, nos. 3–4 (1999), pp. 3–34.
Mijušković, Mirko. "Privreda Crne Gore Prije Ujedinjenja." *Bankarstvo* (1929), pp. 2–45.
Milaković, Dimitrije. *Istorija Crne Gore.* Zadar: n.p., 1856.
Milutinović, Simeon. *Istorija Crne Gore od Iskona do Novijeg Vremena.* Beograd: n.p., 1835.
Milutinović, Simeon. *Pjevanija Crnogorska i Hercegovačka.* 1933. Reprint, Nikšić: NIO Univerzitetska Riječ, 1990.
Mirković, Mirko. *Pravni Položaj i Karakter Srpske Crkve pod Turskom Vlašću 1459–1766.* Beograd: n.p., 1965.
Mitrović, Andrej. *Jugoslavija na Konferenciji Mira u Parizu.* Beograd: n.p., 1969.
Mitrović, Andrej. *Srbija u Prvom Svjetskom Ratu.* Beograd: n.p., 1984.
Nenadović, Ljuba P. *O Crnogorcima: Pisma sa Cetinja, 1878. Godine.* 1879. Reprint, Kraljevo: Unireks, 1997.
Nicolson, Harold. *Peacemaking, 1919.* New York: Grosset & Dunlap, 1965.
Nikčević, Tomica. *Političke Struje u Crnoj Gori u Procesu Stvaranja Države u XIX Vijeku.* Cetinje: Obod, 1958.
Nikčević, Vojislav. *Crnogorski Jezik.* Cetinje: PEN, 1993.
Nikčević, Vojislav. "Istrage Poturica Nije ni Bilo." *Ovdje* 189 (1985), pp. 4–9.
Nikčević, Vojislav. *O Postanku Etnonima Dukljani, Zećani, Crnogorci.* Podgorica: Grafički Zavod, 1987.
Nikčević, Vojislav. *Pravopis Crnogorskog Jezika.* Podgorica: Montenegrin PEN Center, 1997.
Novaković, Stojan. *Zakonski Spomenici Srpskih Država Srednjega Veka.* Beograd: n.p., 1912.

O'Brien, Francis Williams, ed. *Two Peacemakers in Paris: The Hoover-Wilson Post Armistice Letters, 1918–1920.* College Station: Texas A&M University Press, 1978.

O'Grady, Joseph P., ed. *The Immigrants' Influence on Wilson's Peace Policies.* Lexington: University of Kentucky Press, 1967.

Paulova, Milada. *Jugoslavenski Odbor: Povijest Jugoslavenske Emigracije za Svjetskoga Rata, 1914–1918.* Zagreb: Prosvjetna Nakladna Zadruga, 1924.

Pavlović, Srdja. "The Podgorica Assembly in 1918: Notes on the Yugoslav Historiography (1919–1980) about the Unification of Montenegro and Serbia." *Canadian Slavonic Papers* 41 (June 1999), pp. 157–176.

Pavlović, Srdja. "Poetry or the Blueprint for Genocide." *Spaces of Identity OnLine* 1 (January 2001). Available at: http://www.spacesofidentity.net.

Pavlović, Srdja. "Understanding Balkan Nationalism: The Wrong People, in the Wrong Place, at the Wrong Time." *Southeast European Politics On Line* 1 (December 2000). Available at: http://www.seep.ceu.hu.

Pavlowitch, Stevan K. *Anglo-Russian Rivalry in Serbia, 1837–1839.* London: Ernest Benn Limited, 1971.

Pavlowitch, Stevan K. *A History of the Balkans, 1804–1945.* London and New York: Longman, 1999.

Pejković-Aleksić, Ljiljana. *Odnosi Srbije sa Francuskom i Engleskom, 1903–1914.* Beograd: n.p., 1965.

Pejović, Djoko. *Iseljavanje Crnogoraca u XIX vijeku.* Titograd: Istorijski Institut Crne Gore, 1962.

Pejović, Djoko. *Prosvjetni i Kulturni Rad u Crnoj Gori, 1918–1941.* Cetinje: Obod, 1982.

Pejović, Djoko. *Razvitak Prosvjete i Kulture u Crnoj Gori, 1852–1916.* Cetinje: n.p., 1971.

Pejović, Momčilo D. *Školovanje Crnogoraca u Inostranstvu, 1848–1918.* Podgorica: Istorijski Institut Crne Gore and Službeni List Crne Gore, 2000.

Perazić, Gavro. *Nestanak Crnogorske Države u I Svjetskom Ratu.* Beograd: n.p., 1988.

Peric, Zivojin. "Crna Gora u Jugoslovenskoj Federaciji. Posebna Izdanja." Special issue, *Ekonomist.* Zagreb, 1940.

Petranović, Branko. *Istorija Jugoslavije.* Vols. 1–3. Beograd: n.p., 1988.

Petrović, Nikola I. *Cjelokupna Djela.* Cetinje: n.p., 1969.

Petrović, Nikola I. *Pjesme.* Cetinje: n.p., 1969.

Petrović, Petar Njegoš. *Gorski Vijenac.* Vienna: n.p., 1847.

Petrović, Petar Njegoš. *The Mountain Wreath.* Translated by Vasa D. Mihailovic. Belgrade: Serbian Europe Publishing, 1997.

Petrović, Petar Njegoš. *Sabrana Dela.* Vols. 1–6. Cetinje/Beograd: n.p., 1977.

Petrović, Vasilije. *Istorija o Crnoj Gori.* Moscow, 1754. Translated by Radmilo Marojević. Reprint, Titograd/Cetinje: Leksikografski Zavod Crne Gore, 1985.

Petrovich, Michael B. *A History of Modern Serbia, 1804–1918.* 2 vols. New York and London: n.p., 1976.
Petrovitch, Woislav. *Serbia, Her People, History, and Aspirations.* London: Harrap, 1915.
Pisarev, Iu.A. *Velikie derzhavy i Chernigoria v gody pervoi mirovoi voiny.* Moscow: Mezhdunarodnye otnosheniia na Balkanakh, 1974.
Popović, Andra. *Spas ili Propast Crne Gore.* Beograd: n.p., 1928.
Popović, Djuro. *Čitanka za Četvrti Razred Osnovne Škole.* Šesto Izdanje. Cetinje: n.p., 1909.
Popović, Djuro, and Jovan Roganović. *Geografija Kraljevine Crne Gore za Treći Razred Osnovnih Škola.* Cetinje: Školska Komisija, 1911.
Popović, Pavle. *Geneza Srbijansko-Crnogorskog Pitanja.* Rome: Crnogorska Državna Štamparija, 1920.
Prodanović, Jaša M. "Gorski Vijenac kao Vaspitno Delo." *Srpski Književni Glasnik* 2, no. 16.7 (1925), pp. 11, 32.
Radičević, F. *Starine.* Cetinje: Prosvjeta, 1896.
Radojičić, Djordje S. "Biblioteka na Cetinju 1638. Godine." *Istorijski Zapisi*, no. 10 (1954), pp. 11–24.
Radović, Andrija. "L'enigme Montenegrine." *Le Temps,* July 21, 1917.
Radović, Andrija. "La Question du Montenegro." *Gazette de Lausanne*, August 30, 1917.
Radović, Andrija, Radovan Bošković, and Luka Vukotić, eds. *La Questione Montenegrine.* Paris: n.p., 1919.
Radović, Anfilohije. *Vraćanje Duše u Čistotu: Besjede, Razgovori, Pogledi.* Kraljevo: Unireks, 1992.
Rakočević, Novica. *Crna Gora i Austro-Ugarska, 1903–1914.* Titograd: Istorijski Insitut Crne Gore, 1983.
Rakočević, Novica. *Crna Gora u Prvom Svjetskom Ratu, 1914–1918.* Cetinje: Obod, 1969.
Rakočević, Novica. *Politički Odnosi Crne Gore i Srbije, 1903–1918.* Cetinje: Obod and Istorijski Institut Crne Gore, 1981.
Raspopović, Radosav M. *Diplomatija Crne Gore, 1711–1918.* Podgorica and Beograd: Istorijski Institut Crne Gore and "Vojska," 1996.
Rastoder, Šerbo, ed. *Uloga Francuske u Nasilnoj Aneksiji Crne Gore: Dokumenta.* Translated by Marina Vukičević. Bar: Conteco, 2000.
Rastoder, Šerbo. "Tri Jugoslavije." *Vijesti,* no. 204 (1998).
Rastoder, Šerbo. *Janusovo Lice Istorije: Odabrani Članci i Rasprave.* Podgorica: Vijesti, 2000.
Rastoder, Šerbo. *Životna Pitanja Crne Gore, 1918–1929.* Beograd: Biblioteka *Disertatio,* 1996.

Raznjatović, Novak. *Crna Gora i Berlinski Kongres.* Cetinje: Obod, 1979.

Rezun, Miron. *Europe and War in the Balkans: Toward a New Yugoslav Identity.* Westport, Conn.: Praeger, 1995.

Le Role de la France dans l'annexion forcee du Montenegro. Rome, 1921.

Rotković, Radosav. *Odakle su Došli Preci Crnogoraca.* Podgorica: Matica Crnogorska, 1992.

Roucek, Joseph. *Balkan Politics: International Relations in No Man's Land.* Westport, Conn.: Greenwood, 1948.

Rovinsky, Pavel Apolonovich. *Crna Gora u Prošlosti i Sadašnjosti.* Cetinje: n.p., 1993.

Rovinsky, Pavel Apolonovich. *Etnografija Crne Gore.* Vols. 1–2. Podgorica: CID, 1998.

Russinow, Denison. "Nationalities Policy and the National Question." In *Yugoslavia in the 1980s,* edited by Pedro Ramet. Boulder, CO: Westview Press, 1985, pp. 131–166.

Ruvarac, Ilarion. *Montenegrina.* 2nd ed. n.p.: n.p., 1899.

Šaulić, Novica. *Crna Gora.* Beograd: n.p., 1924.

Šaulić, Novica. *Crna Gora i Srbija.* Podgorica: n.p., 1922.

Scott, James Brown, ed. *President Wilson's Foreign Policy: Messages, Addresses, Papers.* New York: Oxford University Press, 1918.

Šekularac, Božidar. *Dukljansko-Crnogorski Istorijski Obzori.* Cetinje: Crnogorska Narodna Biblioteka, 2000.

Šekularac, Božidar. *Vranjinske Povelje.* Titograd: Istorijski Institut Crne Gore, 1984.

Šepić, Dragoslav. *Italija, Saveznici i Jugoslavensko Pitanje, 1914–1918.* Zagreb: Školska Knjiga, 1970.

Seton-Watson, Hugh. *Nationalism: Old and New.* Sydney: Sydney University Press, 1965.

Seton-Watson, R.W. *Disraeli, Gladstone, and the Eastern Question.* New York: Norton, 1972.

Seton-Watson, R.W. *The Rise of Nationality in the Balkans.* New York: Howard Fertig, 1966.

Shoup, Paul. *Communism and the Yugoslav National Question.* New York: Columbia University Press, 1968.

Simić, Andrei. "Montenegro: Beyond the Myth." In *Crises in the Balkans,* edited by Constantine P. Danopoulos and Kostas Messas, pp. 113–135. London and Boulder, Colo.: Westview Press, 1997.

Simić, Andrei. "The Blood Feud in Montenegro." In *Essays in Balkan Ethnology*, edited by William G. Lockwood, special publications no. 1 (1967), pp. 83–94.

Singleton, Fred. *A Short History of Yugoslav Peoples.* Cambridge: Cambridge University Press, 1985.

Sirotković, Hodomir. "Nacrt Frana Supila o Federativnom Uredjenju Državne Zajednice Jugoslovenskih Naroda." *Zbornik Pravnog Fakulteta u Zagrebu* 18, nos. 3–4 (1968), pp. 17–33.
Šišić, Ferdo. *Ljetopis Popa Dukljanina*. Posebna Izdanja. Beograd: SKA, 1928.
Škerović, Nikola. "Njegoš i Jugoslovenstvo." *Nova Evropa* 2.1 (1925), pp. 12–40.
Škerovic, Nikola. *Crna Gora na Osvitku XX vijeka*. Beograd: n.p., 1964.
Škerovic, Nikola. *Crna Gora za Vrijeme Prvog Svjetskog Rata*. Titograd: n.p., 1963.
Skrivanić, Garvo A. *Imenik Geografskih Naziva Srednjovjekovne Zete*. Titograd: Istorijski Institut Crne Gore, 1959.
Sloane, William M. *The Balkans: A Laboratory of History*. New York: Eaton & Mains, 1914.
Šobajic, Simo. *Crnogorci*. Beograd: NB Vuk Karadžić, 1996.
Spasojević, Janko. *Crna Gora i Srbija*. Paris: Informativna Sluzba Ministarstva Inostranih Dela, 1919.
Stanković, Djordjije. *Nikola Pašić i Jugoslovensko Pitanje*. Vols. 1–2. Beograd: BIGZ, 1988.
Stanojević, Gligor. *Crna Gora u Doba Vladike Danila*. Cetinje: Muzeji Crne Gore, 1955.
Stanojević, Gligor. *Šćepan Mali*. Beograd: Srpska Akademija Nauka i Umetnosti, 1957.
Stavrianos, L.S. *The Balkans, 1815–1914*. New York: Holt, Rinehart & Winston, 1963.
Stranjaković, D. "Političke i Kulutrno-Prosvetne Prilike u Crnoj Gori do 1834. Godine." *Cetinjska Škola, 1834–1934*. Beograd: n.p., 1934.
Sugar, Peter F. *Southeastern Europe under Ottoman Rule, 1354–1804*. Seattle: University of Washington Press, 1977.
Sugar, Peter F., and Ivo J. Lederer, eds. *Nationalism in Eastern Europe*. Seattle: University of Washington Press, 1969.
Šuković, Mijat. *Podgorička Skupština*. Podgorica: DOB, 1999.
Temperley, H.W.V. *History of Serbia*. New York: Fertig, 1969.
Terzić, Velimir, and others. *Operacije Crnogorske Vojske u Prvom Svjetskom Ratu*. Beograd: Vojno Delo, 1954.
The Other Balkan Wars: A 1913 Carnegie Endowment Inquiry in Retrospect with a New Introduction and Reflections on the Present Conflict by George F. Kennan. Washington, D.C.: Carnegie Endowment for International Peace, 1993.
Todorova, Maria. *Imagining the Balkans*. New York: Oxford University Press, 1997.
Tomašević, Jozo. *Peasants, Politics, and Economic Change in Yugoslavia*. Palo Alto: Stanford University Press, 1955.
Tomić, Svetozar. *Desetogodišnjica Ujedinjenja Srbije i Crne Gore*. Beograd: n.p., 1929.

Tomović, Slobodan. *Komentar Gorskog Vijenca*. Nikšić: NIO Univerzitetska Riječ, 1986.
Tošić, Desimir. *Srpski Nacionalni Problemi*. Paris: Savez Srpskih Zadruga 'Oslobodjenje,' 1952.
Treadway, John D. *The Falcon and the Eagle: Montenegro and Austria-Hungary, 1908–1914*. West Lafayette, Ind.: Purdue University Press, 1983.
Valenta, Anto. "Podjela Bosne i Borba za Cjelovitost." *Dom i Svijet* 288 (2000). Available at: http://www.hic.hr.dom.
Veliki Rat Srbije za Oslobodjenje i Ujedinjenje Srba, Hrvata i Slovenaca. Vol. 1, 1914. Beograd: n.p., 1924.
Vendel, Herman. *Borba Jugoslovena*. Beograd: n.p., 1921.
Veselinović, Janko. *Hajduk Stanko*. Beograd: BIGZ, 1987.
Vinaver, Vuk. "O Interesovanju Engleske Javnosti za Problem Crne Gore posle Prvog Svjetskog Rata." *Istorijski Zapisi* 1 (1965), pp. 42–68.
Vojinović, Perko. *Crnogorska Inteligencija od Polovine 18 Vijeka do 1918. Godine*. Nikšić: Istorijski Institut SR Crne Gore and NIO Univerzitetska Riječ, 1989.
Vojvodić, Mihailo. "Velike Sile i Crna Gora u Prvom Svetskom Ratu." *Istorijski Zapisi* 76, nos. 1–2 (2001), pp. 9–35.
Vojvodić, Mihailo. *Skadarska Kriza, 1912*. Beograd: n.p., 1970.
Vošnjak, B. *U Borbi za Ujedinjenu Narodnu Državu*. Beograd, Ljubljana, and Zagreb, 1928.
Vrčević, Vuk. *Narodne Pripovijesti i Presude iz Života po Boki Kotorskoj, Hercegovini i Crnogori*. Dubrovnik: n.p., 1890.
Vucinich, Wayne, and T. Emmert, eds. *Kosovo: Legacy of a Medieval Battle*. Minneapolis: University of Minnesota Press, 1991.
Vučković, Vojislav. "Diplomatska Pozadina Ujedinjenja Crne Gore i Srbije." *Jugoslovenska Revija za Medjunarodno Pravo* 2 (1950), pp. 21–40.
Vujović, Dimitrije. *Crnogorski Federalisti, 1919–1929*. Titograd: CANU, 1981.
Vujović, Dimitrije. *Podgorička Skupština*. Zagreb: Školska Knjiga & Stvarnost, 1989.
Vujović, Dimitrije. *Prilozi Izučavanju Crnogorskog Nacionalnog Pitanja*. Nikšić: Univerzitetska Riječ, 1987.
Vujović, Dimitrije. *Ratna Saradnja Crne Gore i Francuske, 1914–1916*. Podgorica: CANU, 1994.
Vujović, Dimitrije. *Ujedinjenje Crne Gore i Srbije*. Titograd: Istorijski Institut Crne Gore, 1962.
Vujović, Dimitrije Dimo. "Borba Rusije i Francuske za Uticaj na Spoljnu Politiku Crne Gore i Kampanja Protiv Knjaza Nikole 1867." *Istorijski Zapisi* 22, no. 1 (1965), pp. 12–56.

Vujović, Dimitrije Dimo. "O Etnogenezi Crnogoraca i Marksističkom Odredjenju Nacije." *Praksa* 2.1 (1981), pp. 25–62.
Vujović, Dimitrije Dimo. "Rad Srpske Vlade u Emigraciji na Ujedinjenju Crne Gore i Srbije." *Istorijski Zapisi* 13, no. 17/4 (1960), pp. 2–36.
Vujović, Dimitrije Dimo. "Saveznici i Crnogorske Finansije, 1914–1921." *Istorijski Zapisi* 39, no. 3 (1986), pp. 34–58.
Vukosavljević, Sreten. *Organizacija Dinarskih Plemena.* Beograd: n.p., 1957.
Vuletić, Savo. *Članci i Rasprave.* Bijelo Polje: n.p., 1998.
Wachtel, Andrew B. *Making a Nation, Breaking a Nation: Literature and Cultural Policies in Yugoslavia.* Stanford: Stanford University Press, 1998.
West, Rebecca. *Black Lamb and Grey Falcon: A Journey Through Yugoslavia.* London: Penguin Books, 1982.
Wolff, Larry. *Inventing Eastern Europe: The Map of Civilization on the Mind of the Enlightenment.* Stanford: Stanford University Press, 1994.
Wolff, Robert Lee. *The Balkans in Our Time.* Cambridge, Mass.: Harvard University Press, 1956.
Žanić, Ivo. *Prevarena Povijest: Guslarska Estrada, Kult Hajduka i Rat u Hrvatskoj i Bosni i Hercegovini, 1990–1995. Godine.* Zagreb: Durieux, 1998.
Zbornik Povodom Pola Milenijuma Crnogorskog Štamparstva. Cetinje: Matica Crnogorska, 1995.
Zelenica, M. "Rat Srbije i Crne Gore 1915." *Vojno Delo* (1954), pp. 35–52.
Živković, Dragoje. *Istorija Crnogorskog Naroda.* Cetinje: Obod, 1989.
Živojinović, Dragan R. "America, Italy, and the Birth of Yugoslavia, 1917–1919." *East European Quarterly* 4 (1972), pp. 22–47.
Živojinović, Dragoljub. "Crna Gora u Borbi za Opstanak: Otvaranje Crnogorskog Poslanstva u Vašingtonu, 1917–1918, god." *Glasnik Cetinjskih Muzeja* 5 (1972), pp. 10–26.
Živojinović, Dragoljub. *Crna Gora u Borbi za Opstanak, 1914–1922.* Beograd: Vojna Knjiga, 1996.
Živojinović, Dragoljub. "Crnogorska Misija u Sjedinjenim Američkim Državama 1915 Godine." *Glasnik Cetinjskih Muzeja* 12 (1979), pp. 2–37.
Živojinović, Dragoljub. "Italija i Božićna Pobuna u Crnoj Gori, 1919, Godine." *Istorijski Zapisi* 38, no. 1 (1985), pp. 24–53.
Živojinović, Dragoljub. *Italija i Crna Gora, 1914–1925: Studija o Izneverenom Savezništvu.* Beograd: n.p., 1998.
Živojinović, Dragoljub. "Kralj Nikola i Teritorijalno Širenje Crne Gore, 1914–1920." *Istorijski Zapisi* 61, nos. 3–4 (1988), pp. 15–39.
Živojinović, Dragoljub. "Pitanje Crne Gore i Mirovna Konferencijia, 1919, Godine." *Istorija XX Veka: Zbornik Radova* 14–15 (1982), pp. 23–58.

Živojinović, Dragoljub. "Prilog Proučavanju Delovanja Crnogorskog Odbora za Narodno Ujedinjenje, 1917–1918." *Glasnik Cetinjskih Muzeja* 14 (1981), pp. 11–29.

Živojinović, Dragoljub. *Vatikan i Prvi Svjetski Rat, 1914–1918*. Beograd and Cetinje: n.p., 1980.

Živojinović, Dragoljub. *Vatikan, Srbija i Stvaranje Jugoslovenske Države, 1914–1920*. Beograd: n.p., 1980.

Živojinović, Dragoljub. "Velika Britanija i Problem Crne Gore, 1915–1918." *Balcanica* 8 (1977), pp. 15, 27.

Žižek, Slavoj. "Yugoslavia: The Burden of Being the Stuff OTHERS' Dreams Are Made Of." Guest lecture, Conference on Construction, Deconstruction, Reconstruction of South Slavic Architecture, Hollis Auditorium, Cornell University, New York, March 27, 2001.

Newspapers and Periodicals

Beogradske Novine, Beograd, 1895–1912.
Cetinjski Vjesnik, Cetinje, 1908–1915.
Crna Gora, Beograd, 1908.
Dnevni List, Beograd, 1887–1914.
Glas Crnogorca, Cetinje, 1903–1919.
Gazette de Lausanne, Lausanne, August 1917.
Kalendar Srbobran, 1907.
Književni List, Cetinje, 1902.
Jugoslovenska revija za medjunarodno Pravo, Beograd, 1950
Le Temps, Paris, July 1917.
Narodna Misao, Nikšić, 1906–1907.
Novo Doba, Cetinje, 1918–1919.
Odjek, Beograd, 1902–1914.
Pijemont, Beograd, 1911–1915.
Politika, Beograd, 1904–1915.
Radničke Novine, Beograd, 1902–1915.
Samouprava, Beograd, 1910.
Slobodna Riječ, Podgorica, 1907.
Slovenski Jug, Beograd, 1903–1912.
Štampa, Beograd, 1902–1914.
Tribuna, Rome, August, 1917.
Ujedinjenje, Paris, 1917.

Index

Albania, 71, 73, 78, 81, 95
Alexander III (emperor of Russia), 97
annexation, 1, 2
Austro-Hungarian empire, 1, 42, 47, 95, 97, 177; declaration of war on Serbia, 66; offensive against Montenegro (1915), 75–76

Bajić, Milan, 154
Bakić, Ljubo, 155
Balkan, 15
Balkan Alliance (1912), 47, 62–63n69
Balkans, the, 43, 96, 116n63, 177; British interests in, 106; nation-building in, 53; Ottoman rule of, 32, 60n9; Russian influence in, 99
Banac, Ivo, 1, 25n26, 25n28
Bećir, Jovan, 47, 68–69, 84n17, 107
Begović, Blažo, 158
Blank Hand (Crna Ruka), 69
Bojović, Petar, 73
Bošković, Radovan, 154
Bosnia, 7, 40, 53, 61n46, 75; annexation of, 44
Boym, Svetlana, 24n9
Božović, Mihailo, 158
Božović, Miro, 68
Božović, Todor, 74
Braćinac, Djoko, 157
Branković, Djuradj, 30
Bulgaria, 47
Bushatlija, Mahmout, 60n21

Car, Marko, 53
Cemović, Nikola, 159
Central Executive Committee for the Unification of Serbia and Montenegro, 148–50, 160, 162
Central Powers, desire of for Montenegrin neutrality, 66
Cerović, Savo, 154, 159
Ćetković, Jovan, 14, 19–20, 153
Christianity, 7
Christmas Uprising, 163–68, 173n88, 175; declaration of the rebels, 166; failure of, 164, 166–68; Italian support for, 165; makeup and number of rebel forces, 165–66; retaliation against the rebels, 168, 173–74nn89–90
Ćirkovic, Petar, 61n30
Clark, George F., 126
Corfu, 89, 119
Corfu Declaration, 94, 129, 132, 143n59, 146
Crna Gora (Montenegro [Śaulić]), 15
Crna Gora i Srbija (Montenegro and Serbia [Spasojević]), 14
Crna Gora u Jugoslovenskoj Federaciji (Montenegro in the Yugoslav Federation [Perić]), 20–21
Crnogorac, 54
Crnogorski Političari (Montenegrin Politicians [P. Jovović]), 15–16, 168
Crnojević, Djuradj, 31–32
Crnojević, Ivan, 31, 52

Crnojević, Staniša, 32, 60n10
Crnojević, Stefan, 32
Croatia, 7, 54
Cross-Bearing Army, 39, 61n38
Crowe, Eyre, 107
Curzon, George, 107
Čuturilo, Stevo, 54
Cvjetiša, Frano, 102

Daković, Marko, 78, 85n47, 132, 158
Dalmatia, 53, 172n68
Damjanović, Lazar, 154, 155, 158, 159
Danak u Krvi (blood tax), 61n41
Desetogodišnjica Ujedinjenja Srbije i Crne Gora (The Tenth Anniversary of the Unification of Serbia and Montenegro [S. Tomić]), 17–18
District of Croatia (Banovina Hrvatska), 19
District of Serbia (Banovina Srpska), 19–20
Djonović, Jovan, 74
Djonović, Nikola, 163
Djurašković, Boro, 114n16
Djurašković, Jovan M., 124, 137
Djurašković, S., 120, 135
Dožić, Gavrilo, 154–55, 156–57, 159
Dožić, Marko, 46
Dragićević, Risto, 85n29
Dragović, Ž., 57
Drljević, Marko, 46
Drljević, Sekula, 132
Dušan, Stefan, 12, 53, 56

Eastern Orthodoxy, 7, 53, 54

Fatić, Savo, 157–58
First Balkan War (1912), 47
France, 39, 61n35, 81, 112, 126; dynamics of Franco-Montenegrin relations, 99–100; financial interests of in Serbia, 105–6; guarantees of to the Montenegrin government, 103–4; influence of on Montenegrin foreign policy, 99–101; and the Paris Peace Conference, 101–2; as a political force in Europe, 99; and the preservation of an Ottoman state, 99, 115n44; support of the Montenegrin government in exile, 87, 90–91, 101, 128; support for the unification of Montenegro and Serbia, 98, 101
Franchet d'Esperey, Louis-Félix-Marie-François, 104, 147; report of on the situation in Montenegro, 105, 116–17n73
Franco-Serbian Bank, 106
Franz Ferdinand (Archduke of Austria), assassination of, 65–66
Franz Joseph (emperor of Austria-Hungary), 78

Gatalo, Danilo, 89, 91, 120, 129, 131, 137
Gazette de Lausanne, 125
Geography of the Kingdom of Montenegro for the Third Year of Elementary School, 57
George, David Lloyd, 128
Germany, 95
Glas Crnogorca, 54, 72, 114n24, 120, 125, 138
Glomazić, Ljubo, 159
Gorštaćka Krv, Crna Gora (Highlanders' Blood, Montenegro 1918–1928 [Štedimlija]), 16–17
Grahame, George, 127–28, 132–33, 136
Great Britain, 17, 72, 126, 133; interests of in the Balkans, 106; and Serbo-Montenegrin relations, 107–8; support of the Montenegrin government in exile, 128
Great People's Assembly of the Serbian People in Montenegro. *See* Podgorica Assembly
Great Powers (Russia, France, Great Britain), 1, 3, 40, 73, 83, 87, 103, 116n63, 117n78, 168; preference for a unified South Slav state, 138–39, 145–46, 147, 175, 178; suspicions of Montenegrin relations with Austria-

Hungary, 107. *See also* Paris Peace Conference (1919)
Greece, 47, 59
Greens (Zelenši), 2, 3, 23, 26–27n51, 170–71n40, 178; origins of, 153–54
Grey, Edward, 107, 117n78
Grgurević, John, 136
Grol, Milan, 102
Gvardija military unit, 36
Gvozdenović, Anto, 88, 94, 102, 133, 135, 137

Hajduković, Jovan, 42, 62n52
Hajduković, Niko, 87, 89, 138
Herzegovina, 40, 53, 61n46, 75; annexation of, 44
History of Montenegro (Dragović), 57
History of the Serbian People for the Third and Fourth Year of the Elementary Schools (Kovačević and Perović), 55
Hrebeljanović, Lazar, 56–57

Istorija o Černoj Gori (History of Montenegro [Vasilije Petrović]), 33–34
Italy, 47, 67, 87, 112; relations with Montenegro, 95–97; support of for an independent Montenegro, 133, 138, 139
Ivanović, Miloš, 120, 136–37, 143n64

Janković, Bozidar, 69, 71, 77, 78
Jelavich, Barbara, 60
Jiriček, Konstantin, 8
Jojić, Risto, 120, 124, 158
Jojić, Velimir, 155
Jovanović, Jagoš, 39
Jovanović, Jovan, 18; opinion of King Nikola, 18
Jovanović, Mihailo, 154
Jovanović, V. J., 57
Jovović, Pantelija, 15

Kadić, Todor, 39, 40
Kalabić, Milan, 173–74n90

Karadjordjević, Aleksandar, 46, 81, 91, 102, 147, 159
Karadjordjević, Petar I, 45, 157
Karadjordjević dynasty, 97–98
Katunjanin, 25n27
Kingdom of Serbs, Croats, and Slovenes, 2, 95, 102, 105, 111, 112, 159, 163, 168, 172n68, 175
Kosić, Mirko, 102
Kosović, Petar, 17, 148
Kosovo, 56, 58
Kostić, Milan, 54
Kovačević, Mile, 55
Krunić, Ljubo, 123
Kulišić, Špiro, 7
Kuluk, 36

La France, 125
"La Question du Montenegro" (Radović), 125–26
Labriolla, Arturo, 133
Latas, Omer-Pasha, 37, 40, 61n41
Le temps, 125
League of Nations, 176
London Conference (1913), 47

Macedonia, 53
Mali, Šćepan, 33, 34–35; assassination of, 35; rule of, 35
Marković, Božidar, 102
Marttinović, Mitar, 67
Matavulj, Simo, 53
Metanović, Milo, 88, 91, 93, 113
Mihailović, Ljuba, 109
Mihailović, Vasa D., 8, 9
Mijušković, Lazar, 43, 78, 87–88
Mijušković, Šćepan, 173–74n90
Mijušković, Stevan, 173–74n90
Milaković, Dimitrije, 8
Milanović, Boža, 90
Miles, Sherman, 107–8
Milošević, Radivoje, 69
Milošević, Slobodan, 27n54, 116n63

Milutinović, Dragutin, 147, 148, 152, 153, 170n30

Mitrović, Andrej, 145

Montenegrin Bulletin. See *Ujedinjenje*

Montenegrin Committee for Unification of Montenegro with Serbia and Other Yugoslav Lands, 92–93, 94, 109, 119–21, 133, 139, 140, 147, 169n15, 176; activities of among Montenegrin students, 128–30, 142n50; diplomatic activities of, 122–23; financing of, 120–21; and the prisoners of war issue, 130–32, 142n51; program and proclamation of, 121–22, 140n10. See also *Ujedinjenje*

Montenegrin People's Movement, 164

Montenegrin Question, 16, 49, 50, 97, 113, 176, 180; international character of, 99, 110; as a Serbian internal matter, 139, 146; and the United States, 109–11

Montenegrin Warrior, 54

Montenegrins/Montenegrin identity, 2–3, 5–13, 29–30; appropriation of Montenegrins by the Serbs, 12–13; conflicting identities as Montenegrins or Serbs (Montenegrin Serbdom), 6–7, 11; and the Constitutional Assembly, 42–43, 62n53; and conversion to Islam, 8, 10; heroism of, 53, 54; and the ideology of constant struggle, 7; and national categories, 11; perception of as ethnic Serbs, 3, 6, 57–58; political conflict as a factor in determining identity, 12; role of dynastic struggle in, 12; self-centeredness of Montenegrins, 25n28; and the tradition of epic poetry, 7–11; at the tribal level, 6, 11, 132, 143n56; violence of Montenegrins toward others, 10–11

Montenegro, 1–3, 29, 170n39, 176–77; activities in by unionists, 147–54; annexation of by Serbia, 2, 3–4, 99, 138–40, 147 (*see also* Christmas Uprising; Podgorica Assembly); antiunionism in, 152–53; army of (1912), 47; and the coronation of Nikola I Petrović, 44–47, 62n63; delineation and expansion of its boundaries, 39, 61n37; division of into ten *nihijas*, 42, 61n32; division of, 24n7; doubling in size of, 41; early historical references to, 30–31; exile government of under Milo Metanović, 93; exile government of under Evgenije Popović, 93–94; in the first half of the nineteenth century, 9–10; Ottoman attack on, 40; paramilitary forces (*Komite*) of, 151–52, 170n26, 170n28; and the Paris Peace Conference, 94–95, 101; political marginalization of, 111–13; rebel opposition to Serbian annexation, 110–11, 158–59, 173n77 (*see also* Christmas Uprising); relations with Italy, 95–97; romanticized image of, 53–54; secularization of, 38, 43; security measures in against Serbian terrorists, 44; social mobility in, 42; territorial expansion of, 66–67; territorial gains of during the Balkan Wars, 47; tobacco monopoly in, 42, 61–62n50; under Danilo I, 33, 38–40; under Nikola I, 40–45; under Ottoman rule, 32; under the rule of the Crnojevićes, 30–31; under the *vladikas*, 32–38; unification of with Serbia, 2, 74–75, 91–93, 113, 115–16n54, 178; war with the Ottoman state (1876), 41–42, 61n46; war with the Ottoman state (1912), 47. See also Montenegro, statehood of; Montenegro, and World War I; Old Montenegro

Montenegro, statehood of, 48–59; anachronistic state models of, 58; and the editorial policy of Montenegrin newspapers, 54–55; and the renewal of empire, 50, 63n78; role of the school system in, 54, 55–58; Russian assistance for, 48–49; and Venetian patronage, 48

Montenegro, and World War I, 66–68, 86n48, 95, 177–78; Allied supplies to Montenegro, 75, 85n43; animosity between Montenegrin and Serbian command structures, 71–72; and the capitulation of Montenegro, 75–78, 80–83; and the capture of Scutari, 71, 73; declaration of war on Austria-Hungary, 67–68; division of into occupational zones after World War I, 104; historical interpretations of Montenegro's capitulation, 81; lack of weapons and equipment for the Montenegrin army, 75, 85n46; Montenegrin prisoners of war, 130–32, 142n51, 163; number of Montenegrin military forces (1915), 75–76; operational plan for Montenegrin military forces, 68–69; proposed neutrality of Montenegro, 66–67; protection of the Serbian army during its retreat, 76, 85n47; refusal of Montenegrin soldiers to fight, 76; role of the Serbian envoy in Montenegro, 72–75; Serbian command of Montenegrin forces, 69–70; takeover of state affairs by Austro-Hungarian military authorities, 80–81; treaty of Montenegro with Serbia, 68–72

Mountain Wreath, The (Petar II Petrović Njegoš), 8–11, 24n16, 25n24, 37; "colonization" of for political ideology, 9; and the dating of the "Christmas Day Massacre," 8; and the reconfiguration of the Montenegrin armed forces, 89–90

Nahija, 24n7
Napoleon III, 52
Naučni Slovnik (Jiriček), 8
Nemanja, Stefan, 56, 57
neopatriarchy, 23, 27n54
New Europe, The, 122, 140n15
Nicholas I (tsar of Russia), 36
Nicolson, Arthur, 117n78
Nicolson, Harold, 126, 136
Nikola I Petrović, 12, 14, 15, 16, 40–41, 54, 62–63n69, 63n71, 83n5, 100–101, 107, 109, 172n60, 177; blaming of Italy for the collapse of Montenegro, 87; as commander in chief, 47; and the Constitutional Assembly, 42–43; coronation of, 44–47, 62n63; desire for territorial expansion of Montenegro, 66–67, 95; Lord Hardinge's opinion of, 128; and Montenegrin statehood, 58–59; opposition to his policies, 74; opposition of to unification with Serbia, 132–38; proposed peace agreement/negotiations with Austria-Hungary, 77–78, 139, 176; reforms of, 42; relationship with Russia, 97–98; responsibility of for Montenegrin capitulation, 81–83; treason of, 128, 130; understanding of Serbia as greatest threat to Montenegro, 66; vanity of, 58, 81; visit of to the front (1915), 76. *See also* Nikola I Petrović, in exile

Nikola I Petrović, in exile, 87, 113, 123, 124, 165, 175–76; assassination plot against, 135–37; attack of on the declaration of the Montenegrin Unification Committee, 137–38, 144n73; complaints of concerning the Allied forces in Montenegro, 104; and the formation of a new government under Andrija Radović, 88–89; territorial aspirations of, 88; on the unification of all Slavs, 146–47

Niš Declaration, 70

Njegoš, Danilo I Petrović, 8, 43, 48, 51, 63nn74–75, 99; assassination of, 39; historical consciousness of, 49; military campaigns of, 38; reign of, 33, 37, 38–40; religious authority of, 33, 60n15; vision of for a Montenegrin state, 52

Njegoš, Petar I Petrović, 35–36, 61n30; historical consciousness of, 51, 53; and Montenegrin statehood, 50–51, 52

Njegoš, Petar II Petrović, 36–38, 52, historical consciousness of, 51; and Montenegrin statehood, 50–51, 52; writings/literary career of, 37–38, 53

Njegoš, Sava Petrović, 8–11, 33
Novaković, Boža, 54

"O Etnogenezi Crnogoraca" (On the Ethnogenesis of the Montenegrins [Kulišić]), 7
Obrenović, Mihailo, 40, 58–59
October Revolution, influence of on young Montenegrins, 129–30
Old Montenegro, 6, 11, 24nn7–8; rule of by the *vladikas*, 32–33
Old Serbia, 53
Omladinski Pokret u Crnoj Gori (Youth Movement in Montenegro [Ćetković]), 14–15
"Onamo 'namo," 54, 63n83
Ottoman Empire, 1, 6, 7, 41, 97, 106, 99, 115n44, 177; rule of over Serbia, 13; Russian influence on, 48–49. *See also* Serbia, war with the Ottoman Empire (1876)

Palikarda, Stanko, 35
Paris Peace Conference (1919), 16, 23n1, 94–95, 99, 110, 175, 176; and the "empty chair," 101–2
Pašić, Nikola, 46, 65, 67, 69, 74, 75, 84n20, 91, 103, 104, 105, 124, 140n1; actions against Paul Plamenac, 109; and the Corfu Declaration, 143n59; financial support of Radović, 147–48; instructions of to the Montenegrin Committee for Unification, 119–20; and the Paris Peace Conference, 116–17n73
Pavićević, Ivo, 160
Pavićević, Mićun, 136–37
Pavlović, Jovan, 54, 55
Pavlović, Vojvoda Peko, 42, 62n51
Pelagić, Vasa, 54
People's Party (Narodna Stranka [Klubaši]), 12, 43
Perić, Živojin, 20–21
Perjanici paramilitary unit, 36

Perović, Danilo, 85n29
Perović, Lazar, 55
Perović-Tunguz, Radovan, 71
Pešić, Petar, 19, 68, 71, 76–77, 105; as commander of Montenegrin troops, 72–73; description of the Montenegrin army, 85; and the distribution of food supplies, 73–74; opinion of King Nikola, 73
Peter the Great, 33
Peter III, 34
Petrović, Božo, 42
Petrović, Mirko (Prince Mirko), 40, 78, 80
Petrović, Nikola. *See* Nikola I Petrović
Petrović, Šako, 43
Petrović, Vasilije, 33–34; model of for a Montenegrin state, 49–50, 52
Petrović, Veljko, 102
Philips, William, 109
Pichon, Stéphen-Jean-Marie, 103
Piletić, Jole, 42, 62n51
Piletić, Spasoje, 158
Piroćanac, Milan, 41
Pišteljić, Luka, 120, 124
Plamenac, Arsenije, 33
Plamenac, Petar, 88, 109–10, 126, 117n78, 141n34
Plamenac, Jovan, 81
Plamenac, Milo, 166
"Plan for the Joint Action of the Serbian and Montenegrin Armies in the War against Austria-Hungary" (1914), 68
Podgorica, 2
Podgorica Assembly, 2, 3, 5, 108, 110, 112, 140, 171n49, 172n58, 176; completion of the unification process, 159–60; and the contravention of parliamentary procedure, 160, 162; debate concerning King Nikola's properties, 158–59, 172n65; debates of at the first regular session, 155–56; deposing of King Nikola I, 157; election and establishment of the Executive Committee, 155, 158, 171n52; elections for, 150, 152, 154;

introduction of courts martial by, 158; negative impact of, 179–80; opposition to preparations for, 153; partisan arguments during, 157–58; preliminary session of, 154–55; preparations for, 147–50, 178–79; and rejection of the Yugoslav idea, 162–63; resolutions of, 156–57, 162–63, 171n54, 179. *See also* Christmas Uprising; Podgorica Assembly, writings on

Podgorica Assembly, writings on, 13–23, 180; on the Allied betrayal of Montenegro, 17; on the conflict between Whites and Greens, 21–23; on economic issues, 16–17; ideological bias of, 13, 19; as propaganda, 13–15; unionist viewpoint, 17–18

Poincaré, Raymond, 103

Polk, Frank, 136

Popović, Djuro, 56, 70

Popović, Evgenije, 93–94, 114n26

Popović, Krsto, 110, 166

Popović, Marko Miljanov, 42, 62n51

Popović, Risto, 78, 80, 84n15

Popović, Simo, 54, 92

Popović, Tihomir, 93, 112

Princip, Gavrilo, 65

Protić, Rista, 169n13

Putnik, Radomir, 68, 73

Radnički Savez (Workers' Alliance), 42

Radonjić, Jovan, 35

Radović, Andrija, 69–70, 84n20, 98, 101, 102, 104, 105, 110, 131, 140n1, 176; allegations of involvement in assassination plot against Nikola I, 135–37; attacks on in the newspapers, 125; authoritarian attitude of, 129; character flaws of, 114n16; criticism of King Nikola, 125, 126, 133, 135, 142n36; formation of the new government under, 88–89; insistence that Serbian troops enter Montenegro, 147; on the Montenegrin Committee for Unification, 122–23; opposition of to Bolshevism, 130; perception of as a traitor, 114n20; and the reconfiguration of the Montenegrin armed forces, 89–90; request for Serbian financial support, 147–48, 169n9; support of Montenegrin unification with Serbia, 91–93, 119–20

Radulović, Marko, 78

Raičević, Miloslav, 148, 149, 159, 169n13, 169n18

Reader for the Fourth Year of the Elementary School (D. Popović), 56–57

Regnum Sclavorum, 176

Romania, 47, 59

Russia, 33, 34, 36–37, 87–88, 96, 112, 115n38, 177; and the formation of the Balkan Alliance, 47; influence of on Montenegrin/Serbian unification, 97–98; relationship with Serbia, 58–59. *See also* October Revolution, influence of on young Montenegrins

Salis, John de, 107–8, 117n78; report of on Montenegro, 108–9, 174n92

Sarajlija, Milutinović, 8

Śaulić, Novica, 15

Sazonov, Sergei, 67, 98

Šćepanović, Novica, 154

"Secret Agreement between Montenegro and Austria, The," 71–72

Serbdom, 6–7, 11, 53, 54, 55

Serbia, 1, 7, 26n30, 43, 45–46, 53, 54, 69–70, 81, 112, 126, 145, 163, 170n27, 170n37, 177, 179; Allied mandate for Serbian troops in Montenegro, 104–5; army units of (Scutari Troops, Adriatic Troops), 147, 151–52, 168n7, 170n28; and the assassination of Archduke Ferdinand, 65–66; attempted annexations in Albania by, 47; propaganda outlets of, 102, 116n56; rule of by the Ottoman Empire, 13; as a Russian ally, 58–59;

Serbia (*continued*)
  Serbia/Piedmont comparison, 25–26n29; as the strongest state in the Balkans after World War I, 175; war with the Ottoman Empire (1876), 41–42, 61n46. See also Montenegrin Question, as a Serbian internal matter; Montenegro, annexation of by Serbia; Montenegro, unification of with Serbia; Niš Declaration
Serbian Bureau for Journalism, 102
Serbs, 2–3; India as ancestral home of, 63n90
Seton-Watson, R. W., 23n1, 122, 126, 140n15
Simović, Nikola, 154
Škerović, Nikola, 132
Šoć, Pero, 135
social poetics, 24n9
Socialist Federal Republic of Yugoslavia (SFRY), 23, 116n63
Sokolović, Mehmed-Pasha, 61n41
Sonnino, Sidney, 72, 96
South Slavic Piedmont, 43
South Slavs, 43, 53, 96, 97, 112, 132; common state of, 1–2, 59, 106, 111, 145–47, 159, 160, 162, 168nn2–3, 175, 179; influence of Russia on, 97–98
Spasojević, Janko, 14, 74, 88, 92, 101, 120, 137, 140n1, 148, 152, 154; and the prevention of Nikola's return to Montenegro, 147–48; on the resolution of the Podgorica Assembly, 157
Štedimlija, Savić Marković, 16–17
Stefanović, Dušan, 90, 147
Stepanović, Stepa, 46
Stojanovich, Traian, 27n54
Stvaranje Zajedničke Države Srba, Hrvata i Slovenaca (The Creation of the Unified State of Serbs, Croats, and Slovenes [Jovan Jovanović]), 18
Sundečić, Jovan, 54

Tanović, Marko, 34

Thessalonica, 89, 90, 102, 119; Allied offensive on the Thessalonican front, 147–48, 175
Tomaović, Lazar, 54
Tomić, Radovan, 158
Tomić, Svetozar, 17–18, 152, 169n8; arguments for the unification of Serbia and Montenegro, 151; and the Central Executive Committee for the Unification of Serbia and Montenegro, 148–49; prevention of Nikola's return to Montenegro, 147–48
Toscović, Janko, 62n61
Treadway, John, 47
Treaty of Berlin (1878), 41
Tribuna, 125, 133
True People's Party (Prava Narodna Stranka [Pravaši]), 12, 43
Trumbić, Ante, 143n59

Udediniteljí Crne Gore i Srbije (The Unifiers of Montenegro and Serbia [Ćetković]), 19–20
Ujedinjenje, 94, 122, 123–26, 131, 141n24; distribution of, 124; poor quality of, 123–24; print run of, 141n19
Ujedinjenje Crne Gore i Srbije (The Unification of Montenegro and Serbia [Vujović]), 21–23
unification, 1–2
United Serbian Youth (USY), 54
United States: and the Montenegrin Question, 109–11, 133–34; reaction to the alleged assassination plot against Nikola I by Andrija Radović, 135–37

Venice (city-state of), 48, 177
Vesnić, Milenko, 89, 91, 92, 96, 119
Vešović, Radomir, 70, 78, 80
Vojvodina, 54
von Hotzendorff, Conrad, 66
von Weisner, Friedrich, 65
Vrbica, Mašo, 42

Vučković, Pero, 88, 120, 124
Vujović, Dimitrije Dimo, 21–23, 123, 140n1, 165–66
Vukmirović, Djuro, 136–37
Vukotić, Janko, 47, 78, 80, 166
Vukotić, Jovan, 165
Vukotić, Luka, 154
Vukotić, Stevo, 158
Vuksanović, Ljubomir, 154
Vuletić, Savo, 18–19, 168, 172–73n74

Whites (Bjelaši), 2, 3, 23, 26–27n51, 178; origins of, 153–54
Wilson, Woodrow, 16, 109, 117n89

Yugoslav Committee (London), 94
Yugoslav Communist Party, 21
Yugoslavia, 162
Yugoslavia (Kingdom of), 2, 99, 179–80

Zakonik Opšti Crnogorski i Brdski (General Law of Montenegro and Brda), 36, 60nn23–24
Zapisi, 18
Zeta, 24n4, 30, 31, 46, 57
Živojinović, Dragoljub, 128, 165
Žižek, Slavoj, 7